FURTHER PRAISE FOR
SHARIAH LAW: QUESTIONS AND ANSWERS

'A clear-eyed, scholarly, thorough and timely general treatment of the most pressing questions an English-speaking layman may have about the Shariah.'

Professor Dr. HRH Prince Ghazi bin Muhammad bin Talal

'A most appropriate book that provides a clear understanding of Shariah law, especially in these times of general misunderstanding about the system in the West. Highly recommended.'

Mashood A. Baderin,
Professor of Laws, School of Law,
SOAS University of London

ABOUT THE AUTHOR

IS He SUNNi or Shia?
IS He using TAQiha To lie?

Mohammad Hashim Kamali is founding CEO of the International Institute of Advanced Islamic Studies (IAIS) at the International Islamic University, Malaysia. He lives in Kuala Lumpur.

Shariah Law

MULTIPLE INTURPATIONS

QUESTIONS and ANSWERS

MOHAMMAD HASHIM KAMALI

ONEWORLD

A Oneworld Book

First published by Oneworld Publications, 2017

Copyright © Mohammad Hashim Kamali 2017

ISBN 978-1-78607-150-7
eISBN 978-1-78607-151-4

Typeset by Siliconchips Services Ltd, UK
Printed and bound in Great Britain by Clays Ltd, St Ives plc

Oneworld Publications
10 Bloomsbury Street
London WC1B 3SR
England

Contents

Acknowledgments

S ince this book is largely based on my general knowledge of Shariah law that I have gained over the years, I owe a debt of gratitude to all those from whom I have learned it. I take this opportunity to thank them all, especially my late father, who was a Shariah scholar and judge and gave me an early grounding in the subject. I take this opportunity also to thank my teachers, students, colleagues and peers whose views and counsel have influenced my own views. In my more recent deliberations, I have learned from Tun Abdullah Ahmad Badawi, former Prime Minister of Malaysia and current Chairman of IAIS, with whom I have sat on numerous consultative sessions. I thank warmly Tun Abdul Hamid Mohamad, former Chief Justice of Malaysia, through many conversations and the exchange of letters we had over matters of mutual interest. I have enjoyed similar relationships with Dr Chandra Muzaffar and Tan Sri Jawhar Hassan, and I thank them both for their valuable views and advice on issues especially of concern to developments in Malaysia. Learned works of outstanding scholars I have consulted include those of Professors Seyyed Hossein Nasr, Mohamed Selim al-'Awwa and John Esposito, all of whom I have personally known, but also the learned Sheikh Yusuf al-Qaradawi whose works I have admired and frequently quoted. I record my profound appreciation for their impressive contributions to the scholarship and the better understanding of Shariah.

Professor Muhammad Khalid Masud read an early version of this work and made many useful comments. I also thank most warmly Novin Doostdar of Oneworld Publications who was supportive not only in facilitating publication of this work, but also that of my previous title, Shari'ah Law: An Introduction, which I published with him back in 2008. He made useful suggestions on both occasions that facilitated the timely publication of these works.

I would also like to mention and thank warmly my friends and colleagues at the Institute here, especially Dr Mohamed Azam Mohamed Adil, for the many beneficial exchanges of views and conversations we had on matters of mutual interest. My colleague Mohd Fariz Zainal Abdullah was most helpful with filling gaps in my own knowledge and checking details, especially in the Arabic sources. Siti Mar'iyah Chu Abdullah has been closely involved in assisting me with manuscript preparation and computer work. Norliza Saleh was ever ready and courteous, helping me with data searches and computer work in Arabic.

Last but not least, I thank most warmly my wife Susannah for taking care of me and providing me with the space and peace of mind to spend so much time on writing.

Any shortcomings that remain are my own.

Mohammad Hashim Kamali
International Institute of Advanced Islamic Studies (IAIS), Malaysia
March 2017

Introduction

The question and answer style information on Shariah provided in this book is intended to inform the reader on the salient aspects of Shariah and its characteristic features, with some information on its sources, its rules and objectives and its internal resources for self-adjustment, without engaging in any detailed exploration of this inordinately rich field of Islamic discipline. The volume at hand is organised in seventeen sections consisting of a total of 190 questions and answers. Some sections are large but most are brief, often no more than a few pages or paragraphs. Some of the more extensive of these sections that occupy relatively larger spaces are the first two about the sources of Shariah, and legal opinion (*fatwa*), followed by the sections on marriage and family, Shariah and science issues, Shariah law and governance, and jihad, war and violence. This is due partly to the topicality of the subjects and the more extensive treatment they have received in both the classical *fiqh* and modern scholarship. The Shariah and science section is concerned mainly with Shariah responses on biotechnology and bioethics, raising issues, for instance, on genetic engineering on humans, or eugenics, human cloning, artificial insemination, surrogate motherhood, euthanasia and abortion. Issues of concern to animals and plants, food safety and genetically modified organisms have also been raised. The section on 'Shariah, Constitutional Law and Civil Liberties' raises questions on Islam and democracy, separation of powers and the status of statutory legislation side by side with the Shariah. Other themes featuring in this section include caliphate and the Islamic state, fundamental rights and liberties, gender equality, and human rights. These last two are exceedingly wide-ranging in themselves but our treatment of them is limited to women's right to work outside the home, their entitlement to education and rights to choose their own marriage partners. We have also discussed issues of concern to gender segregation, women as witnesses and judges, domestic violence and female genital mutilation. Included in our selection of topical issues of concern to Shariah and human rights are also Shariah punishments, namely the *hudud*, which have given rise to questions by contemporary human rights activists. We raise issues and address them while taking into consideration the concerns both of Shariah scholars and those of the proponents of human rights. We have also taken the opportunity in this connection to advance reform proposals that arise from our previous research into the source evidence of Shariah on a number of issues, including the *hudud*. The reader will thus note that our selection of questions on Shariah and the responses they have received are on the whole issue-oriented, as opposed to descriptive expositions, as it were, of the Shariah and Islamic law perspectives. The responses we have presented also echo the concerns of a modern student and reader of Shariah.

The main purpose in all of this has been to provide an inkling for a general-interest reader and one who may be inclined to do further research and take these questions further. We look at the basic contours of Shariah, whether it has the resources to address contemporary issues, and the manner how it may relate to other legal traditions. The first chapter thus provides a comparative overview of the commonalities and differences of note between the Shariah, the common law and the civil law traditions.

As already noted, one of the reasons we have chosen a question and answer format for this book is simplicity and easy access, especially for the non-specialist. The present writer has previously published larger texts on Islamic law and jurisprudence and has found out through years of contact and feedback with his publishers in the UK and elsewhere that there is a demand for easier presentations of Shariah to the average reader of this discipline, especially in the West, and in the English language. My previous works, especially, *Principles of Islamic Jurisprudence* (1991, and 3rd revd edn 2003), and *Shariah Law: An Introduction* (2008) are textbooks on their subjects designed mainly for university students and readers. The second of these two books also has attempted to be less technical. This book follows that trend in a different way and seeks to reach the average educated reader at a time that misinformation on Shariah has proliferated in the mainstream media and amongst the general public. Unlike Orientalism which was confined mainly to academia, the current tide of Islamophobia and misinformation on Islam and the Shariah is more general. That said, the present book still seeks to be more than skin-deep and seeks to combine an academic flavour, as it were, to introduce the thoughtful reader, however lightly, into the characteristics of an exceedingly rich discipline. A yet additional reason for the selection of the present format is to afford an opportunity to engage in issues of contemporary and topical interest. This is not always possible in a textbook or monograph but only when one has the liberty to pose relevant questions of topical interest. We hope that this purpose has been achieved, or at least partially achieved, as unlike a textbook engagement in a measure of speculation is also inevitable in answering unprecedented questions.

Most of the responses given are based on the present writer's general knowledge of Shariah and how that can be related to the concerns of the twenty-first-century world. The age of globalisation has widened beyond prec- edent the scope and level of encounter and interaction between Muslims and non-Muslims. As already mentioned, our responses to some unprecedented issues may be speculative, in certain parts at least, just as the veracity of the responses we have given to questions of concern to technology and science – cloning and genetic engineering for example – may also be open to further research and development and inclined therefore to be open-ended. We have often attempted to combine the scholastic *fiqh* positions with developments in modern scholarship and statutory laws of the present-day Muslim countries. Significant developments in *fiqh* have sometimes been made in the wake of twentieth-century Islamic revivalism on aspects, for instance, of matrimonial law, marriage, polygamy and divorce. We have naturally borne in mind the concerns both of continuity and change, and the truism that certain aspects of the Shariah are not changeable as opposed to those that are open to recon- struction and *ijtihad* (independent reasoning).

Being primarily concerned with a contextualised exposition of the main principles of Shariah, this book establishes a closer contact with the scrip- tural sources of the discipline, especially the Qur'an and Sunnah (sayings and exemplary conduct of the Prophet Muhammad). The learned *fiqh* scholars and imams have themselves drawn from those sources and have often advised their followers to do the same whenever they were unsure of the veracity of their interpretative endeavours. It is therefore a valid approach in many ways to include the source data of the Qur'an and Sunnah/hadith in our synoptic responses to questions. These are, in turn, enriched as and when the context required, by their scholastic developments and interpretations in both the Sunni and Shia schools of theology and jurisprudence.

One other source of information I have utilised fairly extensively is the legal maxims of *fiqh*, known in Arabic as *qawa'id kulliyyah fiqhiyyah* (general *fiqh* principles). Towards the end of each section of this volume, the reader will thus find a list of the Qur'anic verses and hadith, followed by a number of legal maxims of interest to the subject that I was able to find in the sources I consulted. These are presented in bare skeletal form, usually in a bullet-point format, that help to provide the reader with an inkling into the juristic abstractions of the more elaborate articulations of the relevant *fiqh* principles. None of the collections I have presented is, however, exhaustive in the sense of providing relevant answers to all the questions raised, while they do provide valuable information and input. Some of the legal maxims have been explained in the footnotes so as to clarify their main message, for the text may otherwise be too condensed for the non-specialist to understand, and also due to the utmost brevity that is characteristic of this genre of the *fiqh* literature. Often a substantive principle of Shariah is articulated in a few words or phrases rarely exceeding a single sentence. An overemphasis on brevity can at times prove to be less than helpful to the non-specialist. This also explains why we have given the Arabic wording of the legal maxims – and also of the Qur'anic verses and hadith we have quoted – in the endnotes for clarity and easy reference.

For English translations of the Qur'anic verses I have relied mainly on Abdullah Yusuf Ali's translation, but the English translation of most of the hadith and almost all of the legal maxims I have quoted are my own, although I have occasionally consulted other translations that have been available to me. My own translations of the legal maxims and hadith seek on the whole to convey the main message, as opposed to a verbatim translation of the original text.

As a distinctive genre of the *fiqh* literature, legal maxims represent a latent development in the history of *fiqh* that emerged after the crystallisation of the leading schools of Islamic law (*madhhabs*) around the fourth century AH/tenth century CE. Most of the legal maxims consist of rules of general application, although some are more specific and relate to particular themes and chapters of *fiqh*. The legal maxims were extracted from the larger *corpus juris* of *fiqh*, well after the latter was developed and crystallised often for educational purposes as well as providing panoramic and impressionist overviews of an increasingly well-developed discipline. Scholarly writings in the various branches of *fiqh* had, however, grown in the course of time into considerable length and complexity, and a need was felt, therefore, for condensing them into concise abstracts as aids to teaching. The substantive *fiqh* was there, in other words, before the legal maxims could be drawn and extracted from it. That said, some of these maxims were also drawn directly from the Qur'an and hadith. A certain text of the Qur'an or hadith was thus rehashed or paraphrased and made into a legal maxim. The much larger body of the legal maxims (estimated at over 1,200 maxims altogether) have been drawn from the well-recognised manuals and textbooks authored by leading scholars and imams. The maxims so constructed and selected were sometimes revisited and further refined by other scholars thus eventually growing into a distinctive branch of the *fiqh* scholarship. The legal maxims of *fiqh* are also known to be goal-oriented and provide useful pointers to the higher intents and purposes of the law, as well as focusing on the salient principles and ideas that regulate and govern a whole area or chapter of *fiqh*. Scholastic differences among the Sunni schools themselves and also between the Sunni and Shia schools of jurisprudence do exist over details, but the general picture tends to be one of uniformity and concordance across the board.

As a distinctive genre of the *fiqh* literature that has been the focus of renewed attention of Muslim scholars in recent decades, the legal maxims of *fiqh* have remained a relatively less well known aspect of Islamic law especially to its readers in the English language. They are internally diverse and often unusually revealing and insightful. Adding them in the order we have presented may well be seen, it is hoped, as a distinctive feature of the present volume.

And lastly, since a great deal of the responses I have presented have been drawn from my previous works on the various themes of Shariah, I have provided in the bibliography at the end a fairly full listing of my previous publications. Some of these can also be found on the Internet either under the present author's name, the subject matter, or both. Most of the articles and shorter texts I have published can also be accessed on my website page www. hashimkamali.com.

I

Shariah and *Fiqh* – Meaning, Definition, Sources, Salient Features and Comparisons with other Legal Systems

Q1) What is Shariah? Where does the word come from and what does it mean now? What is the difference, if any, between Shariah and Islamic law?

A) Shariah literally means the way to the watering place, or the path, one might say, to seeking salvation and relief. It appears in the Qur'an only once (al-Jathiyah, 45:18) although its derivatives and substantive rules occur more frequently in the Holy Book. In the English language, however, the phrase 'Islamic law' has been used to refer to both the Shariah, which is mainly based on divine revelation, and its interpretation as developed by the jurists, called *fiqh* (lit. understanding), which is a human construct for the most part based on rational thought and interpretation. *Fiqh* refers to the discipline or body of knowledge on how the jurists have understood and articulated the Shariah, especially its practical rules that relate primarily to the conduct of individuals. Shariah is not confined to the legal subject matter as such, which is of concern mainly to *fiqh*. Shariah may thus be said to be the wider source from which *fiqh* has been derived. This distinction is not conveyed in the expression *Islamic law*, but it is important that it is borne in mind. As a path to religion,

Shariah is primarily concerned with a set of values and rules that are essential to the understanding and practice of Islam. Whereas Shariah is contained mainly in the Qur'an and the exemplary sayings and conduct of Prophet Muhammad, known as Sunnah, *fiqh* refers mainly to the *corpus juris* that is developed by the legal experts and schools (*madhhabs*), individual jurisconsults, scholars and judges by recourse to independent reasoning (*ijtihad*) and the issuance of legal opinions (*fatwa*). *Islamic law* may thus be said to be generic and over-arching in that it ignores the lines of distinction between Shariah and *fiqh*, the revealed and man-made components of Shariah, as already explained. Islamic law suggests no well-defined boundaries, yet it is most likely to mean the applied laws of Shariah.

Q2) Is Shariah the same as positive law, or law proper, in regards to its purposes and characteristics?

A) Shariah is a wider source that encompasses different purposes and characteristics than positive law. By positive law is mainly meant *applied law* duly ratified by the law-making authority of the community or state, which is also cognisant of the lines of distinction between law, morality and religion. In its broader sense, Shariah includes law, morality and dogma all together in the belief that all of these must go hand-in-hand towards the construction of a holistic legal order that seeks to integrate all of these various dimensions. Shariah thus proceeds on the assumption that law alone is not the only effective instrument for the formation of a holistic legal order and the development of wider human potentialities, even though it plays an important role in regards to both. Law has a limited power in regards to making men accomplished individuals and useful members of society. This is because law sets minimum standards and defines broad guidelines for individuals and institutions. One may be observant of the law and yet be an objectionable character, a bad actor in a certain role or even generally. Shariah is different in this respect in that it incorporates the moral aspects of behaviour into the fabric of its rules and values to guide individuals and institutions, and yet it also draws certain lines of distinction between law and morality proper for purposes of enforcement and the formalities of court proceedings, as we will elaborate.

Q3) When was Shariah/Islamic law created? How? By whom?

A) Shariah is mainly contained, as already mentioned, in the Qur'an, which according to Muslim dogma is God's revealed speech to Prophet Muhammad, received over a period of twenty-three years of his prophetic mission in the early seventh century CE. It was further developed and supplemented by the Prophet himself through his sayings and exemplary conduct, or Sunnah, which is conveyed and recorded in the hadith. The interpretation of Qur'an and hadith and extraction of the more specific rulings (*ahkam*) of Shariah, especially with reference to newly arising issues were generally developed over time, mainly by the jurists (*fuqaha'*). This also gave rise to a degree of convergence between the divinely revealed and the juristic components of Shariah that were developed through interpretation and rational construction. Thus, the lines of distinction between Shariah and *fiqh* tended to become increasingly less obvious. All one can say is that interpretation which adds no new elements to the text of the Qur'an and the explicit words of hadith is an extension of the same and the core embodiment of Shariah, whereas *fiqh* subsumes interpretation that involves recourse to independent reasoning (*ijtihad*), juristic opinion and *fatwa*.

Shariah courts also played a role in the development of Shariah, but it was the work mainly of individual jurists who acted in their private capacities as pious individuals in the various parts of Islamic lands. That is why Islamic law is often referred to as 'jurists' law' and is similar in this respect to Roman law. Almost all of the leading eponyms and imams of jurisprudence, including Imams Abu Hanifah, Malik, Shafii, Ibn Hanbal, Ja'far al-Sadiq, and others, were private individuals and teachers. They wrote little themselves but their teachings were subsequently developed by their learned disciples, many of whom authored works that represented the authoritative articulation of their particular teaching circles that eventually developed into schools, or *madhhabs*. These works became well-known over time and further refined, expanded, annotated, abridged and elaborated by reference to practical incidents and cases by subsequent scholars and commentators, and most of their contributions are with us to this day. Shariah is, as such, exceedingly rich and resourceful in scholarly writings: each of these terms I have used (in the previous sentence) actually refer to a separate but distinctive genre of literature in Shariah scholarly works, known by their various Arabic terms as *Mutun* (original extant texts of the leading figures and imams, also known as *zahir al-riwayah*), *Hawashi* (annotations and explanatory works), *mukhtasars* (abridgements for teaching purposes), *al-nawadir* (works on practical incidents and developments akin to case law) and *fatawa* (legal verdicts and opinions) given by individual jurisconsults, or Muftis, often in response to particular questions they were asked.

Q4) Is the concept of Shariah solely Islamic? Is there a Jewish Shariah? A Christian Shariah?

A) The Qur'an says that each community has been given its own law, including the people of Moses and Jesus (peace be on them). The validity of revealed laws preceding the Shariah of Islam, especially of Judaism and Christianity, is explicitly recognised in the Qur'an and also in the detailed articulations of Islamic jurisprudence (*usul al-fiqh*). There is no mention in the Qur'an though of any Shariah for these other religions: the text often uses expressions such as guidance, light, open way (*huda, nur, minhaj*), and so on. Those revealed laws are not, however, practiced by Muslims as the latter are not bound by them unless explicitly affirmed and articulated in the Qur'an. This is so mainly because the Shariah of Islam became gradually self-contained. Some of the laws of Judaism, to which the Qur'an has made references, have survived, however, under the Shariah of Islam, but which were integrated in due course and became an integral part thereof. The Jews have a similar legal system, which they refer to as Halakha and has many aspects in common with the Shariah. Christianity is basically not a law-based religion and has no elaborate legal system of its own. The Roman law which developed in Christian lands does not claim a divine origin in the religion. prior to Christianity

Q5) Being divine law, Shariah is often said to be immutable. Do you agree?

A) This characterisation is not entirely accurate. This is because the Shariah itself integrates adaptability and change in its principles and methodologies. *Ijtihad* (lit. striving – independent reasoning and interpretation) is the main vehicle of adaptation and change of the Shariah rules, pertaining especially to civil transactions, *mu'amalat*, in tandem with the changing conditions of society. It has already been indicated in answers to the previous questions, that the text and language of the Qur'an is open to interpretation for the most part. The Qur'an, especially the legal verses, occur in several genres that have been classified for purposes of interpretation into such categories as the general (*'aam*) and specific (*khass*), ambiguous (*mujmal*) and clarified (*mubayyan*), and so forth. The general verses and proclamations of the Qur'an occupy an estimated ninety per cent of the entire text, although it may be less so in regards to the legal verses. But even so, a smaller portion of the legal contents of the Qur'an, in the areas, for instance, of worship matters, inheritance, family law and penalties are specific (*khass*). In general, the Qur'an is on the whole open to interpretation, although its more particular rulings may be less so, even the latter portions, or *khass* of the Qur'an, are not entirely closed to interpretation. Interpretation may either be confined to the words and sentences of the text, that is *tafsir*, or go beyond the confines of words and sentences and engage with what is known as allegorical interpretation (*ta'wil*). This can be said, *mutatis mutandis*, of the division of the Qur'anic text and rulings into the various other categories of absolute (*mutlaq*) and qualified (*muqayyad*), manifest or apparent (*zahir*) as opposed to clear and categorical (*nass*), as we will elaborate.

The general, the absolute and the manifest parts of the Qur'anic rulings remain open on the whole to specification, qualification and clarification respectively according to context and purpose. With regard to civil transactions (*mu'amalat*), for instance, the textual rulings of the Qur'an on the fulfilment of contracts, the legality of sale, the prohibition of usury (*riba*), respect for the property of others, documentation of loans and other forms of deferred payments, etc., are conveyed in broad and general terms, which may be specified and qualified, as they have been in fact, with reference to particular modes of transactions and contracts, reflecting in the meantime the custom and usage of people, and the changes and developments in the marketplace. This can also be said with regard to the numerous Qur'anic dispensations on justice, advocacy of truth and methods of proof, some of which are conveyed in the form of specific rules but the much larger part consists of general guidelines and no specific details are provided, in which case the ruling authorities ('*ulu al-amr*), jurists and judges may develop and interpret them in the light of the general guidelines of Shariah and the legitimate needs and aspirations of society. In sum, there is a core part of the Shariah in the area of specific rules and those pertaining to ritual performances that may be seen as immutable, but the larger part of the Qur'an, as also of Shariah, in the sphere especially of civil transactions, and the parts that are open to interpretation and development are, on the whole, capable of adaptation and change. They are not, in other words, immutable. Neither the Shariah nor *fiqh* can therefore be said to be immutable. What is immutable is the wording of the Qur'an, as God's words, but since they too are to be understood by the human intellect and in rational ways, interpretation and analysis become inevitable. In sum, Shariah is immutable in some respects but mutable and subject to interpretation in others.

Q6)   What parts of the Shariah can be said to be adaptable as opposed to those which are not?

A)   From the viewpoint of adaptability and change, the rules of Shariah may be divided into two types, namely those that are constant and unchangeable (*thawabit*) and those that are changeable (*mutaghayyirat*). Broadly the clear injunctions of Shariah with regard to devotional matters ('*ibadat*), definitive prohibitions (*muharramat*) and its religio-legal obligations (*wajibat*) are permanent and unchangeable. The Shariah is adaptable, on the other hand, in the areas of civil transactions, or *mu'amalat*, criminal law, government policy and constitution, referred to as *siyasah shar'iyyyah*, fiscal policy, taxation, and economic and international relations. On many of these themes, the Shariah only provides general guidelines and their relevant details can be determined, adjusted and modified, if necessary, through the exercise of human reasoning and *ijtihad*. I may quote in this connection what Muhammad Iqbal (d. 1938) wrote in his renowned work, *The Reconstruction of Religious Thought in Islam*: 'I have no doubt that a deeper study of the enormous legal literature of Islam is sure to rid the modern critic of the superficial opinion that the law of Islam is stationary and incapable of development.' The language of the text, its clarity and decisive tone, and sometimes also repetition for the sake of emphasis, provide the bases of distinction between the changeable and unchangeable parts of Shariah. Islamic jurisprudence also recognises certain concepts, such as general consensus (*ijma'*) and ordinances of the head of state, such as a national charter or constitution, which could play a role and elevate a changeable aspect of Shariah to the rank of unchangeable.

Q7) What is the Qur'an?

A) Islamic dogma maintains the Qur'an consists of the exact words God the Most High has revealed to the Prophet Muhammad through the Angel Gabriel in Arabic over a period of twenty-three years during the Prophet's time in Mecca (about thirteen years), and then subsequently in Madinah (about ten years). The Prophet himself memorised the Qur'an as and when he received it, which he then dictated to his scribes (a total of sixty-five scribes are mentioned as having been employed at various times), who were assigned the task of writing down the text. The entire text of the Qur'an was put in writing by those scribes who then cross-checked and verified it during the Prophet's lifetime, with himself and other fellow scribes. By the time of the third caliph Othman ibn 'Affan, barely two decades after the Prophet's death (632 CE), variations in the pronouncement of some words and expressions of the text in the different Arabic dialects had cropped up among various tribes and regions, which persuaded the caliph Othman to unify the standard text of the Qur'an with the help of the leading Companions who were still alive. He then ordered the variant texts to be destroyed. No part, sentence or words of the Qur'an have since been changed and the text has remained intact down the centuries. This is the text which we have today.

Q8) What is the Qur'an all about?

A) The Qur'an is the first and most authoritative source of Shariah and the primary source of every Muslim's faith, moral guidance and practical conduct. It deals with a wide variety of subjects of concern to human beings in this life and the hereafter: faith and doctrine, morality, worship, creation, wisdom, law, prophethood, life and death, as well as history and narrative of bygone nations and events – all in various proportions. But the most basic yet all-embracing theme of the Qur'an is the relationship between God and man and the rest of the creation. At the same time, the Qur'an provides guidelines for a just social order, proper human conduct in family and society and an equitable socio-economic structure of society.

Q9) Is the Qur'an mainly devoted to legal rules? Can you describe the internal structure and contents of its text?

A) No. Legal rules occupy less than three per cent of the entire text. The Qur'an is a book primarily of religious guidance and morality expounding the essentials of belief, the dogma of Islam, worship matters, and so on. But it also contains legal rules of concern to individual conduct, family relations, marriage, divorce, inheritance and bequest, trading transactions and contracts such as partnership, lease and hire, and agency, and so forth.

The Qur'an consists of a total of 114 chapters, or suras, and 6,235 verses of unequal length, known as *ayat*, all in about 77,000 words. The shortest of these suras consist of three verses (al-Kawther, sura 108) and the longest of 286 verses (al-Baqarah, sura 2). There are an estimated 350 legal verses in the Qur'an, most of which were revealed in response to problems and issues that were actually encountered by the Arab individuals and communities of Mecca and Madinah during the Prophet's life there. The legal verses of the Qur'an lay the foundations of Shariah. The Prophet lived in Mecca during the first twelve years and seven months of the Qur'anic revelation, during which time Islam was a minority movement and was met with strong opposition from the Quraysh tribe of Mecca – the Prophet's own tribe in fact, the leading tribe and aristocracy, so to speak, of Mecca. There was little scope in those situations for a legal code or Shariah while Muslims were only a small minority in the midst of a hostile majority. It was only after the Prophet migrated to Madinah that the Muslim community formed a government of their own. The Prophet continued to receive Qur'anic revelations for the succeeding ten years in Madinah. The Meccan part of the Qur'an (85 out of the total of 114 suras) was devoted mainly to the essentials of belief, morality and general principles of what was lawful and unlawful (*halal* and *haram*) in personal conduct, worship matters, food and social relations. But it was in Madinah that the text paid greater attention to legal matters. By far the larger part of the legal verses of the Qur'an were thus revealed in Madinah.

Q10) How would you characterise the legal contents of the Qur'an and its salient reforms?

A) Some of the legal verses of the Qur'an, which Muslim jurists subsequently labelled as the *ayat al-ahkam*, were revealed with the aim of repealing objectionable practices and pre-Islamic Arab customs, such as infanticide, usury, gambling and unlimited polygamy. Others laid down penalties with which to enforce the reforms that the Qur'an had introduced. But on the whole, the Qur'an confirmed and upheld the existing customs and institutions of Arab society and only introduced changes that were deemed necessary. There are an estimated 140 verses in the Qur'an on devotional matters (*'ibadat*), such as ritual ablution and prayers, fasting, giving of obligatory and optional charities, the pilgrimage of hajj, jihad and self-imposed penalties or expiations (*kaffarat*). Another seventy verses address matters of concern to marriage, divorce, paternity, guardianship, fosterage, child custody, inheritance and bequest. Rules concerning commercial transactions (*mu'amalat*), such as sale, lease and hire, loan, agency and mortgage constitute the subject of another seventy verses. There are about thirty verses on crimes and penalties, such as banditry/terrorism, adultery, theft, false accusation and consumption of liquor. Another thirty verses speak of justice, equality, evidence and proof, consultation in community affairs, basic rights and obligations. Economic matters, workers' rights and social justice issues occupy another ten verses in the Holy Book. That said, it will be noted that Muslim jurists are not unanimous on the precise number of legal verses in the Qur'an, as calculations of this nature tend to differ according to one's viewpoint and approach. Some scholars were inclined, for instance, to extract a legal ruling even from the historical narratives of bygone nations and prophets in the Qur'an, whereas others were inclined to look at the context and exclude narrative and history from the scope of their search for legal verses.

Some of the legal verses are definitive (*qat'i*) and convey a clear meaning and leave little room for speculative interpretation, but there are only a limited number of such verses in the Holy Book. Most of the rest of the legal verses, and in fact also the much larger part of the Qur'an generally, are open to interpretation. The language of the text is of high literary standard; it is explicit and categorical in certain parts, but implicit, general and allusive in others. The Qur'anic language is generally seen to be in need of clarification, in certain parts at least. Some verses are general (*'aam*) whereas others are specific (*khass*), some are absolute (*mutlaq*) whereas others are limited in scope and qualified (*muqayyad*), and so forth. The Qur'an may make a general statement or lay down a ruling of unqualified import in one place and specify or qualify those passages elsewhere in the text, and may be also in a different and unexpected place or context. It is for the jurist and commentator then to provide digested conclusions from a variety of passages that may have implications for one and the same particular text or subject. These and similar other classifications of the words and sentences of the Qur'an have given rise, in turn, to an elaborate science of textual interpretation (*tafsir*), allegorical interpretation (*ta'wil*) and other branches of Qur'anic sciences, such as phenomenology of the Qur'an, or occasion of its revelation (known as *asbab al-nuzul*), division of the Qur'an into the Makki and Madini portions and legal consequences that may flow from it with regard to, for instance, the incidence of abrogation (*naskh*) of the Makki by the Madini verses, rules of interpretation and sentax, incantation (*tajwid*), gradualism in the revealed text (*tanjim*), inimitability (*i'jaz*) of the Qur'an, and so forth. Most of these classifications were attempted for better understanding of the text, mainly by Muslim jurists and commentators, and they influence most of the other branches of Islamic learning, but they are not a part of the Qur'an.

Q11) What is Sunnah – is it also a source of Shariah? Is Sunnah the same as hadith?

A) Yes, Sunnah is the second most authoritative source of Shariah next to the Qur'an. It is the practice, sayings and examples of the Prophet Muhammad in reference often to particular cases or questions he had encountered and was asked about. A hadith (lit. speech or reported speech of the Prophet) is a transmitted report of what the Prophet might have said, did or tacitly approved. Belief in the truth of the Prophethood of Muhammad and his Sunnah is also an integral part of the Islamic faith. The Qur'an and Sunnah together are referred to as the revealed sources (*naqli*) of Shariah, in contradistinction, that is, to the rational sources (*'aqli*), of which there are many. The rational sources include, for instance, general consensus (*ijma'*), analogical reasoning (*qiyas*), considerations of public interest (*maslahah*), precedent or fatwa of the Companions of the Prophet (*fatwa al-sahabi*), general custom (*'urf*), and so forth. The rational sources of Shariah all fall under the general rubric of independent interpretation, or *ijtihad* (see page 17).

Q12) What is the meaning of Sunnah and what role does it play with regard to the Qur'an?

A) Sunnah literally means a clear path, a beaten track and valid precedent. It is the opposite of that which is unfamiliar and harmful (*bid'ah*). A great deal of the Sunnah lays down rules which constitute an integral part of Shariah. It often explains, elaborates and clarifies the Qur'an, but it can also introduce new law that is not found in the Qur'an. The Qur'an provides evidence that the teachings and Sunnah of the Prophet commands obedience and it stands therefore next in authority to the Qur'an itself.

Q13) One often comes across other technical terms side by side with Sunnah, such as hadith, *khabar* and *athar*. Can you explain?

A) Hadith is a near-equivalent of Sunnah, and it refers almost exclusively to the sayings of the Prophet Muhammad. Sunnah is a wider concept, however, that includes not only the spoken word but also acts and tacit approvals of the Prophet. The Arabic word *khabar* (lit. report, news) is sometimes used as yet another synonym to Sunnah and hadith. *Khabar* is commonly used in Shia jurisprudence in reference not only to hadith proper, but also the sayings of the recognised Shia imams. *Athar* (lit. imprint, relic, remnant), refers to the saying and conduct of the Companions of the Prophet.

It so happened that sometime after the death of the Prophet, his sayings and teachings became so common that they dominated the talk of the town, as it were, and the word 'hadith' (lit. speech) began to develop a technical meaning referring exclusively to the speech of Prophet Muhammad. Often the Qur'an lays down a general principle or rule, which is then developed by the Sunnah. With reference to sale and purchase, for example, the Qur'an declares them lawful and lays down a few basic rules to regulate a fair exchange of values and avoidance of usury, etc., in a sale transaction. The Qur'an also lays down a handful of general rules with reference to contracts, such as the requirement of mutual consent and also that contracts must be free of wrongful appropriation of the property of others. The Sunnah/hadith has elaborated the varieties of sales and contracts, their conditions and requirements, and so on, often by way of giving specific examples and declaring certain practices as violations of the general guidelines of the Qur'an. The explanatory role of Sunnah/hadith to the Qur'an is even more prominent in the sphere of devotional matters, such as the ritual prayer (*salah*). The Qur'an merely lays down the obligation that Muslims must pray. The Prophet supplemented this by asking his followers in a hadith to 'pray the way you see me praying'. Then a great number of details arose and developed concerning the obligatory prayers, its various parts and manners of performance, mostly by the Sunnah or hadith, but also through the sayings of the Companions, who would say, for instance, after the Prophet's death, that we saw the Prophet doing this or heard him saying that and would even specify the occasion and context. The more learned Companions developed the Sunnah further through juristic interpretation and *ijtihad*. It is sometimes difficult therefore to draw clear and categorical lines of distinction between the Prophetic Sunnah, hadith and the sayings of the Companions.

Q14) Has the hadith/Sunnah been also documented and written down like the Qur'an?

A) Yes, the Sunnah was reduced to words and documented, but not with the same degree of accuracy as that of the Qur'an. Initially the Prophet himself did not encourage the writing of his Sunnah, presumably so that people did not confuse his own sayings with the Qur'an. But it is reported that after some time when the accuracy of the Qur'anic text was assured, the Prophet permitted his Companions to write down his sayings if they so wished. Since writing down the Sunnah was not a requirement, weaknesses over the veracity of belated writings and reports of what the Prophet had said or done became somewhat problematic, as it became difficult to prevent incidents of fabrication and false reporting.

Literally thousands of hadith are on record. The two most authoritative collections of hadith are those of Muhammad b. Isma'il al-Bukhari (d. 256 AH/870 CE), known as *Sahih al-Bukhari*, and that of Muslim b. Hajjaj al-Nishapuri (d. 261 AH/875 CE), known as *Sahih Muslim*, each recording about 3,000 hadith, without repetitions, but much larger numbers of hadith have been collected and recorded in other collections. The six authoritative collections of hadith, known as *al-sihah al-sittah* (lit. the six sound collections) are, in addition to these two, those of Abu Daud al-Sijistani (d. 275 AH/889 CE), also named after him as *Sunan Abu Daud* (Sunan, as a technical term, signifies that the collection consists mainly of legal hadith), Ahmad b. Shu'ayb al-Nasa'i's (d. 303 AH/915 CE) *Sunan al-Nasa'i*, and another Sunan collection by Muhammad b. Yazid al-Qazwini b. Majah (d. 273 AH/887 CE), known as *Sunan Ibn Majah*, and *al-Jami' al-Thirmidhi* (*jami'* signifying a comprehensive collection not confined to legal hadith) by Muhammad ibn 'Isa al-Tirmidhi (d. 279 AH/892 CE). There are literally dozens of other hadith collections of various sizes offering different perspectives on their collections and the types of hadith they may have recorded, signifying a continuous effort, in the meantime, to leave out spurious and unreliable hadith, isolate and identify those that were doubtful or suspected of forgery, and so on.[*]

Q15) Do the Sunni and Shia use the same collections of hadith?

A) The Shia school or *madhhab* has four authoritative collections of their own. These are: Muhammad b Ya'qub al-Kulayni, *Kitab al-Kafi*; Muhammad b 'Ali al-Babauyah, *Man la Yahduruhu al-Faqih*; Muhammad b 'Ali al-Tusi's *Tahdhib al-Ahkam* and *idem, al-Istibsar*. The Sunni and Shia collections do not differ a great deal in respect of contents and over the essentials of Islam or the Shariah, but they differ mainly in respect of the narrators and transmitters of hadith. Some individual transmitters of hadith that may be acceptable to the Sunnis are not acceptable to the Shia and vice versa. The Shi'i collections also include the sayings of their imams into the body of hadith, whereas this is not the case with the Sunni collections. The Shi'i imams themselves usually attribute their statements and positions to the Prophet and it is often the same message that is recorded through a different route or channel of transmitters. That said, there are also differences in respect of principles, for example concerning the Imamate as a theological principle and certain legal details in respect of marriage, guardianship, inheritance, etc. When

---

[*] For the various other collections of hadith and other information on this subject see Mohammad Hashim Kamali, *A Textbook of Hadith Studies*, Leicester, UK, 2005, p. 22 f.

all these differences are put together, the idea of a separate collection of hadith in the Shi'i *madhhab* acquires its own characteristics.

Some examples of hadith:

'None of you truly believes until he wishes for his brother that which he wishes for himself.'

'God has no mercy on one who has no mercy for others.'

'Harm may neither be inflicted nor reciprocated in [the name of] Islam.'

'Powerful is not he who knocks another down, but it is he who controls himself in a fit of anger.'

'Actions are judged by their underlying intentions.'

'He who eats his fill while his neighbor goes without food is not a [true] believer.'

Q16)   Is Shariah the same or different from other legal systems?

A)   Shariah may be described as a 'legal system' in a broad sense but it is perhaps more accurate to say that it lays down the fundamental principles of law, religion and ethics all combined. This can give rise to different legal structures, as it has indeed historically given rise to a variety of legal systems, all of which can be said to be based on Shariah, though not synonymous with it. In many cases the Shariah coexisted with an already existing legal order, such as the *adat* (custom) in the Malay world, the *zawabit* (subsidiary rules) during the Mughals and the *qanun* (statutory law) during the Ottomans. Governments throughout the long history of Islam also issued ordinances and administrative regulations establishing procedural guidelines, regulating customary practices and setting jurisdictional limits for the various sectors of government under the rubric of *Siyasah* (lit. policy), or *Siyasah Shar'iyyah* (Shariah-oriented policy), which operated either as supplementary to Shariah or side by side with it, especially when they consisted of extra-Shariah subject-matter and rules.

Q17)   How does the Shariah compare with common law?

A)   There are similarities and differences between these two legal tradi-
     tions. Substantive similarities in the values upheld by both systems
     relate to the fact that the Qur'an endorses Christianity and Juda-
     ism as valid religions and concurs to a large extent with the essence
     of morality, upholding justice, basic rights and obligations that may
     flow from this. Both the Shariah and common law are concerned
     primarily with the interests of private persons and are therefore
     more closely associated with the concept of 'private law'. The legal
     tradition in both systems focus more on relations among individuals
     than between the individuals and the state.

Since the Shariah predates common law, it may have influenced the development of legal concepts after the Norman conquest of England in the eleventh
century CE, which is when common law began to develop. The Normans also
conquered and inherited the Islamic legal administration of the Emirate of
Sicily, followed by a series of hostile encounters that took place during the
Crusades. Common law has also influenced Islamic law, much later during the
colonial period in the eighteenth and nineteenth centuries, but this was more
through imposition and official policy rather than natural flow and influence
of ideas. Yet the common-law rules that were adopted in the laws and practices
of the colonies eventually became entrenched and persisted even during the
post-colonial period. Common law is currently applicable in Muslim countries including Malaysia, Nigeria, the Sudan and Pakistan, and in the case of
India the influence was more widespread, thus leading to the emergence of
what became known as Anglo-Muhammadan Law. Yet the tendency began to
be one of a mixed pattern of legal developments in the many Muslim countries
that combine common law, statutory legislation, the Shariah and some aspects
also of the Continental legal system associated with the Code Napoleon.

The common law of England refers primarily to the ancient customary
law of the land. It is the body of law based on customs and court decisions
which gave rise, in turn, to the principle known as *stare decisis* (lit. stand
on things as decided). The decisions of earlier judges became the law for
later ones. The Shariah does not, on the other hand, recognise the binding
authority of judicial precedent in that order and holds instead to the unfet-
tered freedom of the jurist-*mujtahid* and judge to decide based on their own
conviction and understanding of the law. Whereas custom and experience

rather than theorising constitute the basic postulates of the development of common law, by contrast, Shariah law originates in the revealed text of the Qur'an, which is then supplemented by the sayings and exemplary practice of the Prophet Muhammad. That said, the Shariah also recognises custom as a source of law, and twentieth century legal developments in some Muslim countries tend to take cognisance of the inherent merit of the doctrine of *stare decisis*.

Q18) Can you be more specific about commonalities and differences between the Shariah and common law?

A) One cannot be certain, but it is noted that the English trust and agency institutions in common law might have originated and possibly adapted from the *waqf* and Hawalah institutions of Shariah respectively during the Crusades. Trust law is by and large a creature of equity, which is attributed to the parallel jurisdiction of the Lord Chancellor to decide matters independently of the Royal Courts.

Other English legal institutions, such as the scholastic method, the license to teach, the law schools known as the Inns of Court and the European commenda (Islamic *mudarabah*, or *qirad*) may have also originated with and taken adaptations from Islamic law.

Differences are also noted, for instance, between the Shariah principle of *khiyar al-'ayb* (lit. option of defect – the customer's option, that is, of revocation of a sale due to defect subsequently discovered in the subject matter of sale) and the common law concept of *caveat emptor* (buyer beware). The former is basically saying 'seller beware' and makes it a responsibility of the seller to declare all the (hidden) defects he may know to the buyer, whereas the latter effectively makes it the buyer's responsibility to investigate and inform himself – and the two concepts can generate differential results.

Q19) What about the civil law? How does it compare with the Shariah?

A) Civil law is mainly a product of developments in eighteenth- and nineteenth-century Europe. As a body of law, civil law is based on Roman law, both dealing with private rights and claims between individuals, as opposed to criminal law and offences against the state and matters of concern between the individual and state. After the fall of the Roman Empire, the customs of the ruling tribes developed into customary law throughout most of continental Europe. Roman law was rediscovered when European jurists began to codify the existing legal systems with Roman additions. The *Corpus Juris Civil* of Justinian I (sixth-century AD) was of special importance for these evolving legal systems. The development of civil law was further enhanced by the Code Napoleon 1804, which gave France a unified national code. Other countries of continental Europe and Latin America also followed the French lead. The French civil law tradition effectively maintains that the elected legislature is the decisive arm of public opinion and should be the sole law-making authority in the land. Judicial decisions flow from this law, and the judge is guided by the legal text, rationality and logic, not by the influence and authority of powerful rulers, or customs of ruling groups.

As for comparison between the Shariah and civil law, Muslim thinkers tend to find considerable common ground with the basic notions of civil law and Shariah. Even though the Shariah is grounded in the authority of both revelation and reason (*wahy* and *'aql*), the notions of objectivity, rule of law and impartial enforcement of the law by a competent court are nevertheless entrenched in the Shariah.

One of the institutions developed by classical Islamic jurists that might have influenced civil law was the Hawalah, as already mentioned, an early informal value transfer system, which is mentioned in the texts of Islamic jurisprudence as early as the eighth century CE. Hawalah is known to have also influenced the development of the Aval in Italian law. The European commenda which limited partnership (Islamic *mudarabah*) used in civil law as well as the civil law conception of *res judicata* may also have traceable origins in Islamic law.

Q20) Do Muslims want Shariah law in their countries? Which Muslim countries today use Shariah law?

A) Most Muslim countries apply Shariah law in various proportions, often side by side with statutory legislation. The applied family law, inheritance law and bequest in the majority of present-day Muslim countries are on the whole based on Shariah. These aspects of the Shariah have represented the living law and much of it is also customarily entrenched in the practice of Muslim societies, which they often follow even without recourse to official proceedings and intervention by government agencies. This part of the Shariah is closely associated with its devotional corpus and Muslims usually follow it as an extension of their faith and dogma. Even European colonial rulers who dominated legal institutions in Muslim countries under their rule and tried to replace the Shariah with Western laws left worship matters, as well as the family and personal laws, largely uninterrupted as they knew they would be very difficult to replace.

Other parts of the Islamic law in the areas of public law, taxation, criminal and commercial laws, etc., were either replaced by modern laws of Western origin or modified and mixed with them under colonial rule. In the post-colonial period, and after the onset of the so-called Islamic revivalism and resurgence of the 1960s and 1970s, many countries of the Muslim world either amended or replaced parts of those laws – yet the parts that had become entrenched, as well as those aspects of Western laws that were deemed to be compatible with the Shariah were retained. Certain aspects of civil laws and statutory legislation may to this day be also said to be extra-Shariah in parts, but much of it is also taken from the Shariah with necessary adjustments and codified for purposes of enforcement. Thus, the picture that emerges is a mixed one, which includes laws, some based on Shariah and others derived from external sources as well as local customary practices.

Saudi Arabia, Afghanistan, Iran, Pakistan, the Sudan and many other countries use Shariah law more widely than most. Turkey has ceased to apply it, and some countries in the MENA region have also replaced parts of the Shariah with modern laws, while others are bringing in more of the Shariah into their legal systems, especially as a result of the Islamic revivalism and more recently also of the so-called Arab Spring. Although the Arab Spring phenomenon has not yielded its expected results, it has increased general awareness in many Muslim countries of the importance of their Islamic heritage and Shariah.

The onset of Islamic revivalism during the latter part of the twentieth century was to some extent expressive of a public demand by the Muslim masses for a return to their Islamic heritage, and Shariah has been a major component of that demand and their quest for authenticity and self-image. This has remained a continuing process in many Muslim countries. Islamic banking and finance, Islamic laws of property and contract have also been the focus of attention of this latent Islamisation of segments of the economy and

finance in many Muslim countries. The latest phase of this revivalist movement is not only one of bringing back the older laws but also of their revision,
adjustment and reform so as to accommodate new developments, market
trends and realities.

Q21)   Is it possible to modernise or reform the Shariah?

A)   The parts of Shariah that are based on clear injunctions of the Qur'an
may be more difficult to change, but a great deal of the Qur'an is
open to interpretation – even with regard to its specific injunctions
and its legal verses – as already discussed. One who is knowledgeable of the rules of interpretation, the structure of words, commands
and prohibitions of the Qur'an, and has general knowledge also of
the Shariah, would stand qualified to attempt a fresh interpretation
of a text or ruling of Shariah that accommodates a new reality. The
Shariah also validates *ijtihad*, as already mentioned, and a number
of other formulas, such as general consensus (*ijma'*) of the people,
or their representative scholars and *mujtahids*, analogical reasoning (*qiyas*), considerations of public interest (*istislah* or *maslahah*)
and juristic preference (*istihasan*, which is roughly equivalent to the
Western law concept of equity), etc., all facilitating accommodation
of new realities and reform. The Shariah has in principle remained
open to interpretation and *ijtihad* by qualified scholars according to
context and peoples' needs. Yet in reality *ijtihad* has had a chequered
history and succumbed at an early stage in the history of Islamic
legal thought to scholastic developments and the formation of the
schools of law (*madhhabs*) and eventually to the practice of imita-
tive scholarship, or *taqlid*, which has arguably continued with varying
degrees of intensity to this day.

There are also areas and features of contemporary studies and practices of
Shariah, which were altogether absent, or were present on a smaller scale,
in the past, such as codification, law reform through parliamentary legislation and the development of institutions such as *fiqh* councils, academies
and specialised institutions of research in Shariah law. These learned academies and institutions, which currently operate in many Muslim countries
and sometimes even in minority Muslim communities, look into new issues,

investigate and formulate suitable responses that may constitute the basis of issuance of appropriate opinions or *fatwas* that provide the needed responses, or provide input for new legislation and law reform.

Q22) Were there instances of Shariah law reform in the past, and what factors, if any, are associated with the reform of Shariah?

A) Fresh research and reformist thought in Shariah has been an integral part, in fact, of the call over a century ago for the revival of *ijtihad* by Jamaluddin al-Afghani (d. 1897), and his disciples Muhammad 'Abduh (d. 1905) and Muhammad Rashid Rida (d. 1935). Shariah law reform has also been influenced by the patterns of socio-political stability, or the lack of it, in Muslim countries, such that it tended to decline during turbulent times. This has been especially the case since the closing decades of the twentieth century, and more recently of the September 2001 terrorist attacks that brought a particularly turbulent period of military aggression and vicious circles of violence to the Muslim world. Yet the scope of *ijtihad* is also bound to expand further due to the rapid pace of social change and new challenges presented by scientific developments, globalisation and new modes and varieties of transactions in the market place. Certain areas of Shariah law have also remained underdeveloped in relation, for instance, to constitutional law, the Islamic state ideas and the jurisprudence of minorities. This last is designed to look into issues and challenges facing Muslim minorities which reside in non-Muslim majority countries.

Q23) Do Muslims want to impose Shariah law in the West?

A) Muslim minorities in the West have practiced parts of the Shariah pertaining to worship, food and beverage, and have often expressed the wish to practice the Shariah in personal law matters, such as marriage, child custody and divorce, but there is no public demand on their part, or that of the majority Muslim countries and their ruling authorities, for Shariah to be imposed in the West. Following the advent of Islamic revivalism in the latter part of the twentieth century, Muslims in the West have become more widely observant of

Islamic principles in personal lifestyle, financial transactions, clothing, etc., but in the public sphere they have, on the whole, followed the laws and mores of their country of domicile. This is also in keeping with the Islamic position which requires them to observe those laws and live in harmony with the dominant culture and custom as law-abiding citizens, provided they do not violate Islamic religious injunctions. Western laws and constitutions are, on the whole, observant of the basic rights and liberties of their citizens, often more so than some Muslim countries themselves. Muslims in the West are not required, on the whole, to dissolve their identities and assimilate in an oppressive way.

Q24)   What is the relationship between Shariah law and theology?

A)   Before the systematisation of the different theological doctrines under the umbrella of 'ilm al-kalam (also known as 'ilm al-'aqa'id or theology) and crystallisation of the schools of law (madhhabs) around the fourth AH/tenth century AD, the various branches of Shariah were still not separated from one another. Shariah consisted of three major but undivided components to begin with, namely dogma, ethics and law ('aqidah, akhlaq and fiqh respectively). It was during the late second and early third century of the advent of Islam that the three branches were separated, and the fiqh, or Islamic law, as we know today began to operate in many ways separately from theology and ethics. Over time, aspects of Islam pertaining to beliefs were also systematised into the science of theology ('ilm al-kalam), while those relating to human conduct and practical concerns of the applied law fell under law or jurisprudence (fiqh). The parts of Shariah that related to behaviour but was primarily addressed to individuals and not adopted into positive law were placed under the umbrella of morality/akhlaq. That said, law, theology and ethics are intertwined in Islam so much so that theological suppositions, such as the nature of the God-Man relationship, the attributes of God, Prophethood, the role of human intellect ('aql) as well as moral positions on good and evil are not entirely separate from the legal discourses of fiqh. Questions of morality and religion are, in other words, often intertwined with aspects of legal responsibility (*taklif*) and the consequences of conduct that may well constitute the starting points of legal inquiry in the works of jurisprudence. Broadly speaking, *fiqh* consists of a concretised articulation of the religious and moral norms of Islam. These latter two are the mother sources whereas *fiqh* is basically meant to translate their value structures into practical rules of conduct for purposes of enforcement.

Q25) Where and how did one study Shariah or Islamic law in the past? How are they studied today?

A) Some of the basic tenets of Islamic law were taught to Muslim children from early childhood by their parents, or local mosque and imam, but this mostly involved knowledge which is deemed obligatory upon the individual (*fard 'ayn*) such as the manner of performing the ritual prayer and observance of fasting and other acts of worship, rules pertaining to cleanliness and ablution for prayer and other religious occasions. Formal study of the Shariah varied from student learning and apprenticeship with individual scholars (*'ulama* and imams) at informal study circles (*halaqah*) in the mosques, to religious seminaries (*madrasah*) and larger schools and universities (*jami'ah*). Today Islamic law is also studied in the West and elsewhere as part of the 'Islamic Studies' or 'Middle Eastern Studies' courses side by side with other Islamic disciplines such as history and languages. The Shariah is sometimes studied, in modern Islamic universities, as an independent subject in its own right, leading to degrees, for example, in *fiqh* and *usul al-fiqh*. The renowned al-Azhar University of Egypt has evolved over the years in both directions by offering full degree courses on Shariah and modern laws on one hand and a range of non-Shariah studies including engineering and medicine on the other. Islamic law is often studied, in other words, side by side and in combination with other disciplines. This is more so in places where inter-disciplinary approaches to academic courses are being increasingly recognised as preferable. A need was felt during the closing decades of the twentieth century to offer teaching of Islamic law and other disciplines in the English language leading, in turn, to the establishment of Islamic universities, or International

Islamic universities, in various Muslim countries, including Malaysia, Pakistan, Jordan, Morocco, and so on.

SUPPORTIVE EVIDENCE

What we have quoted below, and in most other sections that follow, are passages from the Qur'an and hadith on certain aspects of the Shariah that we have touched upon, beginning, for instance, with passages that praise those who have faith and knowledge, and a directive that one should not take a position over a matter without having the required knowledge of the subject. Then follow passages establishing the authority of the Prophet and his Sunnah as well as a certain order of priority that is ascertained among the various sources of Shariah. This is followed, in turn, by a number of legal maxims on a variety of Shariah subjects. All of this provides additional yet optional information for the reader, as they generally support or provide a certain insight into our responses. That said, the passages we quote are for general interest, and are not tied to all the particular themes we have featured or touched upon in our responses.

⎕ Qur'an and Hadith

- ✦ 'God will elevate in ranks those of you who have faith and have been granted knowledge.' (Q al-Mujadilah, 58:11)[1]
- ✦ 'And take not a position over that of which you have no knowledge. Truly the hearing, the sight and the intellect are all accountable (before their Creator).' (Q al-Isra', 17:36)[2]
- ✦ 'And whatever the Messenger gives you, take it, and whatever he forbids you, avoid it.' (Q al-Hashr, 59:7)[3]
- ✦ 'When the Messenger of God decided to send Mu'adh ibn Jabal (as judge) to the Yemen, he was asked about the sources on which he would rely in making judgment. In reply Mu'adh said: I will judge based on the Book of God. He was asked then: but if you did not find! He said: on the Sunnah of God's Messenger. But if you did not find in the Sunnah! He said: I will do *ijtihad* based on my considered opinion.' (Hadith)[4]

+ 'I have left two things behind: the Book of God and my Sunnah. You shall not go astray if you hold on to them.' (Hadith – note: the Shi'i version replaces the words 'and my Sunnah' in this hadith with 'and my family' thus implying the authority of their recognised imams.)[5]
+ 'Pursuit of knowledge is an obligation of every Muslim, man and woman.' (Hadith)[6]
+ 'Pursuit of knowledge acts as an expiation (*kaffarah*) to what has taken place (of sin) preceding it.' (Hadith)[7]
+ 'Wisdom is the lost property of a believer. He is entitled to it wherever he finds it.' (Hadith)[8]
+ 'It is unbecoming of a person gifted with knowledge to waste himself (by abstaining from teaching it to others.' (Hadith)[9]
+ 'People are of two types: they are either the learned, or the learners, and no good will come out of those who belong to neither.' (Hadith)[10]

☐ Legal Maxims

Legal maxims are useful on the general characterisation of the various aspects of Islam, the Qur'an, Sunnah and the Shariah. We quote below a selection of the relevant legal maxims to convey a general picture of how Muslim scholars throughout the ages have spoken in the briefest proverbial style on these subjects. Our selection also supports may of the details we have given in our foregoing descriptions. The reader may, however, skip this part if so wished as the legal maxims we quote merely support our otherwise self-standing responses.

+ 'Shariah is revealed in order to secure and accomplish the benefits and prevent and minimise prejudice and harm.'[11]
+ 'The whole of the Qur'an is like a single indivisible speech in that some parts of it are necessarily dependent on its other parts.'[12]
+ 'Shariah vindicates and preserves the pristine natural state of *fitrah* [or enlightened human nature].'[13]
+ 'The Islamic Shariah permits all that which is pure, and prohibits all that is impure.'[14]
+ 'No reward and no punishment accrues in the absence of intention.'[15]

+ 'Permissibilities acquire different attributes depending on their underlying intention. If they are intended for piety and devotion, or on how to secure them, they turn into devotional acts.'[16]
+ 'Shariah is brief on the changeable and detailed on that which is unchangeable.' (Note: thus leaving the former open to reconstruction and *ijtihad*.)[17]
+ 'Shariah opts for the most just and moderate positions.'[18]
+ 'The *mutawatir* (continuously proven) hadith establishes definitive knowledge.'[19]
+ 'The pristine Sunnah is an independent source of legislation.'[20]
+ 'What may be exonerated in customary matters could be reprehensible in matters of worship.'[21]
+ 'Analogy (*qiyas*) does not establish the fundamentals of worship.'[22]
+ '[*The ruling of*] Analogy may be abandoned in favour of custom ('*urf*).'[23]
+ 'Custom has no credibility if it contravenes the rules of Shariah.'[24]
+ 'The norm is that the status quo remains as it is unless evidence establishes its opposite.'[25]
+ 'The norm is that the rules (of Shariah) collapse when their effective causes are no longer present.'[26]
+ 'If the prohibition of something is founded in two effective causes, it does not collapse with the collapse of only one while the other still subsists.'[27]
+ 'A prohibition is not decisive on anything unless it is founded in decisive evidence.'[28]
+ 'That which is null and void is abandoned without recourse to authorisation by the ruler (or judge) or anyone else.'[29]
+ 'Permissibility is the norm in all things unless there be evidence as to its prohibition.'[30]
+ 'The norm (of Shariah) is freedom from liability.'[31]

II

Legal Opinion (*fatwa*) and Independent Reasoning (*Ijtihad*)

Q26) What is a *fatwa*? Who can issue a *fatwa* and what are the consequences of *fatwa*?

A) *Fatwa* is a legal/religious opinion issued by a qualified jurisconsult
(*mufti*) in response to a particular question or issue. Anyone with a
question about an aspect of Islamic law and religion can request a
qualified scholar for a *fatwa*. The *fatwa* issued in response is essentially non-binding, and the person to whom it is addressed is free
to dispense with it and seek the opinion of other *muftis* – unless, of
course, the *fatwa* in question merely reiterates a decisive injunction
of the Qur'an or hadith and clarifies its application to the issue at
hand. A voluminous genre of literature under the rubric of *fatawa*
(pl. of *fatwa*) has developed over time and the tradition continues to
this day. It has now become a familiar practice of prominent scholars
at al-Azhar University of Egypt to write or publish a collection of
their *fatwas* and/or write a new commentary (*tafsir*) of the Qur'an,
often after leaving office. Many of the past rectors and prominent
professors of the Azhar have a *fatwa* collection to their names. In the
past *fatwas* were issued mainly for guidance on case by case issues
facing the people, or questions that were sent to learned scholars

by their constituency, mosque circle or disciples, for practical guidance and academic purposes. The *muftis* acted much like the lawyers and legal practitioners of our time as they often wrote detailed case presentations, petitions and also gave *fatwas*. This lay character of *fatwa* is being changed in many present-day Muslim countries, which are regulating the *fatwa* issuance functions of scholars with new guidelines, including statutory legislation or by-laws that seek to prevent possible abuses of a *fatwa* by tendentious figures or those who may be less than qualified for the task and yet can cause harm and disrupt social harmony over sensitive issues.

Q27) Are there any restrictions on the issuance of *fatwa*?

A) *Muftis* are nowadays state functionaries in many Muslim countries with specified statutory jurisdictions, and are no longer allowed to act in their lay capacities as independent religious figures responding to people's needs. Restrictions are also sometimes imposed on their ability to make voluntary contributions in public speeches and mosque sermons to the development of Shariah over specific issues. When a *fatwa* is duly issued by an official *mufti* and gazetted, it often carries a binding force for particular cases, countries and localities. It is debatable whether this can be called a healthy trend insofar as it may be unduly restricting the prospects of scholarly contributions to public discourse and the scholars' freedom of expression. This aspect of contemporary *fatwas* needs to be judged, however, in light of the prevailing conditions of each country and society. Some restrictions are deemed necessary to avoid confusion and misguidance that might be forthcoming from questionable individuals who may be advocating extremist activities and movements.

Q28) Why is a *fatwa* not binding? Can it be turned into a binding law?

A) *Fatwa* is not binding in Islamic jurisprudence, as it is usually based on the personal opinion or interpretation of a jurisconsult (*mufti*) concerning a particular case or question. Since human relations are dynamic and cases or disputes have usually peculiarities of their own, even though they may bear similarities, they are more likely to be different in some respects. It is not always certain either whether the *fatwa* given by a scholar or jurist is reflective of the accurate ruling and position of Shariah pertaining to a particular issue, hence it remains less than definitive and not binding, unless the *fatwa* in question is supported by general consensus (*ijma'*) of the learned or adopted into a government ordinance. The recipient of a *fatwa* is consequently free to go to another *mufti* and obtain a second, or even a third, *fatwa* over the same issue, and it is his choice whether or not to comply with any of them. Only in cases where a *fatwa* consists of a clear injunction of Shariah and the two, three or more views that might have been given on the issue are found to be concurrent would the fatwa be likely to bind its recipient, but not otherwise.

Q29) What other considerations, besides the knowledge of Shariah, should be observed in the issuance of fatwa?

A) *Fatwa* should not only observe the guidelines of Shariah, but also the custom and culture of the place and country where it is issued – hence the jurisconsult would need to know the context well before issuing a *fatwa*. Thus, if a person who resides in another country or a city with totally different cultural characteristics and solicits a *fatwa*, the *mufti* should ask him about the custom of his place first before issuing a *fatwa*. Sometimes linguistic usages, the way people make promises or take oaths and certain other nuances of language differ from place to place and such variations may well play a determinative role in the *fatwa* that may be premised over them.

Q30) Can a *fatwa* over the same question receive different responses with regard to different cases or persons?

A) Yes indeed. A *fatwa* should consider the relevant circumstances and, should there be material variations, they need to be reflected in the *fatwa*. Addressing the role of the effective cause (*'illah*) or a material factor in the *fatwa*, the renowned Abu Hamid al-Ghazali (d. 1111 CE) illustrated it by saying that two persons may approach a *mufti* over the same question and receive different answers. In the case, for instance, of travelling by sea – this may endanger the life of one person but not harm that of another – hence the *mufti* may give a prohibitive *fatwa* to one and a permissive *fatwa* to the other. Having said this, al-Ghazali tersely asks a question that begs a certain answer: then how about the society as a whole? The implication being that the effective cause of a *fatwa* plays an equally important role in reference to the community as well. Another learned figure, Ibn Qayyim al-Jawziyyah (d.1350 CE) also went on record to say that a *mufti* who issues the same verdict in all similar cases is like a physician who prescribes one and the same medicine to all patients that come to him.

Q31) Should the *fatwa* be based on the status quo/present facts or can it also contemplate impending situations that have yet to occur?

A) A *fatwa* is normally founded on existing facts, but the theory of *fatwa* extends its scope also to anticipated situations – if that is deemed to be the only way to secure a benefit or prevent a danger and a harmful situation that is most likely to occur. There is some disagreement among the schools of law over this but the issue can be subsumed under the principle of 'blocking the means' to an unlawful end (*sadd al-dhara'i*), which is one of the recognised proofs in Maliki jurisprudence and assigned a place in *usul al-fiqh* textbooks. There are certain requirements to be met but a *fatwa* in anticipation of an impending harm is valid in principle. Imagine the risk of an impending riot over a sensitive issue that can cause loss of life and the police seek a *fatwa* to stop it even if it has not actually happened!

Q32) What is *ijtihad*?

A) Literally *ijtihad* means striving, intellectual effort or exertion on the part of one or more qualified scholars of Shariah to derive the ruling of Shariah from its valid sources over a new or unprecedented issue. *Ijtihad* is an important source of Shariah and the principal vehicle for its development in tandem with the changing needs of people over time and in reference to new developments, be it in law, culture, technology or science.

Ijtihad is a broad and a fairly well-developed concept that can occur in a variety of forms that are expounded, in turn, under distinctive methodologies and formulas, such as analogical reasoning (*qiyas*), juristic preference (*istihsan*), considerations of public interest (*istislah*), etc., which constitute separate proofs and chapters of the science of *usul al-fiqh*.

Ijtihad is a collective obligation (*wajib kifa'i*) of all those who are capable of conducting it. They are strongly advised thus to attempt *ijtihad* whenever they think it necessary and beneficial or when they can respond to the pressing challenges of the people and societies in which they live. *Ijtihad* has its limitations with regard to that aspect of the Shariah which is decisive (*qati*), and its application is also limited in respect of devotional matters (*'ibadat*) as well as matters of dogma and belief, but its scope remains open with regard to the wider sphere of civil and commercial transactions, technology and science, economic development, international affairs and so forth.

Q33) Who is a *mujtahid?*

A) The person who carries out *ijtihad* is known as *mujtahid* (lit. a striver, highly competent researcher) who has comprehensive knowledge of Shariah and is fully qualified to conduct independent *ijtihad*. This would be an Absolute or Independent *Mujtahid* (*mujtahid mutlaq* or *mustaqil*). The blueprint of *usul al-fiqh* (science of the sources of law) has also listed lower ranks of *mujtahids* whose intellectual attainment and erudition may not reach this level but may still be well qualified in Shariah. Some scholars, known as *ashab al tarjih*, are said to be only capable of making comparisons and preferences and of drawing intelligent conclusions out of complicated writings and scenarios. Some are even said to be only capable of extracting relevant data or responses from a given chapter of law and Shariah and are therefore given the label *ashab al-takhrij*. The lowest degree of scholarship of Shariah, under the traditional rankings of scholars, is that of an imitator (*muqallid*), who may not be qualified to carry out *ijtihad* but may still be able teach and explain the law, and even issue a *fatwa* over a specific issue. These classifications are evidently not always accurate nor can it actually be said that people's intelligence and capabilities naturally occur in that order of classification!

Yet there is probably an element of truth in them that came from actual experience. Some scholars in the same field often tend to have abilities that others may not have.

It is important that the *mujtahid* remains open to healthy adjustment and reform, yet also to have a clear understanding of the principles and purposes of Shariah, including those which may be unchangeable and not amenable to *ijtihad*. Yet the rapid pace of change in the age of globalisation with incessant advances in technology and science tend to emphasise the need for innovative interpretation and *ijtihad* in response to new challenges and issues. No one, including a *mujtahid*, is in principle immune to error, and there is clear acknowledgment of this in the hadith of the Prophet, which acknowledges the possibility that a *mujtahid* may fall into an error of judgment, but also adding that the mere possibility of falling into error should not stop him from making a contribution.

Q34) Are *fatwa* and *ijtihad* the same or different?

A) *Ijtihad* is juridically more substantive in that it must explain its evidential basis and the Shariah principles on which it is founded, whereas this is not a requirement of *fatwa*. A qualified jurist may thus give a very brief *fatwa*, say in a few words, without delving into the source evidence of his opinion. But when a *fatwa* explicates its evidential basis in the sources of Shariah, and has an element of originality that adds to existing knowledge or understanding of issues, then it is about the same as *ijtihad*. Another difference concerns the qualification and standing of the issuer. One who attempts *ijtihad* must be a qualified *mujtahid* who is fully knowledgeable of the Shariah and fulfils a certain number of qualifications. A fatwa on the other hand can be issued by a scholar of a lower standing, even an imitator (*muqallid*) who may or may not be qualified to carry out an independent interpretation but who understands the Shariah well enough to address a particular issue and extract a relevant ruling or response from the source evidence of Shariah.

Q35) Is there any difference between a *fatwa* and a judicial order (*qada*)?

A) Yes there are differences, one of which is that a *fatwa* is basically not binding, whereas a judicial order (*qada*) is. Another difference is that a judicial order can only be issued when a case is brought before the court, and is usually pursued by two parties or litigants. Unless there is a specific case and litigating parties who bring it up before the court, there will be no court judgment or a judicial order as such. The court cannot issue a judgment of its own initiative. This is different in the case of a *fatwa*, which can be issued either in response to a question posed by a questioner to the *mufti*, or indeed in the absence of a question or request. The *mufti* may, in other words, initiate and give a *fatwa* regarding an issue faced by the society in which he lives by way of a scholarly contribution. There need not be two litigating parties challenging one another either, nor there need be an adversarial context to the subject. One other difference between a *fatwa* and a judicial order is that the latter is confined to the issue or case before the court, and is subject to a certain procedure concerning proof and evidence, and it is issued only in matters of practical concern, as is the case also with the *fiqh* generally. A court judgment is not issued on theoretical or academic matters, nor even over matters of concern to the general public unless disputed and taken up for adjudication before the court. Issues of purely religious character of concern to the hereafter, and also purely moral issues usually fall outside the court jurisdiction. A *fatwa* is on the other hand not subjected to any of these restrictions. A *fatwa* can be related to practical issues, religious matters and questions also of concern to morality and even theoretical issues, including matters of purely religious concern. But the history of *fatwa* and the *fatwa* collections we have with us have generally related *fatwa* issuance functions also to practical issues and are not concerned so much with theoretical subject matter.

Q36) Is a *fatwa* issued by a *mufti* (jurisconsult) only? If so, is this a requirement?

A) Governmental approval or official appointment to the position of *mufti* is, from the viewpoint of the theory of *fatwa*, not a requirement of *fatwa*. The *fiqh* blueprint on *fatwa* mainly relates to the qualifications of a *mufti* – chiefly that he or she is knowledgeable and well-informed of the context of the case, custom and conditions of his or her society. The *fiqh* blueprint also provides a number of guidelines on the subject matter of *fatwa*, the conditions of one who solicits a *fatwa* and etiquettes of *fatwa* issuance. *Fatwa* has generally played an important role in the development of Shariah in tandem with the changing conditions of people over time and in relationship also to particular issues and cases.

Q37) How would you compare *fatwa* to judicial precedent in the common-law system?

A) The role *fatwa* has played in legal developments in Islamic jurisdictions may bear some similarity to case law, or judicial precedent, under the commonlaw system. But as already mentioned, *fatwa* is not a judicial decision as such and is not subject therefore to the formalities of court procedures. Yet *fatwa* in the sense of open service and contribution to society also became controversial when unqualified individuals, or those with ulterior motives, began to issue unwarranted *fatwas* over sensitive socio-political and religious issues. It was under the Ottomans (c. sixteenth century CE) that *fatwa* became subject to government supervision, a trendsetting development that has continued and been followed by Muslim countries down to the present day. Many countries, such as Egypt, Syria and Jordan, have established the office of Grand Mufti that supervises the *fatwa* issuance procedures and also advises their respective governments on Islamic affairs. Some official procedures also began to apply to *fatwa* issuance, yet *fatwa* still differs from that of judicial precedent in the commonlaw system.

Q38) Have there been any new developments of concern to *fatwa*-making?

A) The twentieth century also witnessed new developments in *fatwa*-making in regards to the establishment of international *fiqh* academies, or councils, which receive issues from different countries and jurisdictions for consideration and fatwa-based resolutions. Unlike some of the Muslim countries that have legislated on *fatwa* and given *fatwa* a binding character under certain conditions, *fatwas* issued by the international *fiqh* academies are on the whole non-binding and carry a persuasive influence only. Furthermore, the development, more recently, of Shariah advisory councils by the central banks of some Muslim countries, as well as financial regulatory authorities and institutions that regulate Islamic banking and finance may also be seen as an extension of the *fatwa* issuance roles in the more specialised fields of the operation of Islamic transactions and finance. Shariah advisory committees are being set up by financial institutions as well as by Islamic insurance, or Takaful companies, for similar purposes. These Shariah advisory committees are basically *fatwa*-making forums operating in their respective capacities and play increasingly important roles in institutional decision-making in Shariah-related matters, and the trend still continues.

Q39) What sources do Muslim jurists use for their legal rulings and *fatwas*?

A) Muslim jurists mainly rely on two types of sources: revealed and non-revealed. The revealed sources are the Qur'an and the Sunnah (the latter known through the authoritative hadith collections). The non-revealed sources are studied under the science of the sources of law (*usul al-fiqh*), and include a number of methods and formulas for the purpose of extracting legal rules from the revealed sources and those which are endorsed by general consensus (*ijma'*) of the ulama and scholars. The overall exercise of extracting a ruling over a new issue is known as *ijtihad* (lit. striving through research). The sub-varieties of *ijtihad* include, in turn, analogical reasoning (*qiyas*), general consensus of scholars (*ijma'*), juristic preference (*istihsan*), considerations of public interest (*istislah*), blocking the means to an unlawful end (*sadd al-dhara'i*), presumption of continuity of law or status quo ante (*istishab*), general custom ('*urf*), *fatwa* of Companions of the Prophet and unrestricted reasoning in accordance with the general principles of law and religion (*istidlal*). To this one may now add perhaps, parliamentary legislation, and a number of other more recent disciplines of relevance to law-making, even if in a subsidiary capacity, such as science and technology, biological and medical sciences, which enhance and enrich the resources of *fatwa*. For a *fatwa* that is oblivious of related developments in these fields is likely to be less than effective. Most of these Shariah sources mentioned consist of rational principles and concepts that seek to regulate extraction of rules from the primary sources, mainly the Qur'an and Sunnah. All the rest of the proofs and formulas mentioned above constitute subsidiary or secondary sources of the Shariah each in their respective capacities. They are secondary in the sense that they depend for their validity on their proximity to, and support they can find in, the letter and spirit of the data of the primary sources. These doctrines are studied in considerable detail under the rubric of *usul al-fiqh* and each has to qualify a number of requirements for them to offer a valid basis of law and judgment.

Q40) Should a contemporary *mufti* be knowledgeable of newly available data and sources of information?

A) When a qualified jurist/*mufti* resorts to Shariah sources in search of solutions to issues in the issuance of a *fatwa*, he or she normally consults these sources most of which are still, however, only available in Arabic. But this situation began to change when the larger corpus of *fiqh* or Islamic law became available in codified collections and specialised statutory laws, such as civil codes and penal codes, as well as specialised encyclopaedias, etc., during the nineteenth and twentieth centuries, and the scope and size of available information is ever-increasing. It would be strongly advisable also for an Islamic scholar and *mufti* to be conversant in the use of computers and be able to consult available information on the subject of his concern in electronic media and the Internet. In terms of accessibility and speed, the Internet far exceeds the efficiency levels of the previous collections, although it is less reliable at times and falling short of the academic accuracy and rigour of the refereed and verified compilations preceding it. A discerning scholar and jurisconsult can now access a wider range of data of relevance to the formulation and issuance of a *fatwa*.

Q41) How do statutory laws and legal codes impact *fatwa*-making functions?

A) Codification of laws tends to narrow down the role and scope of a *fatwa* and the scholarly calibre perhaps of both a *fatwa* and judicial decision-making. Codified laws did not exist in earlier times. The first comprehensive codification of Islamic law was the *Ottoman*

Mejelle that was compiled by a group of Ottoman scholars in 1876 in about 1,850 articles, published as the *Mujallah al-Ahkam al-Adliyyah*. This has proved to be a reliable source and more easily accessible compared to the *fiqh* manuals, which suffered from poor classification of themes and chapters. The *Mujallah* has also been translated into English and several other languages. During the course of the twentieth century statutory legislation gained momentum in many Muslim countries, and Islamic law, especially in the areas of personal status and matrimonial law, was consequently codified in statutory codes, either separately or as part of the general civil code or civil law as the case may be. These collections provide easy, accessible and standardised references for judges, *muftis* and lawyers, as indeed they are often duty-bound to apply them in the first place. A slight disadvantage of the availability of these codified statutes is that judges, lawyers and *muftis* are distanced as a result from the richer and larger resources of *fiqh* and Shariah.

Historically the *fiqh* sources were also supplemented by administrative ordinances and decrees issued by the ruling authorities in almost every Muslim country within and outside the regular judiciary, often consisting of procedural rules, administrative circulars and guidelines for court practice. As for the sources of Shariah, any standard text on Islamic jurisprudence (*usul al-fiqh*) would refer to the Qur'an and Sunnah as the primary sources of Shariah, followed by detailed sections and chapters on the secondary sources, as well as the many branches of *fiqh* in the sphere of civil transactions (*mu'amalat*). These are the main data that qualified *muftis* and jurisconsults would be likely to consult in the issuance of *fatwas*.* Another development of interest, in addition, that is, to the codification of Shariah laws, is that the substantive and larger corpus of Islamic law, or *fiqh*, has also been compiled in recent decades in better organised and accessible forms in encyclopaedias, manuals and textbooks that have become available in the major Islamic and Western languages, and they are too numerous to mention.

---

* For instance, Mohammad Hashim Kamali, *Principles of Islamic Jurisprudence*, is a standard text on *usul al-fiqh*, which is currently in use in most English-speaking universities and also available in a Malaysian edition.

SUPPORTIVE EVIDENCE

Our supportive evidence on *fatwa* is also compiled in two sections below, beginning with quotations from the Qur'an and hadith, followed by a selection of legal maxims. These are, however, for general information (and can be skipped), but are meant to connect the reader with the tone and tenor of the available guidelines of relevance to our discussions and responses.

▯   Qur'an and Hadith

+ 'Will they not ponder about the Qur'an, or do they have locks on their hearts [and minds].' (Q Muhammad, 47:24)[1]
+ 'Ask those who know if you yourselves know not.' (Q al-Nahl, 16:43)[2]
+ 'And those who strive in Our cause, We shall certainly guide them in Our paths.' (Q al-'Ankabut, 29:69)[3]
+ 'God intends every facility for you; He does not want to put you in difficulties.' (Q al-Baqarah, 2:185)[4]
+ 'When God favours one of His servants, He enables him to acquire knowledge in religion.' (Hadith)[5]
+ 'When a judge/ruler exercises *ijtihad* and gives a right judgment, he will have two rewards, but if he errs in his judgment, he will have still earned a reward.' (Hadith)[6]
+ 'Strive and endeavour, for everyone will achieve something which he is capable of.' (Hadith)[7]

▯   Legal Maxims

+ 'When a qualified *mufti* issues a *fatwa* on destruction/demolition [of something], and only then his error comes to light, he is liable [for damages].'[8]
+ '*Ijtihad* is not overruled by another *ijtihad*.'[9]
+ '*Ijtihad* does not apply to decisive rules.'[10]
+ 'When the follower is faced with diverging *ijtihadi* rulings by two *mujtahids*, he may follow whoever he wishes.'[11]

+ 'One *mujtahid* may not follow another *mujtahid* if they differ in their *ijtihad*.'[12]
+ 'When two indicants are [about] equal, the *mujtahid* selects between them.'[13]
+ 'The *mujtahid* is bound by the result of his *ijtihad*.'[14]
+ 'The *fatwa* follows the public interest whichever direction it takes.'[15]
+ 'It is undeniable that *fatwa* changes with the change of times.'[16]
+ 'The *mufti* declares the ruling (of Shariah) whereas the judge makes it binding.'[17]
+ 'Just character is a prerequisite of *fatwa*.'[18]
+ '*Fatwa* is issued in every city in accordance with the custom of its people.'[19]
+ 'No commitment ensues a *fatwa*.'[20]
+ 'When the *fatwa*-seeker receives diverging *fatwas* from several *muftis*, he may select which one to follow.'[21]
+ '*Fatwa* must address the issue in its own context.'[22]
+ '*Fatwa* that contravenes the scripture and consensus is invalid.'[23]
+ 'Construction of the rules of Shariah such that contravenes the higher purposes of God and the Shariah is invalid.'[24]
+ 'The ruling of Shariah is founded in its purpose not in its apparent verbal form.'[25]
+ 'All aspects of *ijtihad* depend on the knowledge of the *maqasid* (higher purposes of Shariah).'[26]
+ 'Knowledge of the purposes of Shariah is indispensable for *Ijtihad* that addresses determination of meanings, benefits and harms in Shariah.'[27]
+ 'Enquiry and research into the purposes of Shariah are indispensable [to becoming a] *mujtahid*.'[28]
+ 'There is no room for *ijtihad* in the presence of [a decisive] legal text.'[29]
+ 'The opinion of a *mujtahid* stands as valid Shariah evidence.'[30]
+ 'If the *mujtahid* retracts his ruling, it is not permissible [for others] to follow it.'[31]
+ 'Certainty is not overruled by doubt.'*[32]
+ 'Hardship begets facility.'[33]

---

* For instance, if there is a certain marriage and doubtful claim of divorce, the former prevails undisturbed.

+ 'If a lighter [ruling] can secure the purpose, there is no need for a heavier one.'[34]
+ 'It is not the Lawgiver's purpose to impose hardship and go to excess in it.'[35]
+ 'The permissible may be restricted on grounds of safety.'[36]
+ 'Facilitation and ease are the purposes of religion.'[37]
+ 'Credibility is given to what is of common occurrence not to that which is rare.'[38]
+ 'Repelling prejudice and corruption takes priority over securing benefits.'[39]
+ 'The lesser of two evils is to be preferred.'[40]
+ 'Harm is eliminated to the extent possible.'[41]
+ 'Harm may not be eliminated with a similar harm.'[42]
+ 'When an impediment ends, the normal state returns.'[43]
+ 'It is undeniable that changes of rules follow the change of times.'[44]
+ 'The rule stands and falls together with its effective cause ('illah).'[45]
+ 'The norm is that rules collapse with the collapse of their effective causes.'[46]
+ 'When ijtihad relates to evaluation of benefits and harms, knowledge of the purposes of Shariah becomes necessary.'[47]
+ 'The norm [of Shariah] in regard to speech is the real/literal meaning.'[48]
+ 'No attention is paid to inference in the face of an explicit statement.'[49]
+ 'All that which responds to a need in Shariah and is beneficial and not subject to any impediment, it is either permissible or obligatory in accordance with its standing.'[50]

III

Shariah and Acts of Worship ('Ibadat)

Q42) How often do Muslims pray? Are there different types of Muslim prayers?

A) Muslims have a religious duty to pray five times a day. The ritual prayer (*salah*) is the second of the Five Pillars (*arkan*) of Islam, after the testimonial of the faith. Prayers are due at dawn (*fajr* – any time between dawn and sunrise), early afternoon (*zuhr*), late afternoon ('*asr*), after sunset (*maghrib*) and late evening ('*isha*'). These ritual prayers are well-regulated and performing them takes up roughly a few minutes at a time, depending on the number of units involved, but the person must be in a state of purity and take an ablution (*wudu'*) before standing for prayer. One may perform more than one prayer with the same ablution if it remains intact over the intervening time segment.

Apart from the five daily prayers, which are the personal obligation (*fard 'ayn*) of every competent Muslim, there are also prayers which are the collective obligation of the community as a whole (*fard kifayah*), to uphold them as and when the occasion arises, and not allow them to fall into total neglect, but it is not obligatory upon all members of the community to perform them. For instance, the funeral prayer (*salat al-jenazah*), when a person passes away, at least some people from the locality must attend it. If some members of the community perform the funeral prayer, the rest are absolved of the duty.

There are many other optional or supererogatory prayers, which are meritorious and may be offered before and after the obligatory prayers, or at any time. These are known as *salat al-nawafil*: prayers at specific times such as the night prayers during the night or early morning hours (*tahajjud*); prayers at certain specific times of the year, such as the 'Eid prayer (*salat al-'id*) marking the end of the Ramadan fasting month, *tarawih* prayer in late evening during the fasting month of Ramadan; and prayers on certain specified occasions such as the prayer of gratitude (*salat al-shukr*), prayer in time of need (*salat al-hajat*), and a few other varieties.

Q43) How often do Muslims come together as a congregation to pray?

A) The daily obligatory prayers are recommended to be performed in congregation as often as possible, but Muslims are required to pray in congregation at least once a week, that is the Friday prayer (*salat al-jum'ah*) every Friday afternoon (preceded by the Friday sermon) which replaces the regular early afternoon (*zuhr*) prayer. In addition, some non-obligatory prayers, such as the funeral prayers, are usually performed in congregation, and so are the *tarawih* prayers during Ramadan, and the 'Eid prayers.

Q44) What are the laws for cleanliness/purification with regard to prayer and Muslim life?

A) Cleanliness in Islam is a part of the faith (*iman*) and Muslims are as such required to be in a state of cleanliness, not only for ritual prayers, but also generally as it is recommended to observe cleanliness in one's daily life. Some specific rules are also laid down for certain types of ablution, such as the ones before ritual prayers. This ablution is taken with water (*wudu'*), or it may be a dry ablution (*tayammum*), such as with clean sand, in the event water is not available. The ablution involves washing the hands, face, nose, arms (up to the elbow), feet up to the ankles, gargling and wiping of one's ears and head. In addition, the clothes one is wearing and place of prayer must be clean and free of impurities. A purificatory bath (*ghusl*) is also required after sexual intercourse.

Spiritually, purification of the self (*tazkiyat al-nafs*) is a continuous part of the religion, and this typically involves self-appraisal (*muhasabah*), repentance (*tawbah*), seeking forgiveness ('*afwa*) from God Most High (*istighfar*) and one's fellow humans, constant remembrance of God (*dhikr*) and avoidance of sinful conduct. Asking for forgiveness from those one might have offended is also highly recommended.

Q45)   Are Muslims required to fast? When and how?

A)   Muslims are required to fast during the month of Ramadan (according to the Hijri or Islamic calendar) as one of the Five Pillars of Islam. An aspect of the Hijri/lunar, as opposed to the solar, calendar is that it rotates over the years and allows different geographical regions of the planet to experience different lengths of the daytime and seasonal changes. Fasting involves abstinence from food, drink and sex from dawn to dusk. The daily fasting is preceded by a pre-dawn meal (*sahur*) and ends with the breaking of fast (*iftar*) after sunset. While fasting, one is advised to also abstain from other sins such as lying, cheating, backbiting, acts of oppression, gambling, obscenity, etc. As an expression of piety, fasting is also recommended outside the month of Ramadan, as many pious Muslims fast on Mondays and Thursdays, or any other day any time of the year. The rules of religion also make fasting a form of expiation (*kaffarah*), when for instance, someone breaks his fast for no valid reason during Ramadan, he or she is required to free a slave (when this was an option; nowadays it may be replaced by its near-substitues such as helping a poor patient with an expensive surgery), or feed sixty poor persons, or else observe two months of fasting after Ramadan. Taking of a false oath also invokes an expiation of either three days of fasting, or feeding of ten poor persons. Fasting is also recommended on certain other occasions, such as on the day of '*Arafah* as a part of the hajj rituals.

Q46)   Are Muslims required to give to charity?

A)   Muslims are obliged to pay the alms tax (*zakat*), which is a poor-due to be given annually at the rate of about 2.5 per cent of one's income on assets, and on certain assets such as gold and silver. Muslims must also give to the poor the religiously obligatory alms marking the end of Ramadan, known as ending-the-fast charity (*sadaqat al-fitr*), which is equivalent to a bowlful of dates, or a quantity of wheat, or their equivalent monetary value. There is no limit otherwise to supererogatory charity that helps the poor, promotes a good cause, or contributes to a welfare objective and it is highly recommended that one be generous in giving it. In institutional terms, giving of charity (*sadaqah*) is nowadays widely recognised as a means of cleansing impermissible incomes and profit that may have been realised through certain types of proscribed business transactions by Islamic banks and financial institutions. This is quite frequent as many of the existing investment portfolios in Islamic financial institutions involve a margin of, and often unavoidable, impermissible income, or interest-based income. For instance, an Islamic financial institution buys another business or property which may be involved in interest-based loans or mortgages, and it takes time for the inherited impermissible part to be off-loaded. When this is the case, the portion so earned has to be channeled to charity, and this is often stipulated in the applied regulatory regimes of Islamic banking and finance in many Muslim countries.

Q47) Does the Shariah require the pilgrimage to Mecca?

A) Pilgrimage to Mecca, known as haj, is also one of the Five Pillars of Islam. It is obligatory, once in a lifetime during certain times of the year, upon those who are physically fit and can financially afford to make the journey. A supererogatory minor pilgrimage to Mecca, known as *'umrah*, may also be performed at any time of the year by those who can afford it, but this is not a requirement. All pilgrims must wear the *ihram* clothes, just two pieces of unsown white garment. This helps to eliminate distinctions of race, rank and status among the pilgrims, an aspect of Islamic ritual that is inherently egalitarian and internationalist.

Q48) Do the Sunni and Shia *madhhabs* differ over the acts of worship?

A) With the exception of the doctrine of Imamate, which is a Shī̈ite principle and has certain devotional manifestations, the basic outline of the required ritual acts of worship are almost identical on both sides. The one exception of note on the Shi'i side is the requirement of an obligatory charity, known as the imam's portion, or *sahm-e imam*, according to the Shia Imamiyyah, of one-fifth tax payable to the imam. This is not a requirement under Sunni law. Acts of devotion according to Shi'i jurisprudence appear under ten headings as follows: ritual purity (*al-taharah*); prayer (*salat*); obligatory alms (*zakat*); the one-fifth (*al-khums*) tax payable to the imam; fasting (*sawm*); seclusion (*i'tikaf*, which is regarded as a desirable but not obligatory act of devotion – also accepted in Sunni *madhhabs*); pilgrimage to Mecca (haj – the same as under Sunni law); the minor pilgrimage ('umrah – also the same under the Sunni *madhhab*); sacred struggle (*jihad*); and ordering what is good and forbidding what is evil (*amr bi'l-ma'ruf wa nahy 'an al-munkar*). This last too is a Qur'anic principle of equal standing under the Sunni schools.

This outline is perhaps a little more detailed than that of the equivalent Sunni outline of worship. One notable point may be that the Sunnis tend to confine the list of *'ibadat* to obligatory performances thus excluding some of the Shi'i acts of devotion that are optional or recommendable under the Sunni law. In sum the outline of worship is about the same on both sides, albeit with minor differences. If a Sunni Muslim practices the Shi'ite rituals in good faith, the similarities are so predominant that it would not affect the substance of his identity and standing in Islam. The same can be said of a Shia Muslim who practices the Sunni rituals of the faith, or if he prayed behind a Sunni imam. If a Sunni Muslim prays behind a Shia imam, that would also not vitiate his prayer.

SUPPORTIVE EVIDENCE

☐ Qur'an and Hadith

- ✦ 'And be steadfast in prayer; practice regular charity (*zakah*), and bow down your heads with those who bow down (in worship).' (Q al-Baqarah, 2:43)[1]
- ✦ 'And pilgrimage to the House is a duty owed to God – for those who can afford the journey.' (Q Aal-'Imran, 3:97)[2]

+ 'Those who believe and do deeds of righteousness, establish regular prayers and give charity, they will have their reward with their Lord. On them shall be no fear nor shall they grieve.' (Q 2:277).[3]
+ 'One who is compelled [into sin or neglect of duty] without being a transgressor or a rebel, does not incur a sin.' (Q 2:173)[4]
+ 'It is not virtue that you turn your faces [in worship] toward East or West. But virtuousness is to believe in God and the Last Day... to spend of your substance, out of love for Him, on your kin, the orphans and the needy.' (Q 2:177)[5]
+ 'O My servants who have transgressed against their souls! Do not despair of the mercy of God. For God forgives all sins. He is most forgiving, most merciful.' (Q al-Zumar, 39:53)[6]
+ 'God does not burden a soul beyond its capacity.' (Q 2: 286)[7]
+ 'Cleanliness is one half of the faith.' (Hadith)[8]
+ 'Acts are judged by their underlying intentions.' (Hadith)[9]
+ 'You should take advantage of the concessions God has granted to you.' (Hadith)[10]
+ 'It is not virtuous to fast while travelling.' (Hadith)[11]
+ 'God has exonerated my community for their mistakes, forgetfulness, and acts under duress.' (Hadith)[12]

⬚ Legal Maxims

+ 'What can be done is not waived due to what cannot be done.'[13] (Note: one is advised to do even a part of a duty if one is unable to do the whole of it.)
+ 'No reward [accrues to devotional acts] without intention.'[14]
+ 'Islam wipes out [wrongs] previously committed in respect of the Right of God to which no Right of Man is attached.'[15] (Note: sins but not debts owed to others, nor crimes against humans, committed prior to embracing Islam are exonerated. The Right of God may be forgiven but no one other than the right-bearer can exonerate the Right of Man.)
+ 'It is not [advisable] for the competent person to aim at hardship in the discharge of a duty for greater reward.'[16]

+ 'Acting on the primary purposes [of Shariah with good intention] turns all the dispositions of a competent person into devotional acts.'[17]
+ 'The permissible becomes an act of devotion when acted upon for the sake of God.'[18]
+ 'Acts of worship are not justiciable.'[19]
+ 'An act of worship performed prior to its due time does not count either as timely or as belated performance.'[20]
+ 'One who misses a timely act of worship is to do it belatedly.'[21]
+ 'Belated performance does not apply to supererogatory acts of devotion.'[22]
+ 'All acts of devotion have their meanings as the Shariah does not command anything in futility.'[23] (Note: acts of worship have meanings which are, however, not always known to us.)
+ 'A firm resolve to perform an act of worship, which is not actually performed [due to disability], takes the place of performance in the absence of transgression.'[24]
+ 'Customary practices turn into acts of worship with the purity of one's intention.'[25]
+ 'Permissibility granted due to necessity or need is to be accurately measured, and terminates when the necessity comes to an end.'[26]

IV

Schools of Islamic Law, the *Madhhabs*

Q49)   Are there different schools of Islamic law?

A)   Yes. There are different schools of Islamic law within both the Sunni
and Shia branches of Islam. The Sunni schools were initially larger in
number but were reduced over time to only four, namely the Hanafi,
Maliki, Shafi'i and Hanbali, commonly known as *madhhabs* (lit. the
path one treads), named respectively after their eponyms or imams.
These are not only juristic schools but also combine law and theology, although theological schools proper, such as the Mu'tazilah,
the Ash'ariyyah, Maturidiyyah and others are a separate set that are
studied under theology (*'ilm al-kalam* – also *'ilm al-'aqa'id*) and are
mainly devoted to exposition of the attributes of God, the nature of
good and evil, matters of concern to the hereafter, etc.

The schools of law differ from the schools of theology in that the former
expound mainly the practical rules of Shariah (*al-ahkam al-'amaliyyah*)
pertaining to the conduct and behavior of the competent person (*mukallaf*),
whereas theological schools are concerned mainly with dogmatics, matters
of belief and matters pertaining to the world of the unseen, or *ghaybiyyat*.
The Shi'i schools are divided into three, namely the Imamiyah (also known
as Ithna 'Ashariyyah, and Ja'fariyyah respectively – the former because they

believe in twelve imams, and the latter carries the name of their sixth imam, Ja'far al Sadiq), being the largest and has followers mainly in Iran and Iraq; the Zaydiyah (mainly in the Yemen) and the Isma'iliyah (residing mainly in India, East Africa and dispersed elsewhere). The Shi'i schools are at once both theological and legal. For they combine the teachings of their leading imams, who are not merely experts on jurisprudence but also theological figures. The doctrine of Imamate in Shi'i Islam is also an integral part of Shia theology.

Q50)   Do the Sunni and Shia follow a different Shariah?

A)   No. Insofar as the Shariah is divinely revealed, Muslims of all schools and sects follow the same Shariah, including Sunnis and Shi'is. They all believe in the Qur'an and Prophet Muhammad, and all pray their five daily prayers in the direction of the Ka'bah without any differ-ence. But their respective schools of law and jurisprudence differ in matters of detail. Such differences are not only seen in Sunni and Shi'i juristic thought and interpretation, but among the four lead-ing schools of Sunni jurisprudence, and those of the Shi'i schools, as well. They all differ over details. That said, since the leading schools of Islamic law recognise one another as valid interpretations of the Shariah, they have much in common and often borrow from one another for purposes of legal reform. This is, in fact, the subject of the principle of selection (*takhayyur* or *takhyir*) in Islamic jurisprudence, which essentially enables all schools to select and adopt formulas and principles from one another, and integrate them into their own school. This happened on many occasions in the twentieth century when Sunni Hanafi countries, for instance, selectively adopted differ-ent interpretations of the Maliki, Shafii or Hanbali schools, and vice versa into their own laws. The relatively more egalitarian treatment of Shia law of female relatives in matters concerning property rights and inheritance provide potential for the future of selection (*takhyir*) in Shariah law reform in the context of Sunni law.

Q51)   Is the plurality of interpretation among the various Sunni schools/ *madhhabs* of Islamic law a source of conflict among them?

A)   No, it is not a source of conflict. Each of the four recognised Sunni *madhhabs* have made a distinctive contribution to the development of legal thought, interpretation and enrichment of the original sources.

These schools emerged in the second and third centuries AH/ eighth-ninth AD in the heyday of scholastic developments when originality of interpretation and novel contribution were the recognised criteria of establishing a new school of thought or *madhhab*.

One may broadly characterise the schools of Islamic law as a diversity within unity. None have sought to break the unitarian character of Islam and its Shariah nor to declare a separate Shariah of its own. Within that umbrella of unity, each has its characteristics that relate to their surrounding geographical factors, their history and the custom and culture of the societies in which they emerged. The early scholastic centres of Islamic law emerged in two different geographical and cultural settings: Iraq (Basrah and Kufa), and the Hijaz (Mecca and Madinah). Those which emerged in Iraq were further away from the Hijaz and more open to the exercise of personal opinion (*ra'y*) and reason in the conduct of *ijtihad* side by side with the revealed text. They had also greater historical exposure to other cultural traditions, in particular the Sassanides of Persia. The scholastic centres of Mecca and Madinah were, on the other hand, more restrictive over the use of opinion and reason in the understanding of the revealed text and in matters of interpretation. At around the end of the eighth century AD these, geographical schools began to give way to schools that bore the personal names of their imams. The four Sunni schools thus became known as the Hanafi, Maliki, Shafii and Hanbali, each after their respective imams; Abu Hanifah Nu'man ibn Thabit, Malik ibn Anas al-Asbahi, Muhammad ibn Idris al-Shafii, and Ahmad ibn Hanbal. This personalised naming is also a feature to a large extent of the Shi'i schools. Some of the distinctive features of the leading Sunni and Shia schools will be highlighted in the following paragraphs. Much to their credit, they have all spoken of their peers and the imams of other schools with great admiration and respect, and none have claimed exclusivity for their own views. When in doubt over an issue or question, they would typically refer to their sources in the Qur'an and Sunnah and ask their followers not to follow their views in the event that they could find better evidence in the higher sources on which they relied themselves.

Q52) How do the various schools law differ over legal doctrines and principles? Can you explain?

A) I shall start by underlining some of the salient features of the Hanafi scool first and then proceed with the others.

The Hanafi school, led by the imam Abu Hanifah (d. 150 AH/767 CE), has the largest following of the Sunni schools to this day, and is seen to be more protective of the personal liberty and choice of the individual compared to the other schools, just as it also tends to be more lenient in matters of crime and punishment. The element of personal consent and freedom of contract, for instance, is recognised for an adult girl who is qualified to conclude her own contract of marriage, whereas the other three schools, as well as the Shia generally, make the marriage of even adult girls subject to the approval of their marriage guardian (*wali*). Guardianship over the person of individuals must be confined, according to the Hanafi school, to the needs of the ward and there is no such need after the minor has attained the age of majority. Textual support for this view has been sought by the Hanafis in the Qur'an where the text grants the adult woman full authority to manage her own property. It has been argued on this basis that there is no reason why this liberty of action should also not be extended to her marriage. Imam Abu Hanifah has similarly refused to validate judicial interdiction (*al-hajr*) of the idiot (*safih*) and the insolvent debtor on the analysis that restricting the freedom of these individuals is a harm greater than the possible loss of property they might otherwise incur. The imam also held that no one, including the judge, may impose restrictions on the owner's absolute right to the use of his or her property even if it inflicted some harm on another person, provided it did not amount to exorbitant harm (*darar fahish*).

With reference to the punishment of adultery/*zina*, which the Qur'an specifies at 100 lashes of the whip, the majority is inclined to extend the same by analogy to sodomy. Imam Abu Hanifah has regarded this as a discrepant analogy which is invalid, in addition to the basic position the Hanafi school takes that in matters of punishment, reference can only be made to the text and not to an analogy to the text, due to the inherent uncertainties of analogical reasoning. Analogical reasoning (*qiyas*) is, in other words, not valid with regard to the prescribed (*hudud*) penalties. The Hanafi school is distinguished by developing analogical reasoning (*qiyas*), juristic preference (*istihsan*) and custom (*'urf*) into the recognised sources of law and judgment, as these are known to be the Hanafi contributions to the legal theory of *usul al-fiqh*.

The Hanafi school has the largest following of all the schools due to its official adoption by the Ottoman Turks in the early sixteenth century. It is now predominant in Turkey, Syria, Jordan, Lebanon, Pakistan, Afghanistan, Bangladesh and among the Muslims of India, and its adherents constitute about one-third of present-day Muslims.

Q53) How would you describe the Maliki school of law?

A) The Maliki school emerged next in chrolnological order to that of its Hanafi counterpart. It was founded by Malik ibn Anas al-Asbahi (d. 179/795) who spent his entire life in Madinah except for a brief pilgrimage to Mecca. The Maliki school has followers in north Africa and is currently predominant in Morocco, Algeria, Tunisia, upper Egypt, the Sudan, Bahrain and Kuwait. It is versatile and may be said in many ways more comprehensive than the other schools. Whereas most of the other schools are expressive of reservation over one or the other of the jurisprudential doctrines for which they became well known, the so-called secondary proofs or sources of Shariah, the Maliki school has validated virtually the entire range of the proofs that are upheld by the other three Sunni schools. Maliki jurisprudence has thus opened the scope and source materials of *ijtihad* more widely than most and it is in this respect distinguished by its comprehensive approach to the understanding of Shariah. In addition, the Maliki school has proposed two new proofs or doctrines, namely the Madini consensus (*ijma' ahl al-Madinah*), and blocking the means to an evil end (*sad aldhara'i'*) to the range of secondary proofs, and it is a strong advocate also of the doctrine of public interest (*istislah*, or *maslahah*) as a source of law and judgment in its own right. In Imam Malik's view, since Madinah has been the place where the Prophet and his Companions lived; just as its customary and cultural practices have been deeply influenced by their teachings, the Madinese consensus is therefore the most authoritative *ijma'*. Imam Malik also preferred the Madinese practice over the weak and solitary (*Ahad*) hadith. This pragmatic feature of the Maliki doctrine is also reflected in the legal practice (*'amal*) of the Maghreb, which takes more notice than the other schools of the prevailing customs and conditions of the community.

The Maliki law of divorce is more flexible than that of the other schools, including the Shia, and it was the first also to recognise judicial divorce on the ground of injurious treatment of the wife by her husband. The majority ruling on this issue entitled the wife to judicial relief whereby the court may punish the recalcitrant husband. Furthermore, the Maliki contribution to this subject is distinguished by its recognition of a type of divorce, known as *khul*, which is initiated by the wife, who proposes dissolution of marriage by mutual agreement and the return of any dower she may have received from her husband. These features of the Maliki law of divorce have been adopted, in turn, by many Muslim countries and jurisdictions in their Islamic family law reform legislations. *Khul* divorce is also recognised by the other schools but they make it dependent on the husband's consent, whereas the Maliki school authorises the court to approve it even without the husband's agreement. The Maliki school also accepts the testimony of discerning children in minor conflicts so long as they have not left the scence of the incident,

None of the leading imams have encouraged unquestioning imitation (*taqlid*) and Imam Malik has made his standing clear in this regard by saying: 'I am only a human, maybe I am wrong or maybe I am right. So, look into my opinions; if they are in agreement with the Qur'an and Sunnah, accept them, otherwise reject them.' It is interesting to note that when the Abbasid caliph al-Mansur offered to adopt Imam Malik's *magnum opus, al-Muwatta'* as the sole guide to court and government practice in the Abbasid empire, the imam declined and responded that the Companions of the Prophet had differed among themselves and tolerated disagreement in matters of interpretation and *ijtihad* and that this should be allowed to continue.

Q54) How would you characterise the Shafii school?

A) The leader of this school and its founder, Muhammad ibn Idris al-Shafii (d. 205/820), was a disciple of Imam Malik but became well-known for his formulation of the legal theory, the sources or roots of the law, the *usul al-fiqh*. Al-Shafii was the first to identify these primarily at four: the word of God in the Qur'an, the divinely inspired conduct or Sunnah of the Prophet, general consensus (*ijma'*), and reasoning by analogy (*qiyas*). He came out strongly in support of the Sunnah, which he elevated in rank almost to the level of the Qur'an, except in matters of belief where the Sunnah did not command an equal authority. In his renowned book, *al-Risalah*, al-Shafii expounded the legal theory of the sources of law in a way that has basically remained unchanged ever since. In its general orientation, Shafii jurisprudence takes an intermediate stance between the two most eminent movements of his time: the partisans of opinion (*Ahl al-Ra'y*) and the partisans of hadith (*Ahl al-Hadith*). Imam Shafii's purpose was to reconcile these two trends and strike a balance between the traditionist proclivities of the Maliki school and the pragmatism of the Hanafi.

Imam Shafii rejected the Hanafi doctrine of *Istihsan* (juristic preference) and the Maliki doctrine of *Istislah* (considerations of public interest) for their heavy reliance on juristic opinion (*ra'y*). For his staunch support of the Sunnah, the imam earned the appellation in Baghdad of the Champion of Sunnah (*nasir al-Sunnah*). He is also known to have developed two different schools, the Old school (*qadim*), which he founded in Baghdad prior to departing for Egypt, and his New school (*jadid*), which he developed during his last five years of residence in Egypt. The imam revised many of his earlier *fatwas* by reference to the culture and custom of Egyptian society, which he found different in so many ways to the cultural setting of Iraq. He also understood, much like Imam Abu Hanifah, the Shariah to be concerned mainly with the evident aspects of human conduct. It was not therefore for the judge and the jurist to inquire into the hidden meanings of the text nor into the undeclared thoughts and motives of individuals. For this reason these two schools (Hanafi and Shafii) are known as the externalists, as opposed to the Maliki and Hanbali schools that pay more attention to the internalities of human conduct. For instance, when a man marries a woman for quick gratification without intending a lifelong commitment of a genuine marriage, and intends it to be followed by a quick divorce – is this marriage valid? For the Hanafis and Shafiis it is, for all that matters to them is whether there is a valid contract that fulfills all the requirements and conditions of a valid contract of marriage, regardless of underlying intentions. The Maliki and Hanbali schools would be inclined, on the other hand, to look beyond the surface and regard this as a corrupt marriage that distorts the intention of that contract. Yet the majority of Muslim jurists, including the Shafiis, maintain that adjudication and court decisions are to be founded on obvious evidence and proof, not on hidden and unproven motives and factors, which cannot be accepted unless there is objective evidence to support it.

The Shafii school is currently prevalent in Lower Egypt, East Africa, Indonesia, Malaysia, Brunei, the Muslim minorities of Thailand and the Philippines and has many followers also in Palestine, Jordan and Syria.

Q55) How would you characterise the Hanbali school of law?

A) The Hanbali school was founded by Imam Ahmad ibn Hanbal (d. 241/855), who took the Shafii emphasis on the authority of

Sunnah a step further and spearheaded a campaign against the Rationalsits or the *Ahl al-Ra'y* so much so that for some time he was regarded more of a traditionist (*muhaddith*) rather than a jurist (*faqih*). His main work, *al-Musnad* (lit. the Verified), is also a collection, the largest in fact, of some 40,000 hadith. He uses analogical reasoning (*qiyas*) very little and relies mainly on the Qur'an and hadith as well as the precedent of the Companions. His teachings were later developed by his disciples and commanded a widespread following for some time, but then the numbers suffered a continuous decline. In the eighteenth century, the Wahhabi puritanical movement in the Arabian Peninsula adopted it and drew inspiration from the works of the leading Hanbali scholar Ahmad Taqi al-Din Ibn Taymiyyah (d. 728/1328). The Hanbali school is currently predominant in Saudi Arabia and has followers in Oman, Qatar, Bahrain and Kuwait. Imam ibn Hanbal has been quoted to have said: 'Do not imitate me, nor Malik, nor [Abu] Thawr [of Baghdad d. 240/855] nor ['Abd al-Rahman] a-Awza'i [of Syria d. 157/774], but take from where we have taken.' This has prompted a twentieth- century scholar, Muhammad Yusuf Musa, to pose the question: 'Where are we in relationship to this now?' pointing at the scholastic tradition of imitation (*taqlid*), which has become so widespread as to characterise the Muslim mentality and scholarship of our time to this day. People have arguably become wont to strictly adhering to their own particular schools/*madhhabs* as if it were an obligation under Shariah.

The Hanbali school's contribution stands out with regard to the Shariah principle of permissibility (*ibahah*), especially in the areas of contracts and transactions, by giving greater scope to the creative will of the contracting parties. Whereas the majority of schools maintained that the basic characteristics of nominate contracts are determined by Shariah and the contracting parties have only a limited scope to change them and insert stipulations of their own, the Hanbali school maintained that the will of contracting parties can create unilateral obligation (*iltizam*) based on the principle of permissibility (*ibahah*). Thus, a man may validly stipulate in a marriage contract that he will not marry a second wife. Since polygamy is only a permissibility, not an obligation, it may be subjected to stipulations. The other schools disallow this on the analysis that Shariah has made polygamy lawful, a position which may not be circumvented, nor overruled by the will of the contracting parties. Ibn Hanbal maintained on the contrary that contractual stipulations must strictly be observed, which in reference to marriage means that any breach of the stipulation by the husband in respect of avoidance of a polygamous union with another woman, would entitle the existing wife to seek annulment of the marriage contract.

Q56)   What of the Shia – is it also a legal school (madhhab)?

A)   Yes. It is both legal and theological. Shia (lit. faction or group of followers) refer to the followers of the fourth caliph, 'Ali ibn Abu Talib, first cousin of the Prophet and husband of his daughter, Fatimah. The Shi'ites maintain that 'Ali was the first legitimate caliph and successor to the Prophet, and therefore reject the first three caliphs, Abu Bakr, 'Umar ibn al-Khattab, and 'Uthman ibn 'Affan as usurpers. The Shi'is also maintain that the Prophet had expressly declared 'Ali as his successor under guidance from God. They are also called the Imamiyyah because they believe that imam is the repository of the true knowledge of Islam, and hold their imams as erudite and infallible (ma'sum). The Sunnis, and also one of the three Shi'i schools, the Zaydiyyah, do not agree with the idea of infallibility ('ismah) for any imam. For the Sunnis, divine revelation (wahy) ceased with the death of the Prophet Muammad. For the Shia, however, divine guidance which they refer to as inspiration (ilham) continued to be transmitted to their imams even after the Prophet's demise, which is why they include the sayings of their imams in the general body of Sunnah. Until the time of the sixth Imam, Ja'far al-Sadiq (d. 765 AH), Shi'ism had remained political in character, focusing mainly on the issue of succession and arguably lacking a distinct juristic doctrine of its own. It was through the works of Ja'far al-Sadiq (d. 147/765) and his predecessor Imam Muhammad al-Baqir (d. 117/735), whose contributions to the legal theory of usul al-fiqh are commonly acknowledged, that Shi'ism also became a school of jurisprudence. Whereas in Sunni law the head of state is an elected office, Shi'i law maintains that leadership, the imamate, descends in the household of the Prophet through hereditary succession. Although the Shia do not claim to have developed a separate science of *usul al-fiqh*, there are many significant points of departure from the Sunni positions that tend to give the Shia doctrines distinctive characteristics of their own.

The Shi'i followers worldwide are estimated at about ten per cent of the total population of Muslims. They reside mainly in Iran, Iraq, Syria and Lebanon and constitute minorities in many other Muslim countries including Afghanistan, Pakistan, India, Saudi Arabia and East Africa.

Q57)   Is there just one or more Shi'i schools, how would you characterise them?

A)   Of the numerous Shi'i schools that emerged at different periods of time only three have survived: Ithna 'Ashariyyah (or Twelvers, also known as Jafariyyah), Zaydiyyah, and Isma'iliyyah. They differ mainly over the line of succession to which they subscribe after the fourth imam. The Twelvers are named for the number of their 'infallible imams'; and the Zaidiyyah — the so-called 'Fivers', are likewise named for the number of their 'revered imams'. The third branch of Shia, the Isma'iliyyah— are also called 'Seveners' — so named because of the number of their 'infallible imams'. The Isma'iliyyah has two branches: (a) the Bohra Isma'ilis who follow the Jafari *madhhab* (with some Shafii laws and some laws drawn from the works of Qadi Nu'man) under the direction of its leader, the Sultan of the Bohra. They follow al-Musta'li, the ninth Fatimid caliph, and reside mainly in southern Arabia and Syria; and (b) the Nizari Isma'ilis who follow their living imam, the Agha Khan, being the forty-ninth imam in the line of succession from 'Ali and Fatimah – without Islamic law as such. The Nizaris mainly reside in India, Pakistan and Central Asia. The Twelver Shi'ite doctrine that commands the largest following was officially adopted in Persia under the Safavids in 1501 CE, and it still has the largest number of followers in Iran, Iraq, Lebanon and Syria.

The Shi'i laws of marriage, divorce, inheritance and bequest differ in some respects from their Sunni counterparts. They accept, for instance, temporary marriage (*mut'ah*) which the Sunnis do not. Their inheritance laws tend to be more favourable to certain women relatives. With regard to parentage, maternity is established, according to Sunni law, by birth alone, regardless of the presence or absence of a valid marriage between the parents. But under Shi'i law maternity is established only through a lawful marriage. Hence an illegitimate child has no descent even from its mother, and therefore no right to inheritance.

According to the Isma'ili dogma, the words and sentences of the Qur'an have both obvious and hidden meanings. The esoteric meanings of the Qur'an and its allegorical interpretation is known only to their imam, whose knowledge and guidance is indispensable to salvation.

The Zaidiyyah follow Zayd ibn 'Ali (d. 740 AD), the fifth imam in order of the twelve Shi'i imams. They endorse the legitimacy of the three caliphs preceding 'Ali b. Abu Talib and their beliefs do not differ a great deal from the Sunnis. They also do not subscribe to the notion of infallibility of the imams and they mainly reside in the Yemen.

Q58) Do the leading schools of law, or *madhhabs*, differ over the subject matter and themes of Shariah?

A) They do not differ over the basic division of the Shariah into the two main areas of devotional matters (*'ibadat*), which regulate man's relationship with God, and civil transactions (*mu'amalat*), which are of concern to human relations and transactions among people. But they do differ over the more detailed divisions of these two broader divisions of the subject matter of Shariah.

Broadly, the Hanafi school divide civil transactions into five headings of transactions involving exchange of goods and values (*al-mu'awadat al-maliyyah*), equity and trusts (*al-amanat*), matrimonial law (*al-munakahat*), civil litigations (*al-mukhasamat*), administration of estates (*al-mawarith*, also known as *al-tarikat*), crimes and penalties (*al-'uqubat*).

The Shafiis divide the *corpus juris* of Shariah into the four parts of *'ibadat*, which pertain to one's well-being in the hereafter, *mu'amalat*, which relate to one's survival and well-being (*baqa' al-shakhs*) in this world, matrimonial law (*munakahat*) which concern the survival of the species (*baqa' al-naw'*), and penal law (*'uqubat*), which concern the survival of society and civilisation (*baqa' al-madinah*). The Maliki school is more detailed: the Maliki jurist Ahmad ibn Juzay (d. 1339 CE) in his *Qawanin al-Fiqhiyyah* has divided the two major themes of Shariah, namely *'ibadat* and *mu'amalat*, each into ten sub-headings, some of which are not included under either heading by the other schools. The Hanbali classification of the subject matter of Shariah resembles that of the Shafiis albeit with minor changes.

Q59) Are the jurists bound to follow the rulings of the legal school/*madh-hab* of their following?

A) A jurist of the highest standing (a *mujtahid*) who is qualified to carry out independent interpretation (*ijtihad*) directly through consulting the original sources of Shariah is not bound to follow the rulings of the legal schools he or she may be attached to. A jurist who has attained this status, that is a full-fledged *mujtahid*, is not even permitted to follow the opinion of others nor to exercise imitation (*taqlid*), but must always act on his or her own understanding of the Shariah based on conviction. That said, it is the tradition of *taqlid* that has for various reasons dominated the much longer stretch of the history of Islamic scholarship, both Sunni and Shia, and has proven difficult also to dismantle its hold over the existing body of Islamic law or *fiqh*. More recently, and ever since the early twentieth century, leading Muslim scholars have called for the revival and rejuvenation of original interpretation and *ijtihad*. One particular area that may be mentioned, however, where *ijtihad* finds a limited role to play, is the *muqaddarat*, or strictly quantified portions of Shariah laws, such as the laws of inheritance, on account of the fact that this area of Islamic law is based mainly in the Qur'an consisting of quantified shares allocated to various relatives. The Qur'anic scheme of inheritance is fairly self-contained, unlike some of the other branches of law which are based on juristic reasoning and rules extracted from the sources through rational methods of enquiry. Thus, a jurist capable of exercising *ijtihad* in other areas of Shariah may still follow the rulings of his school of following when it comes to inheritance.

That said, even a *mujtahid* of the highest rank may on occasions follow the ruling of an established school of Islamic law, or an opinion or interpretation of individual scholars, if he happens to agree with it and understands its evidential basis. This is not blind imitation or *taqlid*. The discredited *taqlid* is one which is based mainly on mimicry or copying and following others without understanding and conviction on the part of the follower.

Q60) How do the scholastic divisions and *madhhabs* reflect on the unitarian character of Islam?

A) The *madhhabs* are more historical than normative as one does not find categorically supportive evidence for their validity as such. There were, in fact, no recognised *madhhabs*, during the first century of Islam, or even longer. If one speculates to find supportive evidence for the development of these schools, then that which is quoted in support of *ijtihad* may also be cited for *madhhabs*. For the emergence of various schools of thought was an *ijtihad*-related phenomenon. The various *madhhabs* differed mainly in *ijtihadi* matters. Another element one may refer to by way of supportive evidence is the recognition in Shariah of reasoned disagreement (*ikhtilaf*), which is also like another name for *ijtihad*. Some have also quoted a hadith, which is a weak hadith, and one which Imam Shafi'i has not quoted in his renowned work *al-Risalah*, the hadith which says: 'disagreement of my *ummah* is a (a source of) mercy (*ikhtilafu ummati rahmah*)'. It is a weak hadith in view of the fact that Islam is strong on unity and *tawhid*. Unity in the essence of belief and the essentials of Islam is not open to any level of disagreement.

The Qur'an has in many places declared the Muslim community as one nation – *ummatan wahidatan* – which is at once the witness and guardian of its own unity. Notwithstanding a certain level of tension that the plurality of *madhhabs* presents to the unitarian spirit of *tawhid*, the various schools of law, it may be added, have actually interpreted the Shariah in light of the needs and realities of their time. Diversity and pluralism in *fiqh* is acceptable, and has proven inevitable, however only in regard to the practical legal rules, but not over the essence of belief or the essentials of Islam. All the leading Sunni schools we have discussed are, in fact united, in the articles of Islamic faith (*iman* – referring to six pillars, namely: belief in God, in His Books, His Messengers, the angels, resurrection, and the Day of Judgment), and the Five pillars of Islam (testimonial of the faith, prayers, charity/*zakah*, fasting/*sawm*, and the pilgrimage of haj). This is also true of the Shi'i *madhhabs*, although one or two differences are noted in regard to the articles of faith. Shia theology records the five pillars or articles of belief as follows: (1) affirmation of the Oneness of God (*tawhid*); (2) justice of God (*'adl*); (3) necessity of prophethood (*nubuwwah*); (4) necessity of imamate (*imamah*); and (5) the Day of Judgment (*ma'ad*).

The *madhhabs* have evidently contributed to the efflorescence of legal and theological sciences and doctrines, and have, to that extent, been a prime mover behind the impressive legacy of scholarship they have developed. On the negative side, the *madhhabs* have also, unwittingly perhaps, become the main instrument of imitation (*taqlid*) and division among Muslims – sometimes condoning unhealthy fanaticism, even factional fighting and fratricide of the kind we have recently been witnessing in Iraq, Pakistan and elsewhere.

☐ Legal Maxims

+ 'Fatwa is not valid if it exits the *mufti*'s own *madhhab* of following.'[1]
+ 'The ruling of his imam for him (follower) is like the ruling of the Lawgiver for the independent *mujtahid*.'[2]
+ 'Every follower must subscribe to a particular *madhhab*.'[3]
+ 'Effect is given to what the upright judge considers preferable in the [rulings of a] *madhhab* in regards to a disputed matter among people.'[4]
+ 'Exiting disagreement is recommendable.'*[5]

Note: The reader will notice that we have quoted no supportive evidence for *madhhabs* from the Qur'an or hadith. This is because there is none, and what we were able to find of legal maxims in support of *madhhabs* is also very little. This goes to show that *madhhabs* are entirely historical without any scriptural support, as they emerged and crystallised well over 200 years after the advent of Islam and the Prophet's death. The pioneering age of Islam and the most important period of its history, incluing the periods of Companions and their Successors, was in other words, without any scholastic divides, or *madhhabs*.

---

* It is on this basis that the *ulama*' have reached a consensus to validate the congregational prayers of a follower of the Hanafi *madhhab* behind a Shafi'i Imam and vice versa, notwithstanding their differences in some aspects of the ritual prayer (*salah*) and that of the ablution (*wudu*') preceding it.

V

The Scale of Five Values (*al-Ahkam al-Khamsah*)

Q61) How does Islamic law categorise human actions? Do the *Madhhabs*, Sunni and Shia, differ over this?

A) Human actions are categorised according to a scale of Five Values, namely those that are obligatory (*wajib*), recommended (*mandub*, also *mustahab*), permissible (*mubah*, also *ja'iz*), reprehensible (*makruh*) and forbidden (*haram*). The first and last of these, namely the *wajib* and the *haram*, are legal categories in that that they are binding and may also be justiciable. These two categories mainly originate in the decisive rulings of Qur'an and hadith and are fairly limited in scope, whereas the remaining three categories occupy a much wide⬤ space, as they are also largely developed through juristic interpretation and *ijtihad*. The *ijtihadi* conclusions and rules concerning the evaluative labeling of human conduct into these categories are, on the whole, instructive and often rationally undisputable yet not binding – unless they are also upheld and endorsed by general consensus (*ijma'*), in which case they become a part of the actionable ruling (*hukm*) of the Shariah and acquire a binding force. These five values, known as *al-ahkam al-khamsah*, constitute the main bulk of the practical or positive law, the *ahkam 'amaliiyyah*, and the main subject matter of *fiqh*. The Scale of Five Values consists mainly of identifiers of the value attached to practical conduct of competent persons. The *wajib* and *haram* pertaining especially to human relations and *mu'amalat* are also enforceable in the courts of Shariah, but those which pertain to the purely religious and devotional aspects of Islam, such as performing the prayer or haj, normally do not give rise to legal action. The other three categories are not enforceable and basically fall outside the ambit of law enforcement. They are matters mainly of personal choice and may consist of advice, encouragement or discouragement, etc., that should be followed, in the case of recommendable/*mandub*, and should be avoided, in the case of reprehensible/*makruh*, whereas the permissible/*mubah* is totally neutral and may or may not be acted upon. The advice contained in these three categories may have cultural import and consequences and may also affect aspects of personal piety, customary and social relations, but it is not actionable in the way the *wajib* and the *haram* are.

Q62) Are these value pointers the same in all *madhhabs*?

A) Broadly they are about the same in all the leading schools, including the Shia, although there are differences of detail among the *madhhabs* over what they may or may not consider permissible or reprehensible for human consumption in animals, birds and sea food and even in the performance of the rituals of worship. Some have added sub-categories to the scale of values and introduced different terminologies for their identification. The Hanafi school has, for instance, divided the *wajib* into the two types of *fard* and *wajib* respectively, a division that refers to the evidential bases of each. If the *wajib* is based on a clear text and is totally free of doubtful elements, it is obligatory of the first order, or *fard*. But if there be an element of doubt in the evidential basis of *wajib*, such as *wajib* that is grounded in a solitary (*ahad*) hadith, then it would be an obligation of the second order, or *wajib*, according to the Hanafis.

A similar approach is taken to *makruh*, which the Hanafi school has subdivided into the two categories of *makruh* that is closer to haram (i.e. *makruh tahrimi*), and *makruh* that is closer to permissible or *mubah* (i.e. *makruh tanzihi*). *Haram* has also been divided into the two types of *haram* for its own sake (i.e., *haram li-dhatihi*), such as murder and theft, and *haram* due to an extraneous factor (i.e. *haram li-ghayrihi*), such as sexual intercourse with one's wife during the daytime in Ramadan, or conducting trade after the last call to Friday prayer – although this last division of the *haram* is adopted by all the leading schools, not just the Hanafis. These classifications have legal and religious consequences that will be taken into consideration in the evaluation of conduct and in court decisions as the case may be. The Shia Imamiyyah use the same five-fold terminology and classification as the majority of the Sunnis, there being very little variation of note in the choice of terms and even their basic definitions and applied consequences.

Q63)   How are these value pointers determined and identified?

A)   The lawful and the unlawful (*halal, haram*) are determined by reference to the clear text of the Qur'an and authentic hadith, known as the *nusus*. The Qur'an often uses the word *haram* or its derivatives in regards to certain conduct or substance, etc., and so does the hadith, which provide the textual authority for the identification of *haram* and *halal*. Pronouncing something *haram*, or *halal* is a sensitive matter due to the fact that the Qur'an warns the believers against declaring things *haram* or *halal* without there being clear evidence for them to do so. This is also true of the obligatory (*wajib*) which cannot be established without a clear text in the revealed sources. What is said here is also extended to devotional matters (*'ibadat*) in toto, which can only be established by the presence of a clear text. Juristic reasoning and *ijtihad* cannot therefore establish an act of worship in the absence of a clear textual authority.

As for the other three categories of reprehensible, permissible, and recommendable, these too are identified by the text of the Qur'an or hadith, but the text in question may be either clear and categorical, or else open to interpretation, and the jurists draw their conclusions from the indications they find in the textual sources. There are many references in the Qur'an, for instance, where God Most High declares that He 'loves' something or that He does not love, or else that He denounces a certain conduct without declaring it either *wajib* or *haram*. There may also be indications that the nature of the conduct referred to may in some ways be shown to fall into the one or the other of these categories: whether it is reprehensible, recommended, or neutral/permissible. If there is a text, for instance, declaring that 'God loves not the prodigals – *musrifin*', it is likely that extravagance is reprehensible/*makruh*, simply because the owner spends of what he owns, and that conduct by itself cannot take the idea of a total prohibition. There are also many references in the Qur'an where God Most High declares that He loves those 'who do good or who are good to others' – *muhsinun* from the root word *ihsan*. Since the act is not specified and it consists of a very large number of things, the jurist is most likely to classify acts of *ihsan* as recommendable (*mandub/mustahab*). In one hadith the Prophet has, for instance, declared that 'divorce is the most hated of all permissible things in the eyes of God'. The only reasonable evaluation pointed at here is that it is a *makruh*. In another hadith, it is said 'whoever makes a [fresh] ablution for the Friday prayer, it is good, but if he takes a full bath, it is better'. The language of the hadith here points at something praiseworthy, most likely a *mandub*.*

SUPPORTIVE EVIDENCE

☐ Qur'an and Hadith

+ 'God has explained to you in detail what is forbidden to you [which you must observe] unless you are compelled into it.' (Q al-An'am, 6:119)[1]
+ 'And say not any falsehood your tongues may put forth that "this is lawful and this is forbidden," for this is tantamount to ascribing lies to God.' (Q al-Nahl, 16:116)[2]
+ 'And he (Prophet) allows to them (the believers) what is good [and pure] and forbids to them what is impure [and unclean].' (Q al-A'raf, 7:157)[3]
+ 'God loves it that His concessions are utilised in the same way that He loves His commands to be observed.' (Hadith)[4]

☐ Legal Maxims

+ 'What is indispensable for the completion of an obligation also becomes an obligation.'[5]
+ 'The norm in regards to [infliction of] harm is prohibition.'[6]

---

* See for further details on the Five Values, Mohammad Hashim Kamali, *Principles of Islamic Jurisprudence*, Cambridge: Islamic Texts Society, 3rd edn, 2003, pp. 413–431.

- 'The rules [of Shariah] proceed on that which is evident. For what is hidden [in the minds and hearts of people] is referred to God Most High.'[7]
- 'The means to all that which is prohibited is also prohibited.'[8]
- 'Whenever an obligation is contingent on two causes, both must be present for the obligation to fall due.'[9]
- 'Obligations are informed by considerations of moderation and removal of hardship.' (Shariah law in other words does not impose impossible nor extremely difficult obligations.)[10]
- 'Recourse is usually made to the moderate position and approach, which is considered to be normative.'[11]
- 'Concessions do not attach to transgressions. (i. a transgressor may not take advantage of a Shariah concession.)[12]
- 'What is permissible may be subjected to safety requirements.'[13]
- 'When the *haram* and the *halal* co-exist, the *haram* prevails.'[14]
- 'The effective causes of [shariah] rules indicate the purpose of the Lawgiver and should be upheld whenever they are known.'[15]
- 'Avoidance of the reprehensible is preferred to securing a recommendable.'[16]
- 'When two obligatory (orders) cannot be observed both, the more preferable is prioritised and the other is omitted in a Shariah-compliant manner.'[17]
- 'Greater caution is in order in exiting the prohibition toward permissibility than the other way around.'[18]
- 'The basic principles of Shariah require that one who has not intended a transgression is not punished.'[19]
- 'The best of every man's conduct is that which is most beneficial to others, most fruitful and most refined.'[20]
- 'The reprehensible is not committed for [the sake of securing] the recommendable.'[21]
- 'What is indispensable for securing a recommendable is also recommendable.'[22]
- 'The obligatory is not abandoned for the sake of recommendable.'[23]

VI

Shariah Court Proceedings, Evidence and Proof

Q64)   What is a Shariah court and how does it work?

A)   In the context of modern legal systems, a Shariah court is the court
of law applying laws derived from the Shariah in places where
Shariah is recognised as applied law under the constitution, basic
law or statutory provisions. The law often specifies the procedure
of enacting legislation or by-laws based on Shariah that will then
be applied in Shariah courts of the country concerned. The functioning of Shariah courts is thus regulated by statutory law, and it
is often the personal law aspects of Shariah that is the applied law.
In arriving at judicial decisions, recourse is made by Shariah courts
to the codified laws and by-laws as well as the *juris corpus* of Islamic
law, including authoritative scholarly views from across the legal
schools (*madhhabs*), and even rules on which there may be differences of opinion (*ikhtilaf*). An official *madhhab* is sometimes adopted
by the state law or constitution but there also exists a degree of flexibility through the principles of *takhayyur* and *talfiq* (selection, and
patching-up respectively), as already mentioned. What this means is
that the Shariah court in say a Hanafi jurisdiction is often enabled
to resort to the other schools of Islamic law in the event where the

court cannot find a relevant solution in the applied statutory laws of the country or those of the Hanafi *fiqh* to the case under its consideration. It may in such situations borrow from the Shafi'i, Maliki or Hanbali sources in order to adjudicate the case before it.

In a country such as Afghanistan which has, under its 2004 constitution (Art. 131) recognised the Shi'i *madhhab* and jurisprudence to be applicable in cases of personal law in which both parties are of Shi'i persuasion, space is created for cross-fertilisation of ideas between the Sunni and Shi'i jurisprudence.* In the past we have seen this kind of exchange on a limited scale in the area of legislation but not much in judicial decision- making. There is no reason why juridical *ijtihad* in a Sunni jurisdiction should not utilise the relevant resources of Shi'i jurisprudence, and vice versa, when such would prove advantageous toward realisation of the higher objectives of justice in a case under court consideration. One can also envisage possibilities for cross-fertilisation of ideas in cases that involve both Sunni and Shi'i parties or litigants, in which eventuality the court may decide to exercise some kind of *talfiq* (patching-up) of the relevant rules of two different *madhhabs* in a case before its consideration.

In countries where Shariah courts are courts of specialised jurisdiction, such as Malaysia, Brunei, Nigeria, Sudan, etc., a Shariah court would typically have limited jurisdiction, for example, only applicable to Muslims, and often confined to family or personal law (marriage, divorce, child custody, for example) and inheritance. In the past, as it is also the case today in some countries (for example Saudi Arabia and Afghanistan), there was no need for specifically designated 'Shariah courts' insofar as the legal system itself was based on the Shariah and Shariah courts were courts of general jurisdiction. Furthermore, the ruling authorities and head of state in Muslim countries are authorised to issue edicts and regulations of non-Shariah origin under the doctrine of *siyasah shar'iyyah* (shariah–oriented policy). Regulations and ordinances of this kind were in the past typically issued on procedural matters of concern to court organisation and practices. The courts of justice in Saudi Arabia are courts of general jurisdiction that apply the Shariah generally and are authorised to receive and adjudicate all types of disputes, and the king has often issued edicts on matters of concern to Shariah court organisation and

---

* This has yet to become a reality due the fact that Afghanistan has ever since the 2004 constitution been embroiled in security problems and bad politics.

procedure. That said, a mixed pattern of Shariah courts, operating side by side with such other tribunals as commercial courts, industrial courts, military courts, etc., tends to prevail in most present-day Muslim countries.

Q65) Who are *qadis* and how do they differ from *muftis*?

A) *Qadis* are formally appointed judges learned in Shariah who preside over judicial proceedings in courts that apply the Shariah. *Qadis* are appointed by the ruler or government and their decisions or judgments are enforceable under the applied laws of the country. *Muftis* were traditionally used like legal advisors or lawyers, private scholars and practitioners not appointed by anyone and gave *fatwa* or legal advice in their traditional capacities. Country-specific differences regarding the role and function of *muftis* do exist among Muslim countries. *Muftis* are able, in Muslim countries that have not totally bureaucratised the office of *mufti*, to give a legal counsel, a response or *fatwa* and expound the ruling of Shariah and religion on a particular issue that is put to them often by private individuals. Thus both *qadis* and *muftis* are qualified to extract the rulings of Shariah from the source evidence to be applied to a particular case or issue presented to them. Both may also rely on each other's input and advice: just as a *mufti* may refer to previous decisions of the *qadis* in issuing a *fatwa*, so too with the *qadi*, who may cite or solicit the *fatwa* of a *mufti* on certain legal or religious issues. A *qadi* is a state appointed official and cannot, as such, be a private or a lay person, whereas this is not a requirement with regard to a *mufti* – although that difference is also disappearing between them as nowadays *muftis* are also state functionaries for the most part. As already stated in a previous section, the *qadi* should not mix the positive laws of *fiqh* with theology and ethics (*'aqa'id* and *akhlaq*), but the *mufti* is expected to offer sound advice regardless of these boundaries. In many present-day Muslim countries, the office of the *mufti* is separate and operates independently of the judiciary and some, including Egypt, Syria, Jordan, have even a designated Grand Mufti who advises the state on Shariah and religious matters. Broadly, judges adjudicate whereas *muftis* give opinion. Whereas giving of opinions in controversial religious matters can jeopardise independence and impartiality of the judicial office, this may not be the same when giving a *fatwa*.

Q66) How many witnesses are necessary for different types of cases? Are female witnesses equal to male, or are they differently treated?

A) The number of witnesses required according to Shariah manuals is as follows. If the testimony concerns property and other civil transactions, the requirement is two men of upright character, or two women and a man, and in some cases it may be one male witness plus a solemn oath by the plaintiff, although this last is accepted only by some jurists, not all. In crimes and punishments, only two male witnesses may testify although the Hanafi school holds that two women and a man may testify for all disputes other than the prescribed *hudud* penalties (see below). If the testimony is about fornication or sodomy, then it requires four male eyewitnesses. If the testimony concerns matters which men do not typically handle, such family matters, childbirth and matters that are considered privy to women, then it is sufficient to have one woman witness, as female testimony in such matters carries greater weight than male witnesses. In the absence of a female witness in such cases, recourse may be had to two male witnesses, or a man and two women.

The stipulation that two women take the place of one man in property and commercial disputes is explained by reference to the fact that in the past, especially in the male-dominated Arab societies, women customarily did not attend to commercial transactions or judicial disputes, and their retentiveness was consequently deemed to be weaker than men. These positions have been changing though, and many Muslim countries nowadays admit not only female witnesses but also appoint female judges. This is reflective of the larger presence of women in the public sphere, in education and employment sectors and other areas of concern to court litigation – hence their competence to act both as witnesses and judges. That said, each country has its own laws and practices that may need to be consulted for a more accurate response.

Q67) Does the Qur'an attach less value to the testimony of female witnesses?

A) There is a verse in the Qur'an on this subject which I shall presently discuss in order to develop a fuller picture of this somewhat contentious issue. I have dealt with this in detail, however, in a book I have previously published which is still in print.* I start by quoting the relevant verse as follows:

When you enter into transactions involving a debt for a fixed period [in the future], reduce it to writing. And let a scribe write it down between you in fairness... And bring two witnesses from among your men. Should there not be two men, then a man and two women of the women that you are pleased with [their uprightness] to be witnesses, so that if the one errs, the other may remind. (Q al-Baqarah, 2:282)[1]

It will be noted that the verse is on a rather specific subject: financial obligations deferred to a future date. According to the Companion ibn 'Abbas and other commentators, this verse was revealed concerning the *salam* forward sale only. *Salam* is a forward sale wherein the price is paid at the time of contract but delivery of the object of sale is deferred to a future date, sometimes for two or three years, as the hadith of *salam* clearly mentions. What is also important to bear in mind is the widespread illiteracy of the Arab society at the time, but which was especially so among women, and there was scarcity of people who were able to write. This concern about the scarcity of writers and scribes is clearly expressed in a subsequent portion of the same verse, which says that the scribes and witnesses should not refuse to write and testify.

Note also that the Arabic dual pronoun *ihdahuma* in the verse *fa-tudhakkir ihdahuma al-'ukhra* can refer either to two male or two female witnesses. The Qur'an laid down the rule that there must be two witnesses to testify, be it male or female, so that the one may remind the other, and that if the witnesses are female, there must be a minimum of two. In this way the text ensured that reminding is not given by a man to a woman or vice versa, but rather by one of the two women to one another. It will be noted also that the verse, in its subsequent portion (this is a long verse, the longest in fact in the Qur'an – almost a full page) makes two exceptions to the documentation of deferred debts: when the parties trust one another, and if the deal is for a short period. In such cases, documentation may be dispensed with. Hence the act of reminding may become necessary even among men, should there be no documentation involved.

---

* Mohammad Hashim Kamali, *Freedom, Equality and Justice in Islam*, Cambridge: Islamic Texts Society, 2002 pp. 65–73.

Two prominent scholars, Ibn Qayyim al-Jawziyyah (d. 1350 CE) and the former Rector of al-Azhar, Mahmud Shaltut (d. 1963), have further observed that the Qur'anic text before us speaks in the language of persuasion and preference and not of laying down a decisive injunction. The text does not preclude, in other words, the possibility of one woman acting as a witness, or women acting on their own without there being any male witnesses. Shaltut thus drew the conclusion that 'the testimony of one woman alone, or of women not accompanied by men, is thus acceptable in order to establish the truth and serve the cause of justice'. It is well known also that the Shariah admits the testimony of one woman and credits it as full proof, in preference even to men, in matters in which women are expected to be better informed, such as pregnancy, childbirth and so forth.

Elsewhere the Qur'an itself (al-Nur, 24:4–6) prefers the testimony of the wife over that of her husband in the context of divorce by imprecations (li'an) where the oaths taken by the husband who charges his wife with adultery are countered by similar oaths taken by the wife, in which case the wife's rebuttal overrules the testimonials of her husband, and the two are separated therewith.

Q68)   Can the decision of a Shariah court be subjected to appellate review?

A)   Yes. Islamic law validates appellate review, especially in cases where the court decision departs from the clear injunctions and rulings of the Qur'an, the Sunnah, and general consensus (ijma'), or when fresh evidence comes to light after the initial court judgment, or indeed when a serious procedural flaw is in the picture. Many of the present-day Muslim countries where Shariah courts operate have also established Shariah appeal courts or tribunals, and often a full-fledged three-tiered structure of Shariah courts equipped with appellate jurisdictions.

Q69)   Does the Shariah permit lying in certain circumstances? What is dissimulation or taqiyyah under Shi'i law?

A)   No. The unqualified prohibition of lying is established by the clear textual rulings of the Qur'an, Sunnah and general consensus. Yet there are three exceptions that originate in the saying of the Prophet: during warfare, when a lie can help save life or settle a raging conflict between two persons; and when a man tells a white lie to flatter his wife. But even then it is with the condition that substantive justice and moral rectitude are not compromised. The Qur'an and Sunnah proscribe, on the other hand, espionage, acting on suspicion, backbiting, and infliction of harm (darar) through false reporting on others. Only the Shi'i jurisprudence has validated taqiyyah (dissimulation) in exceptional situations that may permit one to conceal, for instance, one's religious belief if disclosing it would mean persecution or torture for the individual concerned. Sunni jurisprudence does not recognise the validity of taqiyyah altogether. That said, lying, fraud and misrepresentation are generally forbidden and unacceptable and that goes for all Muslims, Sunni and Shia alike. Judicial decisions must be based on truth and objective standards of evidence and proof under both Sunni and Shia laws.

SUPPORTIVE EVIDENCE

☐ Qur'an and Hadith

+ 'God commands justice and the doing of good, liberality to kith and kin, and He forbids all shameful deeds, injustice and rebellion.' (Q al-Nahl, 16:90)[2]
+ 'God commands you to deliver the trusts to those to whom they are due, and when you judge among people, you judge with justice.' (Q al-Nisa', 4:58)[3]
+ 'O believers! Be maintainers of justice as witnesses to God, even if it be against yourselves, your parents and your relatives, or whether it be against the rich or the poor.' (Q 4:135)[4]
+ 'And let not the hatred of a people swerve you away from justice. Be just for it is closest to piety.' (Q al-Ma'idah, 5:8)[5]
+ 'And the words of thy Lord find fulfilment in truth and justice. None can change His words.' (Q al-An'am, 6:115)[6]
+ 'When the litigants appear before you, do not decide for one until you hear the other. It is more likely that by doing so, the reasons for a judgment will become clear to you.' (Hadith)[7]
+ 'If people were to be granted what they claim, on the basis only of their claims, they would claim the blood and property of others, but [when the claimant cannot bring witnesses] the oath is on the defendant.' (Hadith)[8]

+ 'I am but a human. When you bring a dispute to me, some of you may be more eloquent in stating their cases than others. I may consequently adjudicate on the basis of what I hear. If I adjudicate in favour of someone something that belongs to his brother, let him not take it, for this would be like taking a piece of fire.' (Hadith)[9]
+ 'One who has a right is entitled to speak out.' (Hadith)[10]

[] Legal Maxims

+ 'The norm is equal treatment of the litigants in the court hearing sessions.'[11]
+ 'Evidence is not turned into proof without the court judgment.'[12]
+ 'No judgment is issued until after both the litigants are duly heard.' [13]
+ 'The judge is not permitted to adjudicate over hearsay (evidence).'[14]
+ 'Judgment is not issued in absentia.'[15]
+ 'The judge has no powers of pardon or omission in prescribed penalties but he has that in regards to ta'zir offences.'[16]
+ 'A duly issued judgment may not be reversed unless it contravenes the Qur'an, Sunnah or general consensus.'[17]
+ 'Court judgments are meant to be binding.'[18]
+ 'When retaliation (qisas) is not feasible, [payment of] blood money (diyyah) becomes obligatory.'[19]
+ 'Mental capacity is the prerequisite of obligation (taklif).'[20]
+ 'Irresistible duress suspends obligation.'[21]
+ 'There is no obligation without prior knowledge.'[22]
+ 'There is no obligation except within the limits of capacity.'[23]
+ 'A child bears no obligation.'[24]
+ 'Insanity causes omission of obligation.'[25]
+ 'Natural calamity omits obligation.'[26]
+ 'When action and speech are in conflict, the latter is preferred.'[27]
+ 'Immunity of the judge is guaranteed.'[28]
+ 'The judgment of a judge is not invalidated by death or dismissal.'[29]
+ 'The judgment of a judge is effective until the time he knows of his dismissal.'[30]
+ 'The plaintiff is entitled to speak first. One who makes a demand may speak first even if the defendant has begun to speak.'[31]

+ 'Infliction of penalties and settlement of disputes are the prerogatives of judges.'[32]
+ 'The considered judgment of an impartial judge of whatever *madhhab* is enforceable in matters on which differential textual rulings
  obtain [in the sources].'[33]
+ 'Administration of penalties, removal of conflicts and [adjudication]
  of civil rights disputes and the like are the prerogatives of judges.'[34]
+ 'The judge is not liable for the error he makes in respect of the assets
  of the Public Treasury.'[35]
+ 'It is impermissible to set aside the judgment of a judge after it is
  duly issued.'[36]
+ 'Any transgression for which a quantified penalty is not available is
  liable to (discretionary punishment of ta'zir).'[37]
+ 'One who unknowingly perpetrates a prohibited act that carries a
  specified punishment is exonerated, but if he knew the prohibition
  and was ignorant only of the quantum of punishment, he is liable to
  punishment.'[38]
+ 'People's lives and properties are not appropriated [by others] by
  means only of claims without the supportive evidence.'[39]
+ 'Adjudication proceeds over that which is apparent not over intentions and (undeclared) secrets.'[40]
+ 'The purpose of adjudication is to give the right-bearers their rights
  and to settle disputes.'[41]
+ 'Retraction of testimony is not valid after the judgment but accept-
  able prior to it.'[42]
+ 'Expert opinion is relied upon in judicial disputes and settlements.'[43]
+ 'A judicial order puts an end to disagreement over an *ijtihadi*
  matter.'[44]
+ 'Certainty overrides probability, and the latter overrides doubt, and
  suspicion has no credibility in the presence of truth/fact.'[45]
+ 'No credibility is attached to honour and status with regard to
  [people's] rights except for the father in the right of his offspring.'[*46]
+ 'Testimony of one woman is sufficient in matters on which men are
  usually not well-informed.'[47]

---

* The exception in favour of the father is based on a hadith that says, 'You and your property
belong to your father.'

VII

Shariah, Criminal Law and the Prescribed *Hudud* Punishments

Q70) What are *hudud* punishments? How were they applied in the past? How are they applied today?

A) *Hudud* (sing. *hadd*) literally means 'limits' but in the current legal jargon *hudud* offences refer to a handful of crimes for which punishments have been specified in the Qur'an or authentic hadith, and they are four, namely, theft (*sariqah*) (Q al-Ma'idah, 5:38–39), adultery and fornication (*zina*) (Q al-Nur, 24:2), slanderous accusation of adultery (*qadhf*) (Q 24:4) and highway robbery (*hirabah*) (Q 5:33). Many jurists also include wine drinking (*shrub*) and apostasy (*riddah*) under *hudud*, but this is disputable as the Qur'an merely refers to these as wrongful conduct without, however, specifying a punishment for them. It is of interest to note also that *hadd* and *hudud* are nowhere used in the Qur'an in the sense of fixed and mandatory penalties, something for which they are almost exclusively used in the *fiqh* literature and contemporary writings. Looking at the Qur'an verses on *hudud*, the latter should not be read in isolation from the parallel provisions of the Qur'an on repentance (*tawbah*) and reform (*islah*). Yet the Qur'anic provisions on repentance and reform are routinely being ignored and overlooked by the judges. There should, in other words, be provisions for repentance and reform in the adjudication of *hudud* crimes. This is because virtually every one of the verses on *hudud* referred to earlier specifies the crime and its punishment, followed by a phrase to the effect that if the accused 'repents and corrects himself, then God is Most Forgiving and Merciful'. This phrase appears with a degree of regularity in all the *hudud* verses, yet the juristic blueprint of *fiqh* has almost completely ignored this feature of the Qur'an on the *hudud*. I have addressed this issue in fuller detail in a book published on the subject, with a plea for fresh appraisal and reform that should attempt a long overdue corrective on the subject. This should be taken up perhaps through a holistic approach to the Qur'an such that would make repentance and reform an integral part of the *hudud* laws.* If this is attempted, it would entail a departure, in turn, from the fixed and mandatory understanding of the *hudud* in the existing *fiqh* manuals. In the past, punishment for these offences and judicial sentencing procedures on *hudud* were on the whole based, in our opinion, on a selective reading of the scripture.

In modern legal systems with codified laws and constitutions, provisions are occasionally found in the state laws for offences such as murder, adultery and theft, making some of the *hudud* punishments consequently redundant. Yet the whole subject touches on public sensitivities leading to a notable reticence on the part of present-day Muslim governments and jurisdictions to address the *hudud* laws openly through innovative legislative reforms. Hence a situation prevails whereby ambiguity, and silence, in the laws tend to lead to complications especially in many of the present-day pluralist societies with sizeable non-Muslim minorities. Conflict of jurisdiction between the civil courts and Shariah courts is a familiar aspect of these complications and, unless they are addressed through pragmatic and judicious legislative and policy initiatives, they remain unresolved.

Q71)   What is the punishment for adultery and for the false accusation of adultery?

---

* For a fuller verson of my work and reform proposals see Mohammad Hashim Kamali, *Punishment in Islamic Law: An Enquiry into the Hudud Bill of Kelantan*, Kuala Lumpur: Institut Kajian Dasar 1995, and a revised edn, by Ilmiyyah Publishers of Kuala Lumpur, 2000.

A) The punishment for adultery, stipulated in the Qur'an for both parties to the act, is that they should be flogged 100 lashes of the whip each (al-Nur, 24:2). False and unproven accusations of adultery (*qadhf*) carries the flogging of eighty lashes and it also disqualifies the person so punished from acting as a witness in the court of justice (Q 24:4). Thus if someone accuses a chaste woman of having committed adultery and fails to prove it, he would be liable to eighty lashes of the whip and barred also from becoming a witness. The onset of secularity and exposure to temptations, pornography, the borderless space of electronic media, etc., have on the whole given rise to questions, in turn, as to whether sufficient protective measures are in place for the implementation of these laws.

Questions do arise as to whether the *hudud* laws were actually meant for a society where marriage was made easy, where promiscuity was suppressed, where the poor were protected and where piety and remembrance of God were kept fresh in people's minds, and also where the Shariah was applied, not selectively as it is today for the most part, but in its entirety? Enforcement of the *hudud* should in principle also preclude doubtful applications, and it is difficult to ascertain absence of doubt under circumstances where changed economic conditions and increased promiscuity have placed societies in the grip of a secularist culture which would be difficult to address effectively through a predominantly punitive approach.

Furthermore, for adultery to be punished, the Qur'an requires four eyewitnesses for proof, which is almost impossible, to obtain. In most cases, adultery is proven by confession or through pregnancy, both of which are liable to distortion and caution is advised not to over-rely on them. In rape cases, for instance, the female victim, often a pregnant woman, is charged but she is also required to prove the case against the rapist, which is not only wrong in principle but also patently unjust and impractical. Only in a few Muslim countries is rape a separate offense and is no longer subsumed under *zina*.

Q72) What does Islamic law say about rape?

A) It is forbidden absolutely, and is a punishable offence, yet it is often (erroneously) subsumed under the Shariah offence of *zina*/adultery. For rape has characteristics of its own which differentiates it from adultery altogether. Whereas *zina* or adultery is consensual, rape violates consent and the victim of rape is robbed of dignity and humiliated. Both are forbidden under pain of punishment. The distinction between *zina* and rape is absolutely essential when it comes to matters of proof and punishment as it would be manifestly unjust to apply the punishment of *zina* also to the victim of rape. It is equally excessive and unjustified to expect the rape victim to present witnesses and bear the burden of proof for a crime committed against her. It makes no difference, as far as the enormity of this crime is concerned, whether the victim is a Muslim or non-Muslim, native or foreigner, and whether she is a follower of another religion or has no religion at all – all are forbidden in Shariah. Everyone must be respected and protected against aggression and abuse. No one may outrage a woman's modesty under any circumstances. All promiscuous relationships are forbidden in Islam, irrespective of the status or position of the woman, and whether she is a willing partner to the act or otherwise.

Q73) How does Islamic law treat adultery and fornication? Is stoning to death a prescribed punishment under Islamic law?

A) Islam has completely prohibited both consensual and non-consensual sexual relations between a man and a woman, married or unmarried, who are not bound to each other by a valid marriage, and everything that leads to it or contributes to it also fall under the same prohibition although not all necessarily punished the same way. Islam is also protective of the purity of the child-parent relationship through lawful marriage, which adultery violates. Preservation of lineage (*hifz al-nasl*) is one of the five overriding objectives, or *maqasid*, of Shariah, and a matter of priority in the order of Islamic values. Sexual intercourse which qualifies as *zina* is a punishable offence that carries the punishment, as is mentioned in the Quran, of 100 lashes of the whip for each of the sex partners.

Death by stoning for an adulterous married man or woman is not mentioned in the Qur'an. Stoning was a Jewish practice before the advent of Islam, and it seems that it was initially applied to a few cases at the time of the Prophet, most likely as a stop-gap measure until the revelation of the Qur'anic verse in sura al-Nur, 24:4, which addressed the subject and provided a uniform punishment of 100 lashes for both adultery and fornication. This was possible as the Qur'an itself had recognised the laws of the Torah as valid law for Muslims and made references to it in several places. The understanding thus prevailed that those laws are applicable to cases on which the Shariah of Islam itself was silent. This is the subject, in fact, of a chapter of Islamic jurisprudence under the heading of 'revealed laws preceding the Shariah of Islam' (shara'i' man qablana). After the revelation of the specified punishment for zina in the Qur'an, stoning as a punishment was in principle overruled and or arguably abolished by way of abrogation (naskh), and should have ceased to apply. But space here does not permit delving into the details of this issue. (I have addressed this subject in greater detail.*)

Q74) What is the hudud penalty for theft?

A) The punishment for theft according to the Qur'an is amputation of the hand of the thief, but only when a number of conditions (about fourteen conditions in all) are duly fulfilled. These are not easy to fulfill, and whenever a shadow of doubt exists, the punishment is likely to be commuted to ta'zir, that is, a deterrent penalty determined by the judge in light of the conditions of the case and those of the offender. Generally, the judges have shown reluctance to apply amputation and usually impose prison sentences instead. Twentieth-century codification of laws in Muslim countries that has resulted in the introduction of comprehensive penal or criminal codes tend to impose prison sentences for property offences, including theft, often without making any reference to hudud penalties. There is a demand now by the advocates of Islamisation of laws in many Muslim countries that these secular laws should be replaced with their Islamic equivalents – hence the hudud debate that is still unfolding in many Muslim countries and has yet to find satisfactory responses from the ruling authorities. This debate also runs, in some countries more so than others, an internal critique of the hudud laws on the analysis that certain reforms need to be carried out to guard against misapplications of the hudud as in the case of rape laws in Pakistan under the Hudud Ordinances of the 1970s, and the position also of non-Muslims vis-à-vis the hudud laws in countries with sizeable non-Muslim minorities.

---

* See Mohammad Hashim Kamali, *Punishment in Islamic Law: An Enquiry into the Hudud Bill of Kelantan*, Kuala Lumpur: Ilmiyah Publishers, 2000.

Q75)   What is the penalty for drinking alcohol and for gambling?

A)   There is no fixed punishment for drinking or for gambling in the Qur'an or hadith. The Prophet Muhammad himself did not apply a fixed punishment for wine drinking, but a penalty of forty lashes of the whip was imposed on wine drinking based on the precedent of the Companions. This precedent is also inconsistent insofar as it was initially fixed at forty lashes, which the second caliph 'Umar b. al-Khattab later raised to eighty lashes of the whip. These rulings were retained in turn in the classical *fiqh* manuals and have remained with us to this day. For gambling the judge may apply a discretionary deterrent (*ta'zir*) punishment. This is because the Qur'an has condemned gambling (*maysir*) and described it as 'a dirty work of the devil' but stops short of specifying a punishment for it. Gambling is consequently a transgression (*ma'siyah*) which is punishable under the rubric of *ta'zir*.

Q76)   What evidence is needed to prove *hudud* offences?

A)   Every *hudud* offence except for adultery/*zina* must be proven by the testimony of two adult male Muslim witnesses of upright character. *Zina* is to be proven by the testimony of four adult upright male Muslim eyewitnesses. *Zina* can also be proven by pregnancy and the birth of a child by the accused woman not then married unless she brings proof of rape and overwhelming duress. The irony of this situation is that in principle *hudud* may not be proven by means only of circumstantial evidence whereas pregnancy is actually circumstantial and falls short of providing a definitive proof of *zina*. *Fiqh* rules are also due for adjustment so as to admit female testimony in the proof of *hudud* offences.

Q77)   Can the *hudud* punishments be applied when there is doubt in proof of the offence?

A)   Doubt suspends the *hudud* punishments. In the event there is an element of doubt in the proof or other material aspects of the offence for the purposes of meting out *hudud* punishments, but a strong probability of guilt exists nevertheless, the *hadd* punishment is suspended but the offender may still be punished by a lesser punishment under *ta'zir*. This is due to a renowned hadith directing the judge and ruler to 'suspend the penalities (*al-hudud*) when there is doubt'.

Q78)   Can *hudud* punishments be reduced and adjusted?

A)   *Hudud* punishments are mandatory according to established Islamic law. It is an entrenched feature of the *hudud* punishments that they may not be reduced, substituted, pardoned or stayed, or in any way varied. Nor can the offender be forgiven by the authorities or the crime victim. The *fiqh* blueprint is explicit on this and stipulates that the judge's main task is to verify the evidence and proof and, when a *hadd* crime is duly proven, he has to enforce it and has virtually no discretion to make adjustments. All of this amounts to a remarkable degree of fixation and rigidity that souround the *hudud*, so much so that the judges themselves are often reluctant to enforce the *hudud* due to their severity and lack of any flexibility for the judges in their enforcement.

Q79)   Are non-Muslims exempted from the *hudud*?

A)   In countries with populations that are not predominantly Muslim (for example Nigeria and Sudan, even Malaysia with a sixty per cent Muslim population), the *hudud* laws are not applicable to non-Muslims. In countries where non-Muslims are a very small minority or non-existent and where an Islamic state is established (such as in Saudi Arabia and Iran), *hudud* offences and punishments are incorporated into the law of the land and apply to all citizens, including non-Muslims though with one or two exceptions, as explained below. For most of the other Muslim countries, a mixed situation obtains where statutory laws have been codified for court guidance and legal practice. The statutes often take their data from the Islamic sources. Generally, the *hudud* punishments are often substituted by various terms of imprisonment either under the *ta'zir* formula by the Shariah courts themselves, or under the applied laws and penal codes. The theory of *hudud* makes an exeption for non-Muslims in regards to two offences, namely wine drinking (*shrub*) and apostasy (*riddah*), which does not offend public sensitivities or publicly attack the principles of Islam. Non-Muslims who commit theft and adultery are not an exception.

Q80)   Are the *hudud* in any way subject to interpretation?

A)   The detailed provisions of Shariah on the meaning, scope, types and evidence, etc., of *hudud* have been developed and articulated through the opinion and interpretation of Muslim jurists and *fiqh* scholars of the past. The methodology of interpretation used often involved independent reasoning (*ijtihad*) and reasoning by analogy (*qiyas*). Their views were further strengthened through universal consensus (*ijma'*) of the jurists or through endorsement by the majority opinion of the Muslim schools and scholars (*jumhur*). The founding of the four schools of jurisprudence by the four great imams (Abu Hanifah, Malik ibn Anas, Shafi'i and Ibn Hanbal) were all in the Abbasid period, the earliest of which would still be 100 or more years after the Prophet's death. All development of Islamic law after the death of the Prophet has been through the rulings of *ijtihad* and endorsement, based on merit, of those rulings by general consensus (*ijma'*). Yes, these are juristic interpretations, even though the *hudud* are generally said to be self-evident and scripturally grounded, regardless of any interpretation.

Q81) Does Islamic law uphold 'an eye for an eye'? What is the punishment of someone who causes another personal injury or death?

A) The law of just retaliation or *qisas* – 'an eye for an eye' – exists in the Qur'an but it actually predates the Qur'an and can be traced back even to the laws of Hammurabi and those of Judaism. By Qur'anic standards, just retaliation is provided only for intentional acts of causing death or personal injury (law of retaliation, or *qisas*, refers to offences that involve loss of life and bodily injury). The punishment for deliberate homicide is death, usually by hanging. But retaliation for bodily injury may be imposed as and when it may be feasible, or else a discretionary *ta'zir* punishment which may consist of imprisonment may be imposed. Similarly, in the event of unintentional killing and cases in which the crime victim or his/her next of kin exercises their right of pardon, compensation in the form of a sum of money or property (blood money or *diyyah* for loss of life, and *irsh* for loss of limbs) is accepted, if the next of kin or guardian of the victim exonerates the offender from death punishment.

Retaliation in injuries according to Shariah applies when exact parity in the infliction of injury can be ascertained. This is often difficult to establish, for example, in the case of a broken tooth, leg or even an eye injury. Exact parity in the infliction of injury is difficult to visualise, which is why additional legislation has been necessary to regulate the application of *qisas*. Retaliation by way of *qisas* constituted the mainstay of tribal justice, which was practiced by the Arabian tribes even before the advent of Islam. Retaliation may be commuted to the payment of blood money (*diyyah*) if the family of the deceased person agrees to it. The Prophet Muhammad used to advise forgiveness, peaceful settlement and compromise in most *qisas* cases that were brought before him. Nowadays the state and attorney general representing the community (and the Right-of-God or *haqq* Allah aspect of the crime) may impose additional punishment in respect of the public right aspect of the offence even when the family of the victim accepts a *diyyah* or a peaceful settlement. The *fiqh* manuals specify the amounts of monetary compensation for death (*diyyah*) and for bodily injuries (*irsh*) often in gold and silver quantities, or livestock, such as 100 camels of certain description, as standard *diyyah* for the loss of life and lower figures for bodily injuries. These have often been converted to their monetary equivalents in present-day Muslim countries that apply them. Since *diyyah* is basically for unintentional homicide, this provision has been widely utilised in traffic offences and a basis on which monetary compensation and support can be provided for the victim's family.

As for apostasy, which is often included in the *hudud* offences, the reader may be referred to Chapter XV on Religious Freedom and the Right of Religious Minorities where apostasy is addressed under a separate question.

SUPPORTIVE EVIDENCE

▢ Qur'an and Hadith

+ 'And the recompense for an injury is an injury equal to it. But one who forgives and reconciles, his reward is with God. God loves not the aggressors.' (Q al-Shura, 42:40)[1]
+ 'If you [decide to] punish, then punish with the like of that with which you were afflicted. But if you show patience, that is indeed the best [course] for those who are patient.' (Q al-Nahl, 16:26)[2]
+ 'But he who repents after his crime and amends his conduct, God turns to him in forgiveness. For God is Forgiving, Most Merciful.' (Q al-Ma'idah, 5:39)[3]

+ 'Suspend the *hudud* punishments whenever there is doubt.' (Hadith-cum-legal maxim)[4]
+ 'One who repents from a sin is like one who has committed no sin.' (Hadith)[5]

☐ Legal Maxims

+ 'When the *hudud* offences are brought to the attention of ruler or judge, punishment falls due and no intercession is accepted.'[6]
+ '*Hudud* penalties are not enforced without the order of the head of state [or his representative].'[7]
+ 'The Rights of God are predicated in easiness unlike the Rights of Men [private rights which are not].'*[8]
+ 'The Right of Man is not omitted except by means of pardon or waiver.'[9]
+ 'A person may exercise indulgence [waive or forgive] in his own rights but not with regard to the rights of others.'[10]
+ '*Hadd* punishment is amalgamated prior to enforcement but not after.'[11]
+ 'Retaliation is indivisible.'[12] (Note: if say one of the next of kin, among many, grants forgiveness, *qisas* collapses and gives way to alternative punishments.)
+ 'Retaliation is not omitted by way of expiry but there is disagreement concerning the *hudud*.'[13]
+ '"When the victim of killing has no heir, the head of state retaliates on his behalf."[14]
+ 'When the direct perpetrator and proximate causer are both present, the ruling/*hukm* falls on the direct perpetrator.'[15]
+ 'The norm [of Shariah] is freedom from liability.'[16]
+ '*Hudud* penalties are suspended in the presence of doubt.'[17]
+ 'One who unknowingly drinks alcohol is not liable either to the *hadd* penalty or *ta'zir*.'[18]

---

* Private rights are thus not amenable to pardon and waiver except by the right-bearer himself. Some discretion with regard to the exoneration of public rights offences may be exercised by the judge or head of state (or his representative, the attorney general).

- 'One who doubts whether he did something or did not, the norm is that he has not done it.'[19]
- 'One who is certain on doing something but doubts its amount whether small or large, the smaller is presumed.'[20]
- 'Doubt does not suspend ta'zir (discretionary) punishment, but it does suspend expiations.'[21]
- 'Responsibility for an act does not fall on the commander, unless he has compelled [the doer].'[22]
- 'One who unduly hastens a process [to gain] from it is punished by becoming deprived of it.'[23]
- 'A purpose of the hudud is to inflict pain.'[24]
- 'In what is not amenable to substitution [and divisibility], choosing a part is tantamount to choosing the whole, and omitting a part is also tantamount to omitting the whole.'*[25]
- 'Prevention is stronger than remedy.'†[26]
- 'When two things from one genus co-exist and their purpose is not different, the one is amalgamated into the other.'‡[27]
- 'Settlement of litigations and disputes is an obligation.'[28]
- 'The norm is to prefer the version of one who supports the apparent, and evidence is on the shoulder of one who claims the opposite of that.'[29]
- 'The norm is to hear the word of one who defends his property.'[30]
- 'Enforcement of the prescribed penalties (hudud) is authorised by the head of state.'[31]

---

* Thus if in retaliation/qisas a relative exonerates his/her part, or some relatives do, but not others, the whole of retaliation collapses.

† Prevention is thus preferable to compensation, retaliation and punishment.

‡ Thus if someone is convicted of adultery/zina twice, or of slander more than once, he or she will most likely be punished only once.

VIII

Hudud in the Present-Day Muslim Countries

Q82) Are the *hudud* penalties applied in the present-day Muslim countries?

A) A categorical answer may be difficult to give to this question. *Hudud* tend to touch on religious sensitivities in many Muslim societies and pose difficulties as to the amount of accurate information one can secure on the subject. Governments are also reluctant to take clear positions on *hudud*. Shariah court judges and lawyers are likewise reluctant to pass *hudud* sentences due to their severity and in some cases, as in Malaysia, due to constitutional issues and lack of jurisdiction. *Hudud* are generally not enforced for these reasons, and also because they are often turned into politically contentious media issues which usually translate into a state of indecision and delay on the part of government leaders and parliaments in the enforcement of *hudud*.

Many of the countries surveyed below have, furthermore, a two-track system of courts: Shariah courts and civil courts, such as in Brunei, Malaysia, Nigeria, the Sudan and Pakistan. They usually have two sets of laws, a penal code, which is meant to be for all citizens, and a separate set of Shariah laws, including the *hudud*, that apply only to Muslims and are enforceable only in Shariah courts. Except for Saudi Arabia where Shariah courts are courts of general jurisdiction, in most other countries Shariah courts operate side by side with the civil courts, which are courts of general jurisdiction, and there are often complications over conflict of jurisdiction and legacy issues due to the domination of the common law system that still prevails in many of these countries.

Q83) Is the Islamic Republic of Pakistan practicing the *hudud* laws?

A) *Hudud* laws were introduced in Pakistan in 1979 under the then president General Zia ul-Haq. On 9 February 1979, the general issued five presidential decrees, known as the Enforcement of Hudood Ordinances. The Hudood Ordinance on *zina* was problematic as it subsumed rape as a *hudud* offence. This proved to be unjust to the victims of rape who often became pregnant but were unable to produce the required number of witnesses against the rapist and would consequently end up being themselves convicted for adultery/*zina*. The Protection of Women (Criminal Laws Amendment) Act, introduced in December 2006, put into place a number of significant amendments. This Act differentiates between the crimes of *zina* (adultery and fornication) and *zina bil-jabr* (rape), criminalising rape as an offence under the Pakistan penal code and preventing women who have been raped from being charged with *zina*. Rape was thus removed from the Hudood Ordinances and placed under the penal code of Pakistan 1860 again, and has since been tried by the civil courts until now. Yet the *hudud* still remains controversial in Pakistan. The various initiatives taken by different regimes and leaders, not all of them consistent or in tune with one another, have brought about a mixed picture of developments concerning *hudud*. A degree of variance is also observed in the roles respectively of the two parallel judicial authorities of the land, the Supreme Court of Pakistan, which is the epic court, and the Federal Shariat Court, also possessing exclusive jurisdiction in Shariah matters – sometimes issuing diverging rulings over issues, including *hudud*-related issues.

Q84) What is the position of *hudud* in Nigeria?

A) The introduction of *hudud* was driven by popular demand in Nigeria. The state of Zamfara in the Muslim north enacted the nation's first Shariah penal code in 2000. Zamfara was followed by Niger state. By 2002 twelve Nigerian states out of thirty-six and one territory

had enacted Shariah criminal laws and set up courts to administer them. Each state has its own governor and legislative assembly.
Most of the offences from the 1959 penal code were retained as *ta'zir*
offences. While the penal codes in the various states differ in detail,
by and large they follow the Malikite doctrine. Cases of adultery,
theft and other *hudud* crimes are often prosecuted and sentences are
occasionally passed but not implemented. The legal system is diverse
and judges often find loopholes, substantive or procedural, either to
suspend the *hudud* penalties or convert them to lesser sentences.

In 2002, for instance, two divorced women were convicted of adultery and
sentenced to death by stoning. Safiyyatu Hussaini and Amina Lawal were
convicted by the lower courts for unlawful sexual intercourse because they
were pregnant without being married. The provincial courts of appeal
quashed both convictions on technical grounds. Penal law was not yet prom-
ulgated when the convictions were passed. Both the appeal courts ruled that
pregnancy of an unmarried woman is not by itself sufficient to prove that the
accused committed *zina*. The reason given was that according to Malikite
doctrine, the maximum period of gestation is five years. Since both the accused
were divorcees, they could theoretically have been pregnant from their previous marriages.

The Nigerian legal system is also an amalgam of two component parts, and
anomalies of a dual heritage (Islamic and common law) often cause complications. Observers have similarly noted that some provisions of the 1999
constitution stand at odds with its other provisions, and with some provisions
also of the state Shariah penal codes. The fact that Nigeria is made up of
two distinct communities (Muslim and Christian) also adds complications. It
appears that while the lawmakers attempted to accommodate both communities, the results were met with limited success and compromises were made to
accommodate diverging interests. The challenge is how to harmonise the two
systems in a way that can safeguard the interests of each community without infringing on the aspirations of the other. Further reforms are needed to
systematise the law and iron out relationships of its various components with
one another in a coherent manner.

Q85)   Is Indonesia applying *hudud* laws?

A)   Generally no, but there have been developments in Banda Aceh,
     where the state legislature introduced the *Qanun Jinayat* and *hudud*

in September 2009 at a time when its term of office was about to expire and many commentators thought the state legislature had breached the fundamental rules of procedure. The next legislature did not ratify and there has been, as a result, an extended delay in the implementation of *hudud* in Banda Aceh. According to reports, in September 2014, the local legislature approved *qanun jinayat* in order to implement the Shariah, and it was announced that the *hudud* would be implemented in one year's time, that is, in September 2015. However, the chairman of *Nahdatul Ulama*, Teungku Faisal Ali, went on record to say that the bylaws had failed to have a substantial effect on Acehnese society as they were not strong enough and there was a lack of political will by the local government, adding further that the conditions then and five years earlier were about the same. The Shariah has been going nowhere in terms of regulations and enforcement. He added that the bylaws on crimes could not be implemented when their punishment clauses were considered controversial.

Q86) Are *hudud* laws enforced in Malaysia?

A) *Hudud* are not enforced in Malaysia, but it is a hotly debated subject and has remained in the limelight of media attention in recent decades due mainly to insistence by the powerful Islamic Party of Malaysia (known as PAS) on this as well as the introduction of an Islamic State in Malaysia. Only two of the thirteen states of Malaysia, namely Kelantan and Terengganu, have legislated on *hudud*. The Kelantan legislation, known as the Shariah Criminal Code (II) Enactment 1993 (or the Shariah Criminal Code Enactment), was passed by the Kelantan state legislative assembly in 1993 and also assented to by the Sultan of Kelantan in the same year. In Terengganu the Shariah Criminal Offences (*Hudud* and *Qisas*) Bill was passed in July 2002 and was similarly approved by the Sultan of Terengganu. The two Enactments are not very different in respect of content, each consisting of about seventy sections, and the Terengganu Enactment has closely followed that of its Kelantan antecedant, but the federal parliament in Kuala Lumpur has not consented to either. This consent is needed as the *hudud* punishments exceed the state Shariah court jurisdictional limits as specified in the Federal Constitution of Malaysia and other statutes.

The *hudud* are consequently not being enforced even in the two northen states under review due to constitutional restrictions and lack of jurisdiction on the part of the local Shariah courts.

On a broader note, criminal law in Malaysia is basically a federal matter and is under the control of parliament and the civil courts, which are courts of general jurisdiction. But the power to create and punish offences against the precepts of Islam has been assigned to the states under Schedule 9, List 2, of the Federal Constitution. However, this power is still subjected to several restrictions. Shariah courts in the various states of Malaysia have jurisdiction only over persons professing the religion of Islam, but even that is limited to certain maxima, as they do not have jurisdiction in respect of offences for which the punishment exceeds three years of imprisonment or RM5,000, or both, whereas the proposed *Hudud* Enactments of Kelantan and Terengganu and the *hudud* punishments therein exceed these limitations. The issue came to a head in March 2016 when the incumbent president of PAS, Abdul Hadi Awang, who is also a Member of Parliament, introduced a Private Member's bill in federal parliament to amend the 1965 law (Act 355) on court jurisdiction so as to increase the jurisdiction of the Shariah courts to adjudicate on *hudud*. This was debated for weeks. Non-Muslims, especially the Chinese members of parliament and political parties, put up a strong resistance, and many procedural limitations were subsequently laid down by the ruling party UMNO (United Malay National Organisation) that delayed prompt action on the proposed bill so that the issues are properly deliberated and understood. This was reflective also of Prime Minister Najib Razak's view on the subject. The matter was kept on Parliament's working agenda and was brought up again in Novermber 2016 only to be postponed for another six months for further clarification. This is one of the problems, one might say, about the *hudud* debate in Malaysia and other Muslim countries with sizable non-Muslim minorities; that it has become highly politicised and political parties pal up against one another – sometimes for decades. Politicisation of religious and juridical issues undermines the prospects of advancing thoughtful jurisprudential discourse about them as well, so much so that scholars are also discouraged to say much, as almost anything they say is likely to be subsumed by political controversy.

Q87) Is Brunei Darussalam applying the *hudud* laws?

A) Here too the picture is not very clear. On 22 October 2013 the Sultan of Brunei announced the introduction of *hudud* laws in Brunei, but on 30 April 2014 the sultan announced that the new Islamic criminal punishments would be introduced in phases, phase one beginning on 1 May 2014. The sultan added that Shariah law penalties would be introduced over time and would eventually include flogging, severing of limbs and death by stoning for various crimes. In response to foreign criticism the sultan said: 'Critics state that Allah's law is harsh and unfair, but Allah himself has said that His law is indeed fair.'

On 1 April 2015, the former Chief Justice of Malaysia, Abdul Hamid Mohamad, in a lecture given in Kuala Lumpur on Islamic Criminal Law in Malaysia, said that he wanted to correct a common mistake. Many people thought that Brunei had implemented the *hudud* law. That was not correct. In fact to this day Brunei has yet to enforce that part of the Shariah Penal Code Order 2013 which contains *hudud* offences. Brunei has gazetted the law. The effective date has not been fixed yet. The most recent information I received from the Assistant Solicitor General of Brunei on 15 December 2014 confirmed that the *hudud* law had not been enforced. In fact, the provisions of the Criminal Procedure Code necessary for the implementation is still under discussion.

Subsequent information obtained on this subject indicates, however, that the core *hudud* penalties have been postponed to a later stage, but that some of the lighter aspects thereof, which are strictly not included in the *hudud*, have been introduced and labelled as 'the first phase' of the Islamic criminal law. Reports thus indicate that this phase of the enforcement had started.

The first phase, introduced on 1 May 2014, included fines, imprisonment or both for eating, drinking or smoking during fasting hours, for skipping Friday congregational prayers for men and giving birth out of wedlock for women. According to some reports fewer than twenty people have been convicted for smoking during Ramadan and Khalwat (illicit proximity). All these offenders were apparently fined.

The second phase which includes whipping and the amputation of limbs has yet to be implemented. It will be followed by the third and final phase, which allows for the stoning of those found guilty of homosexuality and adultery.

Q88)   Is the Islamic Republic of Iran applying *hudud* penalties?

A)   After the Islamic Revolution of 1979 and as early as 1981 the courts began to try sexual offenses and impose *hudud* punishments, including amputations and stoning to death. Frequently the charge on which the accused persons were convicted was based on sura 5, verse 33, of the Qur'an:'waging war against God and His Messenger' and 'spreading corruption in the earth', for which the courts imposed alternate amputation or the death penalty.

In 1982 and 1983 four laws were enacted: (1) The Law Concerning *Hudud* and *Qisas* and Other Relevant Provisions; (2) The Law Concerning *Diyat* (blood money); (3) The Law Concerning Islamic Punishments; and (4) The Law Concerning Provisions on *Ta'zir* (deterrent/discretionary penalties). All of these were later replaced and incorporated into the Islamic Penal Code 2013 (IPC 2013). A certain commitment to the rule of law was shown in article (289) of the Code of Criminal Procedure, which stipulated that sentences in criminal cases must identify the specific article on which a conviction is based. Yet in cases where no specific legal provision existed, the court was obliged to apply the Shariah.

The IPC 2013 provides 100 lashes of the whip for *zina* committed by an unmarried person, but when it comes to adultery of a married man or woman, it is interesting to note that contrary to the old code, this chapter of the current code is silent and makes no provision in this regard. It thus appears that stoning as a punishment for *zina* is no longer applicable in Iran.

The IPC 2013 further provides that any person who insults the Prophet of Islam or other Great Prophets shall be considered as *sabb-al-nabi* and punished by death (Art. 260). The note attached to this article stipulates the same punishment for those insulting the twelve Shia imams and the daughter of the Prophet.

Q89)   Has Sudan legislated on *hudud* crimes?

A)   Sudan introduced a penal code in 1983, which ruled on the application of *hudud* crimes and punishments, as well as laws on retaliation and injury. With some exceptions, this code was applied to both Muslims and non-Muslims, including those living in the south, now an independent country. The punishable *hudud* offences included were theft, highway robbery and unproven accusation of *zina* (that is *qadhf*), which were applicable to all offenders regardless of their religion. However, the punishment of *zina* was dependent on the religion of the offender, which meant that the offender was to be punished according to his religious law.

If a defendant could not be punished with a fixed punishment due to uncertainty (*shubha*), he could still be punished in any way the court saw fit, even if the offence was not identified as such in the code. The code thus widened the scope of *hudud* punishments by lowering the standards of evidence, and *ta'zir* punishment could be applied to a number of acts that only resembled *hudud* offenses or were related to them in some way.

The leader of the 1989 coup, General Omar al-Bashir, announced to implement Islamic law more strictly. Al-Bashir's government adopted a new penal code (Law 8/1991), which made provisions for *hudud* punishments and extended the scope to cases of homicide and injury as well as apostasy.

Although the courts in Sudan have convicted accused persons for robbery, apostasy, adultery and other *hudud* crimes, their sentences have either been reduced, quashed or charges dropped in almost all reported cases. In 2007, Sadia Idriss Fadul and Amouna Abdallah Daldoum were sentenced to death by stoning for adultery in the state of Al-Gezira under the 1991 code (Art. 146a). However, their sentences were quashed on the grounds of lack of legal representation at the trial court. In April 2012, Intisar Sharif Abdallah was sentenced to death by stoning for adultery in the city of Omdurman, near Khartoum, under the same article. However, all the charges were dropped after the thousands of letters received from Amnesty International supporters. In May 2014, Mariam Yahia Ibrahim Ishag was sentenced to death and 100 lashes for apostasy and adultery respectively. She was born to a Muslim father and a Christian mother. She was raised in her mother's faith and married to a Christian man. She was given three days to revert back to Islam. However, she refused and was eventually convicted. On appeal, her sentence was quashed due apparently to international protest.

Q90) Are the *hudud* applied in Saudi Arabia?

A) Yes. Saudi Arabia is unique among the Muslim countries in that the Shariah applies not only in selected areas but is the law of the land generally. Enacted laws – known as *nizam* (regulations) – are subordinate to the Shariah, which in theory means that they cannot be in conflict with the Shariah. Saudi Arabian judges adjudicate on the basis of the Hanbali interpretations of Shariah. *Hudud* sentences are pronounced infrequently. All *hudud* offenses are first tried in courts consisting of three judges. Two other bodies review the cases on appeal, which in total amount to a three-tiered adjudication, and finally the king reviews all cases of execution. Stoning to death and amputation are relatively rare: between 1981 and 1992, there were forty-five judicial amputations and four death sentences by stoning. In December 2011, the right hand of a Nigerian man, Abdulsamad Ismail Abdullah Hawsawe, was amputated after he was found guilty of stealing gold, a pistol and a mobile phone.

Death punishment for the capital offence of murder is carried out in Saudi Arabia through beheading. Other countries that use beheading include Yemen, Iran and Qatar. In 2007, there were a total of 151 beheadings in Saudi Arabia, exceeding the previous record of 113 in 2000. Most people beheaded are foreigners, including citizens of Bangladesh, Yemen, Pakistan and Ghana. The crimes so punished include murder, rape, drug trafficking, apostasy and armed robbery. According to Amnesty International reports, there were approximately twenty-six beheadings in 2011, which is the year of the Arab Spring, and ninety in 2014. However, the number has rapidly increased. In the first half of 2015, 100 people, most of them foreign nationals, were beheaded.

As can be seen, a significant diversity exists in the way *hudud* have been implemented in the countries surveyed. The *hudud* debate in the countries discussed are also marked by the existence of vehement currents of opinion for and against them. The *hudud* are not sufficiently well regulated, and loopholes exist in the standards of proof, admissibility or otherwise of circumstantial evidence and also the discretionary aspects of court procedures. There are instances of the same, or very similar, offences being penalised under the national penal code and separately under the *hudud* provisions. Then there are also instances of conflict in the jurisdictions of the civil courts and Shariah courts, as the case may be, which add to uncertainties and often impede implementation.

IX

Shariah, Constitutional Law and Civil Liberties

Q91) What principles govern political life for Muslims? Does Islamic law prescribe a particular political system?

A) Neither the Qur'an nor the legal corpus developed from it prescribe a political system or model, be it caliphate, sultanate or emirate. In their Qur'anic renditions, politics and government, or management of community affairs – as the Qur'an would phrase it – are guided by a set of objective principles, such as justice, common good, basic rights and obligations, accountability, consultation, trustworthiness and respect for human dignity. Looking at the overall picture of Islamic principles, government in Islam may be further character-ised as essentially civilian (*madaniyyah*), which is, however, neither theocratic nor totally secular but has characteristics of its own. It is a limited and a constitutional form of government whose powers are constrained by reference to the injunctions and guidelines of the Qur'an and Sunnah. An Islamic government is also rooted in the notions of trust (*amanah*) and vicegerency (*khilafah*) of human-kind as God's trustees and custodians of the earth (*khilafah* in this sense differs from caliphate as a political structure, which is a prod-uct of historical developments), and its principal assignments are stewardship, building a just social order and securing the people's welfare (*maslahah*). The state represents the community to which it is accountable. The Islamic system of rule may also be described as a qualified democracy which is elected by the people and must conduct its affairs through consultation and representation.

Q92) Does Islamic law accept the separation of religion and state?

A) The answer is a qualified 'yes.' It should be noted at the outset, however, that speaking of the separation of religion and state in Islam is not the same as in the Western context, since Islam has no institutionalised religious authority, such as the pope and institutionalised church, to speak on its behalf, but instead entrusts every believer with moral responsibility as God's trustees and vicegerents (*khalifah*) on the earth. Religious consciousness pervades the life of Muslims. In an essentialist sense, Islam's teaching on justice, fair dealing and moral virtue, etc., does not preclude politics. A functional separation of powers is not only possible but it had arguably existed all along: executive power rested with the head of state and ministers; legislative power essentially with the *mujtahids* and *ulama*; and judicial power with the judges. They all had, as they still do, recognised spheres of operation that they observed on the whole, while the head of state supervised them and had regulatory powers over them all. The state is also not allowed to regulate matters of dogma and belief, nor does it have any powers to determine the acts of worship.

Muslim jurists have, moreover, drawn a line of distinction between religious obligations (*wajib dini*) and juridical obligations (*wajib qada'i*), and the courts of Shariah are supposed to only concern themselves with the latter. Additionally, in the renowned scale of Five Values of Shariah, which was earlier discussed, only two, namely the obligatory (*wajib*) and the forbidden (*haram*) can have legal and judicial implications, whereas the other three (recommendable, permissible and reprehensible) categories are basically nonjusticiable. The ruler is authorised to issue administrative regulations and decrees for the realisation of public interest (*maslahah*) under the doctrine of *siyasah shar'iyah* (Shariah oriented policy), especially in cases where no ruling can be found in the Qur'an and Sunnah or general consensus (*ijma'*) to regulate the matter. The head of state and government authorities have scope to exercise discretion, introduce policy initiatives and regulations to address issues. In matters of concern, for instance, to civilian affairs, economic development, science and technology, and what it takes to offer appropriate responses to the challenges of globalisation and so forth, one would expect the extra-Shariah and essentially civilian authority of the state to fill the space, with the general proviso that the essential tenets and principles of Shariah are not violated. When this is carefully observed, the ruling is likely to qualify as Shariah-oriented policy. But none of these, one might add, is equal to a total 'separation' of religion and state.

Q93) Does Shariah law require the leadership of a caliph, imam or ayatollah?

A) No. There is no such a requirement to have a leadership under any of these designations. This is because the Qur'an and hadith make no explicit reference to a state, government or a particular system of leadership as such, although the Qur'an does make references to 'those in charge of the community affairs (*'uli al-amr*)'. The question as to whether or not the Muslim community is under a religious obligation to form a government or a system of rule – or put differently, is having a government a religious obligation – has been debated among early Muslim scholars, but the balance tilts in favour of the response that formation of a government is a Shariah obligation. This is because enforcement of the Islamic principles requires a system of rule – hence an obligation by inference that there should be a government to implement the Shariah. This is confirmed by the practical example of the Prophet himself. He did form a system of rule in Madinah, which was however combined, in his case, with the more distinctive mission of prophethood. He was a Prophet first and the system of rule he established was subsidiary and not a part of his Prophetic mission. Nor did the Prophet pay much attention to state and government, leaving these almost entirely for the community to determine through consultation, public interest and *ijtihad*. Had the Prophet specifically addressed and regulated these matters, it is often said, they would have presumably become an integral part of the religion, which is probably why he did not address them in any detail. Government in Islam is meant, for the most part, to administer and govern the civilian and community affairs of Muslims, not their beliefs.

The ayatollah is a distinctly Shi'i designation and a religious office under the Shi'i system of religious leadership. It is a rank that is established by the theological seminaries in Qum and Mashhad, an academic-cum-religious title that has no definitive origin in the religious teachings. In his capacity as the deputy or representative of the (occult) imam, senior ayatollahs are entitled to levy a certain religious tax, the imam's share (*sahm-e imam*, as it is known in Persian, not *sahm-e ayatollah!*) with which he discharges certain functions.

The institution of caliphate as a political system, and that of the ayatollah, are subsequent developments, not dictated by scripture. The institution of imamate does have a religious basis in Shi'i theology as was previously explained.

Q94)   Is there a demand among Muslims for return to a caliphate?

A)   There have been voices and movements, especially in the post-colonial period, calling for a return to the historical caliphate. The Khilafat movement that began to gain support after the collapse of the Ottoman caliphate in 1924, especially in the Indian sub-continent and elsewhere, eventually died out under colonial pressure and Western military dominance. Political unity of Muslims, as was the case under the historical caliphate, even if nominal for the most part, does not seem feasible under the currently ubiquitous nation-state model, whereby almost every one of the fifty-seven states of the present-day Muslim world have their own national charters and constitutions articulating the Western concept and institutions of a national state and its various organs – nor is it a requirement under Shariah that there should be a caliphate as such. Yet the possibility exists perhaps for some form of political unity that may unite the world Muslim community (*ummah*) under some kind of an umbrella organisation or leadership, even if it is not called a caliphate. What we have seen of the so-called Islamic State militants, ISIS or ISIL, and its claim to caliphate, has been espoused with so much brutality and violence that they cannot go together with the idea of a legitimate leadership, let alone a caliphate. Caliphate as an institution takes its origin in the thirty years or so rule of the four Orthodox Caliphs, known as the Rightly Guided Caliphs (*khulafa' rashidun*) that had strong republican features and made a lasting impact due mainly to the piety and people-friendly character of their leaders.

That relatively brief period ended with the Umayyad takeover of power, which turned the caliphate into a monarchy, a change that failed to inspire genuine support and loyalty of the *ulama*. What is now heard in the name of the caliphate and that of ISIL, or Daesh renegades, is a total departure from that precedent. Massacre and mayhem, persecution and violence that brutalise people, evict and force women and children out of their homes into a life of misery as unwanted refugees stricken by hunger and disease are absolutely unacceptable to Islam and violate the core principles of Shariah. It is an accepted principle of Shariah that both the ends, and the means towards them, must be lawful and acceptable.

Q95) How does Islamic law relate to the applied law of the (non-Muslim majority) country in which Muslims may be residing permanently?

A) As a general rule, Muslims are not only allowed but required to be law-abiding individuals and citizens, and thus to obey and observe the laws of the country in which they live, and where they have become citizens and given a pledge of loyalty to the ruling system and leadership. According to a legal maxim of Islamic law, which is also a hadith, 'Muslims are bound by their stipulations', provided that these stipulations do not turn the lawful into unlawful, and vice versa. What this means is that Muslims are to obey the laws of the country of their residence if they do not forbid them to practice their faith or make them reject Islam, and its moral and religious principles.

This question also relates to the position of Muslims in the Muslim majority countries that apply dual legal systems, for example, common law and Shariah, as in Malaysia, Nigeria, Sudan, etc. The secular laws of the country may not be in harmony with the Shariah. Insofar as Islamic law operates in a Muslim country or jurisdiction, it can be the guiding principle for the applied law, or civil law, and the two may well be open to receptivity from one another, in which case the two need not be seen as mutually exclusive. For Islamic law itself creates space for the discretionary powers and civilian authority of rulers under the principle of *siyasah shar'iyyah* as earlier explained. During the colonial period, many Muslim countries have in varying degrees taken their laws, borrowed or adopted from British common law and the Code of Napoleon, just as the latter is also known to have taken from Maliki jurisprudence.

Civil law can moreover be the 'matter' upon which the spirit and principles of Shariah can find expression. In all legal systems and traditions – Islamic included – moral values are accorded a high status, which may well be the bridge between the Islamic and civil law. Retaining the ethical content of civil law is undoubtedly important, particularly when strict application of the law produces onerous and unjust results (for example, Nazi law explicitly authorised the Holocaust). Moreover, Islamic law, or at least the part of Islamic law known as *mu'amalat* (civil transaction), which is primarily concerned with the regulation of human relations, is civilian and positivist for the most part. This part of Shariah is not based on dogma and worship, which is primarily religious. Hence drawing a black and white division between Islamic and civil law and the applied law of the land may be less than accurate. Civil law, or statutory legislation in most of the Muslim majority countries, draws heavily from the Shariah, especially in the sphere of matrimonial, property and family laws, and more recently in the spheres of commercial law and contracts – especially with the rapid spread of Islamic banking and finance, as well as the Islamic alternative to conventional insurance (Takaful).

Q96) Does Islamic law encourage Muslims to break the civil laws of the country where they live? Does it force non-Muslims to abandon their own law and culture?

A) No. Islamic law does not mandate breaking the civil law. Islamic law has, in actual practice, always coexisted with some form of civil laws of non-revealed origin throughout its long history. The Shariah has gone further in its explicit recognition of the custom and culture of the non-Muslim residents and citizens of an Islamic polity. Many important cultural traditions, such as the Malay *adat*, the Mughal *zawabit* and the Ottoman *qanun*, not only survived under Islam but found opportunity for their growth. Moreover, the doctrine of judicious policy (*siyasah shar'iyah*) authorises the ruler to issue administrative regulations to further the public interest and social harmony among people, at the expense, if it must, even of departing from some of the *ijtihadi* rulings of *fiqh*.

Obedience to the civil laws of the country, and those which may in one way or another exhibit harmony with the Shariah or which do not go against its principles, is analogous to obedience to the ruler, which is much emphasised in Islamic law and doctrine. Obedience to the lawful leader is a Qur'anic obligation (al-Nisa', 4:59) and the text here is general and unqualified and thus encapsulates all the laws and ordinances of government that do not contravene the principles of Islam. Extra-Shariah laws, bylaws and administrative ordinances, mainly of the civil variety, have thus existed side by side with Shariah. Obedience to the ruler and the ordinances of government is due as long as it does not entail violation of the religious beliefs, obligatory worship and the devotional aspects of Islam. Breaking the civil law is justified under certain conditions when, for instance, civil law mandates or authorises ethnic cleansing, or in the unlikely situation of requiring the Muslim to renounce his faith. Refusal to obey under such circumstances is permitted in Islam based on the renowned hadith: 'There is no obedience in transgression; obedience is required in pursuit of righteousness.'

Q97) Is Islamic law compatible with democracy? With political pluralism? What is *Shura*, and how does it relate to democracy?

A) Yes it is for the most part. A democratic system of rule is on the whole compatible with Islam because democracy is about people's participation, a representative government by the people and for the people, it is also about fundamental rights and liberties, the rule of law, limitations on the coercive power of the state through checks and balances and equality before the law. Broadly, Islamic law approves of most of these and takes affirmative positions on the protection and realisation of people's welfare and their rights. Islam advocates a consultative and also a limited government that does not impinge on people's rights and liberties, one that is committed to accountability and justice. Islam also envisages a service-oriented system of rule that creates no barriers between ruler and ruled, and shuns pomp and ceremony of the kind that came into vogue with the onset of monarchy and dynastic rule under the Umayyad and Abbasid dynasties. What is just said here is mainly meant to depict a general picture – let it be said, however, that Islamic history in almost every period and dynasty has also known many good and upright, indeed exemplary, rulers who inspired the confidence of their people and left an impressive legacy of dedication to public service.

Political parties are acceptable if they are deemed to be effective means of protecting people's rights and interests and committed also to the principles of good governance and justice, advocacy of people's rights and the fight against dictatorship and corruption. Islamic law also recognises the validity of all monotheistic religions and allows their followers to practice their own personal laws and customs. Political pluralism in the sense of power sharing and recognition of different voices, political parties and associations are important to consultation (*shura*), which is a Qur'anic requirement for the management of public affairs. Additional support for an open and consultative system of rule is also found in the Islamic jurisprudential principle of reasonable disagreement (*ikhtilaf*), which is not only recognised but encouraged if it would lead to more refined and inclusive solutions to issues. Reasoned disagreement is not only allowed in politics, but also in jurisprudence and in regards to issues of concern to the interpretation, implementation and development of Shariah that accommodate social change and people's welfare.

A visible manifestation of *ikhtilaf* is found in the plurality of schools of thought and *madhhabs* that are accepted and exist in almost all Muslim societies to this day. In the end it must be remembered, however, that it is general consensus (*ijmaʿ*) that should be nurtured more. The basic idea is that reasonable disagreement should lead to feasible solutions and consensus-based responses, as no community can be expected to live comfortably with endless *ikhtilaf*. General consensus or *ijmaʿ* is admittedly a jurisprudential principle of some complexity but its inherent strength and appeal in the political life of people is also undeniable. By saying this, I do not necessarily mean the *usuli ijmaʿ*, one that is expounded in the manuals of *usul al-fiqh*, which is somewhat technical and difficult perhaps to obtain. Rather I am supportive of the idea of relative consensus that can be achieved by countries and communities for their own needs and their own issues – the relative *ijmaʿ* that has found support, for instance, in the writings of Shah Waliullah Dihlawi (d. 1762), Muhammad Iqbal (d. 1937) and many others. Ascertaining this kind of relative consensus in modern times is through voting in parliament, in consultative committees and forums, general elections and other democratic procedures.

Shura (consultation) is a Qur'anic principle, which lays down a requirement that Muslims must manage their affairs through consultation. It is particularly relevant to the roles and responsibilities of political leaders and parliamentarians to engage in consultation and exchange of views with community leaders and the general public. Since *shura* in the Qur'an occurs in the context of the ruler and ruled relations, and that the one must consult the other in public affairs, it is concluded that an Islamic government must be participatory and consultative.

Q98) Are Muslim countries under an obligation to become Islamic states?
What are the rights and duties of non-Muslims in such a state?

A) There is no mandate as such for the formation of an 'Islamic state'
(al-dawlah al-Islamiyyah) per se in the sources of Islam, a phrase
which fell into vogue only in the early twentieth-century discourse
in the works of Muhammad Rashid Rida (d. 1935), then followed
also by Abu'l A'la Mawdudi of Pakistan (d. 1979) and Sayyid Qutb
of Egypt (d. 1966).

The rights and duties of non-Muslims living under Muslim rule are basically the same as those of the Muslims. This is the purport of the renowned
saying of the fourth caliph of Islam, 'Ali b. Abu Talib, who said in reference to non-Muslim citizens that, 'They are entitled to what we are and
they bear the same obligations as we do – lahum ma lana wa 'alayhim ma
'alayna.' That said, as a matter of historical and academic interest, classical jurists have differentiated some of their rights and responsibilities. For
instance, non-Muslims (called the dhimmis in classical literature, a term
which is now suggested is replaced by compatriots/muwatinun) – were
required to pay the jizyah (poll-tax in return for state protection), which
is parallel to the Islamic obligatory tax of zakah, and payable also roughly
at the same rate of about 2.5 per cent per annum. The differential ruling
here is founded in the analysis that zakah is one of the Five Pillars of Islam
and non-Muslims should not be expected to comply with it. They were not
allowed to proselytise Muslims, and they were exempted from participating
in military mobilisation and jihad, which was also a religious duty applicable to Muslims only.

Both zakah and jihad are important Islamic principles and it was deemed
improper that non-Muslims should not be bound by them. But those conditions have changed and the poll tax is no longer required due to the introduction of uniform taxation laws in most of the present-day Muslim countries.
Yusuf al-Qaradawi, the author of a two-volume work on zakah, has advanced
the view that if non-Muslim citizens volunteer to pay the zakah as a contribution to their community and in a quest to combat poverty, there is no objection
for them to do so. This is now justified perhaps under the otherwise egalitarian system of rights and duties adopted under the modern constitutions that
currently obtain in most Muslim countries and jurisdictions.

Q99) Does Islamic law curtail certain freedoms protected by most Western countries?

A) Yes there may be some curtailment regarding freedom of speech on highly sensitive religious matters, but Islamic law generally stands for the principle of personal liberty. Islamic law is protective of the personal liberties of individuals much along the same lines as those of the Western democratic and legal regimes. The state and courts of law are not allowed to interfere in the private and personal rights (*huquq*) or liberties (*hurriyat*) of individuals so long as they are exercised within the limits of the law and observance of peace and public order in society. The one limitation Islamic law is known to impose is on freedom of religion, or at least one aspect of that freedom: the freedom to renounce Islam is also debatable, simply because the Qur'an explicitly recognises the freedom of conscience and declares more specifically that 'there shall be no compulsion in religion' (Q al-Baqarah, 2:256).* Women also suffer from certain restrictions on their freedom of movement compared to men. Both of these issues have, however, come under fresh scrutiny by Muslim scholars and jurists, including the present writer, in recent decades. In some instances, the restrictions were elaborated, extended and given juridical grounding by medieval scholarship. A restrictive climate of opinion gained ground due to the so-called 'closing of the door of *ijtihad*' as early as the fifth/eleventh century which remained basically intact until it was revisited by twentieth-century Muslim scholars and researchers. Statutory legislation of twentieth-century origin in many Muslim countries took measures to address relevant issues and introduce reforms towards the realisation of an egalitarian system of family law, although the challenges of innovative *ijtihad* still remain. If Islamic scripture is emphatic on human dignity, fairness, *ihsan* and justice, as it is indeed, there should be ways to articulate them into the details of women's rights to equality as well

---

* I have discussed freedom of religion in two chapters in *Freedom of Expression in Islam*, Cambridge: Islamic Texts Society, 1997 – 'Freedom of Religion' pp. 87–106 and 'Blasphemy', pp. 212–50.

as a more balanced recognition of personal liberty over matters of conscience and religion.*

Q100) Is freedom of speech protected in Islamic law?

A) Yes. Islamic law is affirmative on freedom of speech and expression and protects it in much the same way as do other major world traditions. It also regulates the valid exercise of freedom of speech, encourages it as a matter of principle but also places restrictions on it, for instance, in respect of blasphemy, defamation, slander, obscenity, lying, sedition and incitement to crime. On the affirmative side, Islamic law devotes separate chapters to freedom of opinion (*hurriyat al-ra'y*) whose historical advocates are known as *Ahl al-Ra'y*, promotion of that which is good and rejection of what is unethical and harmful (*amr bi'l-ma'ruf wa nahy 'an al-munkar*), giving of sincere advice (*nasihah*) including to the rulers, consultation (*shura*) in public affairs, freedom to offer a constructive criticism (*hurriyat al-ta'arud*, also known as *hurriyat naqd al-hakim*) and independent interpretation (*ijtihad*) – all of which are premised in the recognition of freedom of speech and expression. These are principles of general application for the most part with few formalities attached to them – hence every competent individual should be able to act on them and use them for his or her own good and the community at large.[†]

Q101) Does the Shariah protect freedom of religion? What does it say about apostasy?

A) The Qur'an is affirmative on religious freedom and maintains that faith must be through one's own free will and conviction without imposition of any kind. Protection of religion (*hifz al-din*) is also one of the higher purposes of Shariah (*maqasid al-shariah*). The Qur'an declares, as already noted, that 'there shall be no compulsion

---

* The reader may be interested in finding details in Mohammad Hashim Kamali, *Freedom, Equality and Justice in Islam*, Cambridge: The Islamic Texts Society, 1999, especially in its chapter on equality that addresses gender equality issues.

† The reader might be interested to know that my award-winning book, *Freedom of Expression in Islam*, expounds most of these concepts in separate chapters and considerable detail.

in religion' (al-Baqarah, 2.256).[1] This is endorsed in a number of other places in the Holy Book to substantiate freedom of religion. This can be seen, for instance, in Muhammad's prophetic mission in respect of da'wah (call to the faith) when the Qur'an explains it to him in a question that begs the intended answer, as in the following verses: 'If God had willed, everyone on the earth would have been believers. Are you then compelling the people to become believers? (Yunus, 10:99).[2] In other verses one reads the following proclamations: 'Let whosoever wills — believe, and whosoever wills — disbelieve' (al-Kahf, 18:29),[3] 'And you [O Muhammad] are not to compel the people, so remind by means of the Qur'an those who take heed' (Qaaf, 50:45),[4] and lastly when the Prophet is instructed to 'Say to the unbelievers: unto you is your religion, and unto me, my religion' (al-Kafirun, 109:1 & 6).[5] The Qur'an thus speaks for itself and leaves little room for doubt in its unequivocal recognition of the freedom of religion.

Q102)   Are human rights protected in Islamic law? Is the concept of human rights different in Islamic law?

A)   If by human rights one means the rights a person is entitled to by virtue of being human, then Islamic law does protect and promote human rights, but the manner of their articulation may differ from the articulations of human rights in other legal traditions and secular law codes. The concept of human rights itself may be said to be diverse enough to accommodate a variety of perspectives and interpretations. Human rights as articulated in the Universal Declaration of Human Rights (UDHR) 1948 are not only acceptable to Islam but one finds in the Islamic sources and doctrine much support for a wide range of the fundamental rights of the individual. The Shariah's position on these rights preceded the UDHR by many centuries but even so show harmony with most of the human rights principles. In modern times and since the adoption and prevalence of the Western nation state and formal constitutions in the Muslim world, the state is generally obligated, under the respective constitutions of Muslim countries (in particular in their chapters on fundamental rights and liberties) currently in force, to guarantee and protect them. The Shariah goes a long way also to protect essential human rights. If there are differences, such as regarding the *fiqhi* articulations of the freedom of religion and those of women's right to equality, as explained earlier, they are also challenges for the future of reformist *ijtihad* and law-making for the Muslim leaders and societies themselves. Many Muslim countries have taken constructive measures, and are still engaged, in varying degrees, to support human rights in their applied laws.

Freedom of conscience is protected in the Qur'an, as explained above. The life and property of all persons are protected and considered sacrosanct under Shariah. Protection of life and property are also recognised as the overriding objectives of Shariah (*maqasid al-shariah*) which must be respected and observed as a matter of priority. The Qur'an speaks emphatically on human dignity and equality and, together with the Sunnah, reject racism and discrimination based on colour, language and status. All members of the human fraternity are declared equal, as in the following:

'O mankind! We created you from a single pair of a male and female, and made you into nations and tribes, so that you may come to know one another. Truly the most honoured of you before God is the greatest of you in righteous conduct.' (al-Hujurat, 49:13)[6]

'We have bestowed dignity on the children of Adam.' (Q al-Isra', 17:70)

Q103) Have any Western countries considered adopting aspects of Islamic law or instituting Shariah courts?

A) The issue does not arise within the Shariah itself as there is clear recognition that Shariah should be implemented within Muslim territories and jurisdictions. In the present setting, while Western countries do not officially recognise the Shariah as a source of law, Shariah courts do exist in some Western countries nevertheless, though not as part of the regular judiciary, which is why their decisions are not legally binding. In addition, the emergence in recent decades of Islamic banking and finance in many Western countries has given rise to court litigation, thus making it obvious that those countries will require some form of adoption or incorporation of Islamic law in their own laws, which may even lead to enabling legislation to recognise or allow parties to settle relevant disputes via arbitration under Islamic law and not always through court proceedings. Many Western countries have allowed the opening of Islamic banks in their territories just as many well-established banks such as HSBC, Citibank and others have established Shariah and Islamic banking windows and units within their organisational structures, and the trend is likely to continue.

Added to this is the large scale migration of Muslims in the latter part of the twentieth century, and then during the second decade of the twenty-first to Western countries, especially Germany. These developments have made possible the presence of Muslim tribunals in some non-Muslim majority countries such as India and Singapore. Some Western leaders, such as the former Archbishop of Canterbury, Dr Rowan Williams, and Lord Phillips, a senior English judge, have even hinted at adopting some parts of the Shariah relating especially to matrimonial law.

Q104)   What is the Constitution of Madinah? Is it relevant today?

A)   The Constitution of Madinah (*dustur al-Madinah*, also *sahifah al-Madinah*) is a document, perhaps the earliest of its kind, that Prophet Muhammad signed with the native tribes of Madinah, mainly Jews and pagans, the resident nascent Muslims of Madinah (the *ansar*) and the newly arrived Muslim migrants (the *muhajirun*) in 1 AH/622 CE. The document consists of about forty-seven clauses or articles that grant certain protections, as well as rights and duties to its signatories and all the residents of the newly established state of Madinah under the Prophet's leadership. The constitution regulated relations between the newly created Islamic government and the citizens of that state, both Muslim and non-Muslim. A new community (*ummah*) was formed in which, as the constitution provided in one place, 'The Jews of Bani 'Awf constitute one community (*ummah*) with the believers' (Art. 26). The succeeding eight articles of the constitution gave other Jewish tribes the same status as that of the Bani 'Awf, which was the main tribe. This obviously meant that the Jews constituted a part of one and the same community. In the preceding clause, the constitution provided: 'For the Jews is their religion and for the believers their religion' (Art. 25). The Jews and other non-Muslims were entitled to assistance and protection, just as they were also required to contribute to the defence of the new state. All the signatories were required to submit to the authority of the new government, to defend Madinah against outside attacks, against criminality from within and to support the new government in pursuit of the stated objectives of the document.

The Constitution of Madinah is as relevant, for the most part, today as in its creation so long ago, of a territorial state, a new community, an early concept of citizenship, a set of commitments on the part of the new leadership, and also a network of rights and duties on the part of the residents and citizens of Madinah.

SUPPORTIVE EVIDENCE

☐ Qur'an and Hadith

+ 'God commands you to render the trusts to those to whom they are due, and when you judge among people you judge with justice.' (Q al-Nisa', 4:58)[7]
+ [God praises] 'those who observe the trusts placed upon them and abide by their promises.' (Q al-Mu'minun, 23:8)[8]
+ 'O believers! Do not betray God and His Messenger by betraying your trusts while you know it.' (Q al-Anfal, 8:27)[9]
+ 'And obey not the command of those who go to excess and who make mischief in the land and mend not (their manners).' (Q al-Shu'ara', 26:151& 152)[10]
+ 'And obey not one whose heart We have permitted to neglect the remembrance of Us; one who follows his own desire and whose case has gone beyond all bounds.' (Q al-Kahf, 18:28)[11]
+ 'One who seeks succor after suffering oppression has nothing to be blamed for.' (Q al-Shura, 42:41)[12]
+ 'And eat not up your properties wrongfully among yourselves, nor influence the rulers with the intention that one party devours sinfully the property of another while you know it.' (Q al-Baqarah, 2:188)[13]
+ 'A Muslim is under duty to listen and obey [those in authority] even if he (or she) likes or dislikes it unless he is commanded to indulge

in transgression, [in which case,] he is under no obligation to listen nor to obey.' (Hadith)[14]

+ 'One whom God has entrusted with managing the affairs of Muslims, and then he distances himself from them and refuses to be involved in their needs, their helplessness and their poverty, God will turn away from his needs, poverty and helplessness on the Day of Judgment.' (Hadith)[15]

+ 'The best *jihad* is to utter a word of truth to an oppressive ruler.' (Hadith)[16]

+ 'Every one of you is a custodian and responsible for that which is under his custody. The head of state is a custodian and he is responsible for his subjects; a man is a custodian and responsible for his family and what is under his charge; a woman is a custodian of her husband's family and children and she is responsible. A servant is a custodian and responsible in his master's property under his charge.' (Hadith)[17]

+ 'The ruler is the guardian of one who has no guardian.' (Hadith)[18]

+ 'One who leaves behind property and assets, they would belong to his heir, but one who leaves a debt or dependants [in penury], they shall be for me and become my responsibility.' (Hadith)[19]

+ 'The Messenger of God, pbuh, cursed one who gives a bribe and one who takes it.' (Hadith)[20]

+ 'The bribe-giver, the bribe-taker, and one who facilitates it are all doomed to Hellfire.' (Hadith)[21]

+ 'Gifts given to [government] employees partake in dishonesty and betrayal.' (Hadith)[22]

[] **Legal Maxims**

+ 'The Head of State is not authorised to take away anything from anyone unless it be through a lawfully proven right.'[23]

+ 'The Head of State may not discontinue that which is indispensable for the Muslims/community.'[24]

+ 'All those who have a right remain as they are unless the opposite of it is proven with certainty.'[25]

+ 'A group of upright Muslims replace the ruler when he is disabled/incapacitated.'[26]

- 'The dispositions of the Head of State over the citizens are based on public interest.'[27]
- 'Command of the ruler does not apply to devotional matters in a primary capacity but may apply in a subsidiary capacity.'[28] (That is in a supportive and regulatory sense such as regulating the mosque affairs or those of the haj pilgrimage.)
- 'Government leaders do not stop short at a [minor] benefit when they are able to secure a greater benefit [for the people].'[29]
- 'Priority in all public appointments is given to ones who are best suited to secure their related [priorities and] interests.'[30]
- 'The head of state has no authority to supervise the private property of individuals.'[31]
- '[Possession of] just character is required for [appointment to] all government positions.'[32]
- 'When the requirement of just character cannot be secured on the part of leaders and judges, priority is given to ones that are the least [guilty] of transgression.'[33]
- 'All those who act on behalf of other persons must do so in accordance with the latter's best interest.'[34]
- 'Private authority [for example like that of the father over his child] is stronger than the public authority.'[35]
- '[loss of something placed with another by way of] Trust is not compensated for unless there be transgression [on the part of trustee].'[36]
- 'Management of citizens affairs must be based on public interest.'[37]
- 'The norm is that consultation is binding on the ruler.'[38]
- 'Consultation is impermissible in that which is regulated by a clear text.'[39]
- 'Assets deposited in Public Treasury are to be expended for public interest purposes.'[40]
- 'All dispositions that give rise to harm/corruption or obstruct a benefit are prohibited.'[41]
- 'The norm with regard to clothing/dress is permissibility.'[42]
- 'The norm with regard to [human] actions and customary practices is permissibility and absence of prohibition.'*[43]

---

* It is typical of the *fiqh* language on the endorsement of basic liberties to say that people are normally free in what they do or say and the decisions they make in their daily lives.

+ '[The basic norm of] permissibility in human activities is contingent on avoidance of harm to another person.'[44]
+ 'The norm [or presumption /with regard to all persons] is [that they possess] integrity [or innocence] unless the opposite becomes known.'[45]
+ 'The norm [of Shariah] is absence of defects.'*[46]
+ 'The norm in the dispositions of Muslims is validity.'[47]
+ 'The norm [or normative presumption] in regards to Muslims is uprightness.'†[48]
+ 'The right of Man takes priority in the event of a conflict [over the Right of God].'[49]
+ 'The right of the living takes priority over the right of the deceased in the event of a conflict.'[50]
+ 'In the event of a conflict between guilt and innocence, the latter take priority over the former.'[51]
+ 'The affairs of Muslims are presumed to be valid and permissible and may not be deemed invalid and corrupt so long as validity seems appropriate.'[52]
+ 'A person's proven right on another is not omitted by [the latter's embracing of] Islam.'†[53]
+ 'That which is not tolerated in the marriages of Muslims may be tolerated in the marriages of non-Muslims.'[54]
+ 'What is prohibited to Muslims in marriage is also prohibited to non-Muslims.'§[55]
+ 'The non-Muslim is included in what is addressed to the people in general [and unspecified] words.'[56]
+ 'Avoidance of oppression [and its cessation] is an obligation.'[57]

---

* People's affairs, exchange of goods and transactions that take place between them are, in other words, presumed to be free of fraudulent dealings and defect unless the contrary is proven.

† Muslims are, in other words, presumed to be of just character unless proven otherwise. This and many of the other norms preceding it on this page are tantamount to legal presumptions, such as the presumption of innocence in Western jurisprudence, in Islamic law. The language may be a little different to constitutional declarations, or those of the basic liberties in a contemporary human rights instrument, but there are credible and interesting similarities.

‡ What this maxim means is that a person's conversion to Islam cannot be used as an escape from his proven liabilities. Another parallel maxim to this of yet wider scope says that, 'The Right of Man is not omitted by Islam – haqq al-adami la yusqat bi'l-Islam.'

§ The main reference is to the prohibited degrees of relations, or marriage among close relatives.

X

Jihad, Violence and War

Q105) What is jihad – is it a form of religious violence?

A) Jihad (lit. striving) also means making an effort, but juridically it can mean two things: struggle to discipline one's own self, one's ego, selfishness and base desires that come in the way of one's moral and spiritual refinement, and the other is military jihad for self-defence and repelling of aggression. The former is described, according to a renowned hadith as the 'greater jihad', in contradistinction to armed combat against the enemy, which is described as the 'lesser jihad'. Jihad in the former sense is an all-embracing concept and a lifelong effort for self-refinement and control. Thus for a person to be engaged in the struggle to educate and discipline oneself and fight for a just and fair social order is tantamount to jihad. This can also be said of a person who toils to earn a living to support himself and family and one who strives to improve and build a healthy environment for himself and others – all are different aspects of peaceful jihad in Islam.

The Qur'an (al-Hajj, 22:78) thus addresses the faithful to 'Strive for God with a worthy effort (jihad).' This verse does not refer to any particular type of struggle, and the 'worthy effort' mentioned is evidently not referring to armed combat but one that can mean efforts which help to improve knowledge of religion and general standards of literacy and education among people.

These peaceable meanings of jihad are all too often distorted by hardline and radical interpreters of the religion. Almost all conditions of a valid jihad are being regularly ignored by the present-day self-styled jihadists, who involve themselves in unjustified violence and the killing of innocent civilians. One of the conditions of military jihad, for instance, is that it must be declared by the lawful leader otherwise it could be a recipe for chaos. This is an important condition which is, however, completely ignored.

Q106)   Would you describe jihad as 'holy war'?

A)   Jihad is often translated as 'holy war' but it is inaccurate and misleading. The literal translation of 'holy war' would in Arabic be *al-harb al-muqaddas*, which is not used by Arab speakers and is totally unidiomatic. 'Holy war' also suggests that jihad is a sacred act, like the *bellum sanctum* (holy war) fought by the medieval crusaders. No war is holy in Islam. Rather it is the objective aspired to by a just war which may be holy, not the war itself, which is inevitably destructive and abhorrent. Classical Muslims thus describe jihad as 'good not in itself but for what it brings'. For this reason, 'holy war' is a mistranslation of the word 'jihad'. Incidentally *ijtihad* (intellectual effort to extract the ruling of Shariah for a particular, new and unprecedented issue), which I have frequently mentioned in my response to previous questions, and *mujtahid* (one who carries out *ijtihad*) are from the same Arabic root *jahada* (to make an effort). Jihad is thus a character development concept, whereas *ijtihad* signifies intellectual development. Both have strong social dimensions for development and growth. The larger Islamic principle of the vicegerency (*khilafah*) of man can hardly be comprehensively fulfilled, it is believed, without persistent effort for improvement of oneself and one's society and environment.

Q107)   Is there anything like peaceable jihad in Islam?

A)   Yes. Just as was explained in the answer to the last question, the peaceful dimensions of jihad, the mainstay of all jihad, one might say, is almost completely ignored and marginalised in the mainstream media and common parlance of people, Muslims and non-Muslims alike.

The misunderstood jihad has nowadays become the main propeller of Islamophobia for what it has become – for it is based mainly on misunderstanding and fallacies concocted by hostile journalism. Jihad consists of the effort one makes to do something good and to prevent or oppose evil. The effort may be directed towards oneself or the outside world. The struggle to control oneself, to conquer ignorance, to excel in the work undertaken to the best of one's ability are the jihad of the self (jihad *al-nafs*). In a similar vein, the Sufi contemplation in combating the distractions of the soul are called *mujahadah*. To combat poverty and disease, to build housing for the poor and to fight corruption and abuse would all qualify as jihad that serves a social purpose of great benefit, and they are all instances of peaceable jihad.

We are cast into a world in which there is disequilibrium both externally and within ourselves, to which jihad serves as a corrective and offers a potent counter-narrative. For ordinary Muslims, praying five times a day regularly all their lives, or fasting from dawn to dusk during Ramadan are certainly not possible without great effort, or jihad. It is now common to hear Muslims speak of jihad in various ways, referring to jihad in the acquisition of knowledge, and jihad against social ills afflicting the youth, drug abuse and Aids; 'business jihad', which is to conduct sound ethical business that is clear of exploitation and support for harmful activities; and even 'gender jihad' in the sense of promoting and vindicating the legitimate and neglected rights of women. Understood in its comprehensive sense, jihad is an inherent aspect of the human condition in facing the imperfections of this world. The Prophet Muhammad has said that 'the *mujahid* is one who wages a struggle against himself'. In a hadith which both al-Bukhari and Muslim, the two most relied-upon hadith collections, have recorded, a young man asked the Prophet: 'Should I join the jihad?' that was apparently in progress at the time. In response, the Prophet asked him a question: 'Do you have parents?' and when the young man said 'Yes', the Prophet told him, 'then strive by serving them'. The Prophet also spoke of jihad which involves combating falsehood to vindicate the truth where he is quoted in a hadith: 'The best jihad is a word of truth spoken to an oppressive ruler.'

Q108)   What is the main issue over jihad?

A)   The main issue concerning jihad is its widespread distortion, misunderstanding, and abuse. The concept of *jihad fi sabil Allah* (striving in the path of God) as contained in the Qur'an and Hadith has often been distorted and misused by the perpetrators of military violence and terrorism, Muslims and non-Muslims alike. It has become the principal tool of the proponents of Islamophobia in the West to the extent that it prompts security firms and businesses to sell their wares by raising the fear of imminent jihadist violence in the neighbourhood. Radical Islamic groups are, on the other hand, recruiting young people to join the 'jihad' by going to Syria and becoming ISIL militants. 'Jihad' is thus equated with terror on one side and with 'radical Islam' on the other – both misrepresenting what jihad actually stands for.

Q109)   Are the Muslims required to engage in jihad?

A)   Jihad in the sense of self-control and self-improvement and improvement of one's society and environment is a requirement for all Muslims at all times. In classical jurisprudence, jihad in the sense of military engagement is a personal obligation (*fard 'ayn*) of Muslims in only one situation, when the enemy has actually besieged the Muslim territory and homeland, in which case everyone must join the effort to confront the enemy. Otherwise jihad is a collective obligation (*fard kifayah*) of the community, which means that when it is carried out by some, the rest are exempted from the obligation. But today the military aspect of jihad is almost everywhere assigned to professional armies and soldiers. The most meaningful jihad in the sense of striving for a good cause would be, for instance, to engage in efforts that would stem damage to the environment, upgrade education and knowledge of the beneficial sciences at all levels and fight corruption. These can still be pursued by individual Muslims and groups wherever they are. This would qualify as an aspect of contemporary jihad. Fighting poverty and disease, building homes and schools for the poor would also qualify, whether performed individually or collectively in cooperation with others.

Q110)   What limits, if any, does Islamic law place upon the use of violence?

A)   The leading schools of law, or *madhahabs*, have held that jihad is legitimate in defence against aggression. They also maintain that jihad must be declared by the legitimate leader. Hence no group, party or organisation has the authority to take up arms in the name of jihad without the authorisation and consent of the head of state. This consent may be given when the country is under imminent threat of an invasion, for there will otherwise be disorder and anarchy. This is the purport of the hadith which provides that:'A Muslim ruler is the shield [of his people]. A war can only be waged under him and people should seek his shelter [in war].' This permission should always be sought and obtained from the lawful authorities. According to a Qur'anic address to the faithful: 'Fight in the way of God against those who fight you, but do not commit aggression. Truly, God does not love the aggressors' (al-Baqarah, 2:190).[1]

During the first thirteen years of his mission in Mecca, the Prophet and his followers were not permitted to engage in fighting nor even to reciprocate the violence they were subjected to by the pagans of Quraysh. Only after the Prophet's migration to Madinah, when they were again attacked, was permission granted for the Muslims to defend themselves – as the Qur'an expounds in the following verse:

'Permission is given to those who have been fought against because they have been wronged, and verily God is able to grant them victory. They are those who have been unjustly expelled from their homes only for having said, "God is our Lord."' (al-Haj, 22:39, 40).[2]

Unlike the Romans, who subscribed to the notion that *silent enim legis enter arma* (laws are silent during war), Islamic law regulated war and proscribed acts of oppression and injustice before the onset of war, during it and after the end of the war. Hostile action may be taken only against armed combatants. Civilians and persons who are not involved or trained to be engaged in combat may not be targeted. Killing and harming women and children and the elderly is strictly prohibited. Animals, crops and trees are to be spared unless it be for sustaining life – which evidently means that in Islam laws are not silent during war. For these reasons, many modern Muslim thinkers, including the present writer, regard the use of nuclear weapons as incompatible with Islamic principles, as such weapons are totally destructive and blind to any such distinctions.

Under normal circumstances, the rule of law and Shariah generally envisage a law-abiding citizen who shuns violence and observes peace and order at all times. Violence against persons without a just cause is an offence, and it is the duty of lawful government, law enforcement agencies and the judiciary to uproot all unlawful violence.

Q111)   How does jihad feature in the Qur'an and in Islamic history?

A)   The Qur'an refers to jihad in twenty-four verses, most of which emphasise the spiritual and non-violent manifestations of jihad, such as being steadfast in the faith and sacrifice in its cause, migration from Mecca to Madinah when the Prophet himself migrated and peaceful propagation of the faith. Jihad as armed struggle against the aggressor occurs only in the Madinan verses of the Qur'an. As already noted, during the first thirteen years of his campaign in Mecca, the Prophet was not permitted to use force even for self-defence. Islam, which literally means peace, was propagated through peaceful methods. The idolaters of Mecca persecuted and forced a number of the Prophet's Companions to migrate, initially to Abyssinia, and later to Madinah. The Meccans not only continued but stepped up their hostility and attacked the Muslims, some 270 km away in Madinah, in the battles of Badr (624 CE) and Uhud (625 CE), with superior forces and inflicted heavy casualties on them. Only then was the permission granted for them to: 'Fight in the way of God those who fight you, but begin not hostilities. Verily God loves not the aggressors' (Q al-Baqarah, 2:190).[3]

Q112)   Is the Shia concept of jihad the same as that of the Sunni?

A)   Broadly speaking yes. Sunni and Shi'i theories of jihad are very similar. One crucial difference of note is, however, related to the Shi'i doctrine of Imamate. As already noted, jihad is one of the ten headings of the Shia acts of devotion ('ibadat) and thus an explicitly designated aspect of piety. The Twelver Shi'is hold that jihad in its military sense can only be waged under the leadership of the rightful imam. After the occultation of the last imam in 873 CE, theoretically no lawful jihad can be fought. However, as defence against attacks remains obligatory and the ulama are regarded as deputies of the Hidden Imam, several wars were fought in the nineteenth century under the rubric of jihad, between Iran and Russia for instance.

Furthermore, the Shi'i concept of non-military jihad is closely related to three principles: jihad in the sense of 'enjoining the good and forbidding the evil': befriending (*tawalla*) those who befriend the Prophet and his descendants; and disassociation (*tabarra*) from those who hate them. But since only a defensive form of jihad is permissible in the absence of the twelfth (Hidden) imam, 'enjoining' and 'forbidding' by use of force is limited to the legitimate Shi'i authority.

Q113) Does Islamic law permit terrorism or suicide bombing?

A) No it does not. Protection of life (*hifz al-nafs*) – of all human life is one of the overriding goals and purposes (*maqasid*) of Islam and the Shariah. Human life must be safeguarded as a matter of priority. 'One who saves the life of another', says the Qur'an, 'it would be as if he saves the life of the whole of humankind' (al-Ma'idah, 5:35).[4] The text also declares in the same verse: 'And one who kills a human being without the latter being guilty of murder or corruption in the land, it would be as if he has killed the whole of humankind.' Elsewhere the Qur'an enjoins: 'Slay not the life which God has made sacrosanct unless it be in the cause of justice' (al-Isra', 17:33).[5] Slaying without a just cause and outside the due process of law and Shariah is prohibited, be it out of despair, ignorance or adventurism. These prohibitions subsume all forms of violence and self-destruction, including suicide bombing. Under no circumstances is suicide, let alone suicidal terrorism and bombing, permitted in Islamic law. These are violations of the principles of Islam.

Al-Bukhari and Muslim, the two most authoritative collections of hadith, have recorded the following hadith from the Prophet:

'One who raises arms against us ceases to be one of us';[6]

And a rehash of the same in another hadith reads:

'One who unsheaths his sword against us is not one of us.'[7]

In yet another hadith, it is provided:

'All that belongs to a Muslim is forbidden to other Muslims [read other persons]; his blood, his property and his honour.'[8]

Terrorising innocent people which may or may not lead to loss of life and limb constitutes the crime of *hirabah*, which carries the death penalty by the clear text of the Qur'an (al-Ma'idah, 5:33). The prohibition of *hirabah* in this text is conveyed in general and unqualified terms that subsume individuals, groups, state and non-state parties all alike.

Those who deliberately kill innocent people commit cowardly murder behind the mask of 'Islam' and delude themselves to think they are taking revenge and waging jihad; they are in fact, in the eyes of the Islam, murderers. It is despicable to hunt down defenceless innocent people and shoot them in a vicious act of terror simply because they think wrongly, or are hostile to Islam.

As for those who have been forced to leave their homes and live in refugee camps, decade after decade, without hope for a solution to their pitiful conditions, they resort to violence and give vent to their rage out of total helplessness. Refugee populations have been steadily rising in the Middle East and elsewhere especially since the ISIL rampage became more extensive and more violent. The plight of these refugees and victims of horrendous violence hardly fails to shake our conscience and every one of us has a moral responsibility to assist in the pursuit of peace and justice. Those in position of authority in the UN, the OIC, powerful world leaders and organisations have a humanitarian and, calling and in some cases, are legally accountable, to help their condition in any way possible. That said, it would still be wrong to condone resorting to suicide bombing, blowing up innocent persons engaged in pursuit of their daily living, women and children who are caught unaware and had never been part of any hostile action. This can never be justified in the name of Islam.

Q114) How is jihad and violence projected in the writings and *fatwas* of Muslim leaders today?

A) The former Shaykhs of al-Azhar, Mahmud Shaltut (d. 1965) and Muhammad Sayyid Tantawi (d. 2010), the former Grand Mufti of Egypt, and also Sheikh 'Ali Gomaa, Grand Mufti of Egypt after Tantawi, have all shown in their writings that the Qur'an only allows war for self-defence. They have condemned the September 11, 2001 attacks as acts of terrorism.

The Jeddah-based Islamic Fiqh Academy affiliated to the OIC, in its sixteenth session (5–10 January 2002) vehemently condemned all manifestation of terrorism and its attributions to Islam:

> Terrorism is an outrageous attack carried out either by individuals, groups or states against the human being. It includes all forms of intimidation, harm, threats, killing without a just cause, all forms of armed robbery, banditry, every act of violence or threat intended to fulfil a criminal scheme individually or collectively, terrify and horrify people by hurting them or by exposing their lives, liberty, and security to danger – all are resolutely forbidden in Islam.

Q115) Is Islam a religion of peace?

A) The answer to this question is undoubtedly 'yes,' for the following reasons:

- Islam advocates values such as human unity and equality, love of the Creator, compassion, subjugation of passion and accountability for all actions. These values are supported by innumerable verses in the Qur'an, enjoining believers to be righteous, compassionate and moderate their conduct in their dealings with their fellow humans. All the Five Pillars and core values of the faith, such as submission to God and prayer, giving to charity, fasting (which involves self-restraint, suffering and self-sacrifice) and pilgrimage of the haj (which involves acts of devotion to God and expresses unity and brotherhood with one's fellow humans) are non-violent, humanitarian and peaceful. Islam is also a strong advocate of justice ('adl), benevolence (ihsan) and wisdom (hikmah), and is inherently moral when it prioritises obligations, or one's duty to others, over one's own rights. Islam is emphatic on social justice, abolishment of all forms of slavery, racism and discrimination. These are all premised in peace and provide a favourable framework for social harmony.
- Islam proposes several principles that support non-violent resistance to adversity, such as patience, persuasive engagement, consultation and dialogue, sincere advice (nasihah),

withdrawal from situations of injustice and boycotting all acts of aggression. It also recommends emigration and exit from war and oppression, prioritises diplomacy, and readiness to seize all opportunity for peacemaking, as well as designating special prayers for ending fear, conflict and incitement to sedition.

- Patience and perseverance in its Qur'anic perspective is not mere passivity. It is active striving in the way of truth. Patience and self-restraint is far better and preferable than taking revenge. The Prophet Muhammad has said that 'power resides not in being able to strike another, but in being able to keep the self under control when anger arises.' Patience is most praiseworthy when it comes from those who are able to take revenge but who exercise restraint.

- The emphasis in Islam is on the doing of good (*khayr, ihsan, birr*) and not on power. *Khayr* and *ihsan* in Islam underline support for the poor and charity. Charity is prescribed in at least twenty-five places in the Qur'an, and occurs in many varieties, all encouraging the faithful to assist the underprivileged and help in the removal of injustice in society. Justice and the doing of good are expected to prevail in all interactions with one's fellow humans, Muslim and non-Muslim alike.

- Islam's vision of the human life on earth is underlined by harmony and peace with other creatures and inhabitants of this planet. Peace (*salaam*) in Islam is not merely an absence of war; it is the elimination of the grounds of violence and conflict, of futility and waste, oppression and corruption (*fasad*). Peace, not war or violence, is God's true purpose for human life and for humankind's vicegerency on earth.

- Islam takes an unequivocal stance on the unity of all humanity and on essential human dignity, which are central to Islam's order of values. Humankind is also an integral part of an ocean of creation, and is the most dignified and exalted of them all, the prize indeed of God's creation. This can best be preserved and further enhanced through peaceful coexistence.

- While Islam stands for peace, it needs to be added that it does not subscribe to pacifism. War is clearly permitted in self-defence, defence of one's homeland and manifest aggression against oneself or others who may be helpless in the face of overwhelming acts of aggression. Absolute non-violence is therefore unrealistic and cannot be envisaged by a religion that is characterised as an uprising for justice. Limited use of force is therefore permitted under certain conditions for which there are rules designed to contain and control violence and unwarranted aggression.

SUPPORTIVE EVIDENCE

☐ Qur'an and Hadith

+ 'We have bestowed dignity on the children of Adam.' (Q al-Isra', 17:70)[9]
+ 'We have indeed created man in the best of moulds.' (Q al-Tin, 95:4)[10]
+ 'And the servants God are those who walk the earth with humility, and when the ignorant address them, they say *peace*.' (Q al-Furqan, 25:63)[11]
+ 'Nor can goodness and evil be equal. Repel with what is better; then will he between whom and you was hatred become as if he were your friend and intimate.' (Q Fussilat, 41:34)[12]
+ 'Let there arise from among you a nation who invites to goodness, enjoins right conduct and forbids indecency. Such are they who are successful.' (Q Aal-'Imran, 3:104)[13]
+ 'God commands justice, the doing of good, and liberality to kith and kin, and He forbids all shameful deeds, injustice, and rebellion.' (Q al-Nahl, 16:90)[14]
+ 'Whenever they (mischief makers) kindle the fire of war, God extinguishes it. They strive to do mischief on earth and God loves not those who do mischief.' (Q al-Ma'idah, 5:64)[15]
+ 'If they incline to peace, you should also incline to it, and place your trust in God.' (Q al-Anfal, 8:61)[16]
+ 'O you who believe! Seek help with patience and persever-ance and prayer. For God is with those who patiently persevere.' (Q al-Baqarah, 2:153)[17]

+ 'If you persevere patiently and guard against evil, then that will be the determining factor in all affairs.' (Q 3:186)[18]
+ 'O you who believe! Persevere in patience and constancy; vie in such perseverance; strengthen each other and fear God that you may prosper.' (Q 3:200).[19]
+ 'Fighting is prescribed for you, even though it be hateful to you; but it may well be that you hate something that may perhaps be good, and that you love something that may perhaps be bad for you. And God knows, whereas you know not.' (Q 2:216).[20]
+ 'Keep to forgiveness, enjoin kindness, and turn away from the ignorant.' (Q al-A'raf, 7:199)[21]
+ 'Repel evil [not with evil] but with something that is better (i.e forgiveness).' (Q al-Mu'minun, 23:96)[22]
+ 'I have not been sent to curse anyone but to be a source of mercy and compassion.' (Hadith)[23]
+ 'God has mercy upon those who are merciful to others.' (Hadith)[24]

Legal Maxims

+ 'Human dignity is a foundational purpose of the Shariah.'[25]
+ 'All that which cause sedition/tumult is impermissible.'[26]
+ 'The principle of reciprocal treatment among nations is bound by considerations of moral virtue.'[27]
+ 'Hardship begets facility and ease.'[28]
+ 'The obligation of jihad partakes in the obligation of means and not of the ends/purposes.'*[29]
+ 'Shariah advocates equality among people unless there be evidence to justify specification [of this general principle].'[30]
+ 'Shariah is founded in legislating on the benefits of people in this world and in the next.'[31]
+ 'In regards to the [basic] rights of people in war, the belligerents under safe conduct and non-Muslim permanent residents are all equal.'[32]

---

* Jihad is a means, in other words, with which to repel aggression and injustice, and if these objectives can be met by other means without recourse to military jihad, there shall be no necessity for jihad.

+ 'Property that is not guaranteed in respect of a Muslim [such as property temporarily deposited with one for safe keeping] is also not guaranteed in the respect of an unbeliever.'[33]

+ 'Everyone who works for Muslims [Muslim and non-Muslim alike] is entitled to support from the Public Treasury.'[34]

+ 'Muslims, *dhimmis* and temporary residents are all equal in respect of enacted rights that protect against harm.'*[35]

+ 'Peace among Muslims is permissible provided it does not turn the *halal* into *haram* nor the *haram* into *halal*.'[36]

+ 'Avoidance of hostility as far as possible is an obligation.'[37]

+ 'Elimination of injustice as far as possible is an obligation.'[38]

+ 'Elimination of harm as far as possible is an obligation.'[39]

+ 'Settlement/cessation of disputes as far as possible is an obligation.'[40]

+ 'When defence is possible by lighter means the more difficult/heavy ones may not be attempted.'[41]

+ 'Safe conduct is not granted to one who harms the Muslims.'[42]

+ 'The norm [a normative Shariah presumption] is absence of duress/ compulsion.'[43]

+ 'The norm is absence of hostility.'[44]

+ 'The norm is absence of treachery.'[45]

+ 'Liability [for compensation] falls on the aggressor.'[46]

+ 'Aggression does not acquire a right for the aggressor.'[47]

+ 'Punishment is co-related to prohibition.'[48]

+ 'The norm with regard to life, property and honour is inviolability.'[49]

---

* Everyone is, in other words, protected against hostile action to their persons and properties. 'Enacted rights' mostly imply recognised rights and those under man-made laws and treatises. The substance of this maxim is endorsed by at least three other similarly worded maxims.

XI

Shariah, Gender and Family

Q116) Does Islamic law require the segregation of men and women?

A) Segregation is neither a genuine Islamic nor Arab tradition. It was originally an ancient Persian practice that was adopted by some Muslim communities and became widespread in the course of time. During the time of the Prophet, women had freedom of movement, work and even took part in military expeditions. Yet, Islam discourages free mixing between men and women, especially in situations of privacy, but not all forms of social interaction. They may socialise and work together within the bounds of dignified decorum free of promiscuity, touching, secret meetings or flirting, according to the general rules of interaction between the genders that emphasise modesty and restraint against temptations. Some of these rules are referred to, and understood under, the prevailing custom (*'urf*) and culture of the community, just as they are also liable to change in the course of time. According to a legal maxim of *fiqh*, 'Custom is [a valid] basis of judgment – *al-'adatu muhakkamatun*.'

Q117) Are there any requirements in Shariah regarding how women should dress? Are men also required to dress or groom themselves in certain ways?

A) Shariah requires covering of the private parts (*'awrah*) of both men and women, and there are some detailed rules on this subject which the *fiqh* manuals elaborate. In the case of women, it is clear that the face and the hands are not included in *'awrah*. Wearing the *hijab* is recommended if it is conducive to modesty but the more conservative version, the *niqab*, (as opposed to *hijab, purdah*, scarf, *tudung* (this last as known in Malaysia, etc.) which covers the face completely is an exaggeration, not a requirement, and can sometimes give rise to awkward situations.

I know from personal experience at the International Islamic University of Malaysia that the exam invigilators had difficulty identifying the students who were donning the *niqab*, a situation which led the university authorities to ban *niqab*-wearing in the examination halls.*

For men, their *'awrah* refers to part of the body from the navel (not inclusive) to the knees (inclusive). Religion advises cleanliness of body and attire. Men should not indulge in decorating themselves by wearing feminine clothes, gold jewellery and silk garments that are neither customary nor dignified. What is modest and dignified in clothes and appearance is also to some extent determined by reference to the prevailing custom (*'urf*) of particular societies, and in our time also to some extent by technology and science. What the society considers decent is also deemed, on the whole, acceptable to Islam. This is the purport, in fact, of the often-cited hadith (although most likely to be the saying of the prominent Companion, 'Abd Allah b. Mas'ud) providing: 'What the Muslims deem to be good is good in the sight of God – *ma ra'ahu al-muslimuna hasanan fa-huwa 'ind Allahi hasan.*'

---

* I also happened to interview via Skype a young lady PhD in a foreign country who had applied for an academic post. It was our first encounter and the lady was wearing the *niqab*. At the end of the interview neither I nor my two other colleagues were able to form a clear impression of the candidate's character and opinions. And we put it down partly to the *niqab*. It is remarkable how much simple body language and facial appearance can convey in such situations.

Q118)   What is the Shariah position on marriage?

A)   Shariah is a strong advocate of marriage to the extent that there is no place for celibacy in Islam. Marriage is considered as a religious duty of all able-bodied youth and decent individuals who can make responsible spouses and parents, especially in situations where there is a fear of them falling into sinful conduct, promiscuity and *zina*. The Qur'an views marriage as a sign of God's favour and blessings on humankind. The Prophet of Islam declared that 'marriage is my way; and whoever shuns my way is not of me'. He has also said that 'marriage is one half of the religion', thus signifying marriage as the training ground for many moral virtues including selflessness, patience, steadfastness, accountability, compassion, generosity and more. It is also considered a moral safeguard as well as a social necessity for the health and stability of the family unit.

Marriage is a contract signifying a lifelong commitment between a man and a woman to live as husband and wife in a life of mutual friendship and devotion to one another. It is primarily a civil contract concluded by mutual agreement of two competent persons, but one which also has a religious aspect and this is why marriage is often regarded as a holy union of a man and wife for noble purposes. This contract may, nevertheless, be terminated by divorce or judicial separation on certain grounds, which the law has specified. This is basically in situations where the marriage no longer fulfills its valid objectives and turns, on the contrary, into an instrument of prejudice and abuse (*darar*). The *fiqh* manuals also record serious disease, infertility, failure to provide financial support by the husband, criminality, desertion, dishonourable behaviour and irreconcilable differences as valid grounds for the dissolution of marriage. There may be some variation over the modes of dissolution among the various schools of Islamic law but all have in principle concurred on the possibility of dissolution of marriage when it has reached the point of virtual breakdown.

Q119)   Are men superior to women under Shariah?

A)   Not in the essence of humanity, but there are differences in their rights and obligations. Both genders are seen as equally noble creatures of God. Men and women are different in important ways but are equally accountable before their Creator for their conduct. They are both morally autonomous and the ordinances of religion and Shariah do not treat them differently in regard to their essential human dignity. Women as well as men may attain the highest degree of spiritual eminence, and there have been many women throughout Muslim history who became revered and famous for their good works and scholarly achievement and leadership. Men and women are each rewarded for their good deeds without discrimination.

Q120) How does the Qur'an position women?

A) The Qur'an provides in a verse that men are maintainers and protectors of women, which is on account of the obligation that men provide financial support to women, but the implications of this verse have often been exaggerated so as to say that men are superior.

To quote the verse:

'Men are the maintainers (*qawwamun*) of women because God has made some of them excel others and because of what they spend of their wealth on one another.' (al-Nisa', 4:34)[1]

Another verse often quoted in this connection provides that:

'Women have rights similar to those that men have over them in a just manner, and men are a degree above them.' (Q al-Baqarah, 2: 228)[2]

Both of these passages have come under scrutiny by many observers including the Federal Shariat Court of Pakistan (FSC), which generated, in a leading case in 1983,[*] considerable debate about the precise meaning of the word *qawwamun* in the first verse that may be summarised as follows:

The petitioner Ansar Burney filed a suit to challenge the appointment of women judges and argued before the FSC that the appointment of women as judges was repugnant to the injunctions of Islam. The counsel for the petitioner argued that since the testimony of two women is equivalent to that of one man, at least two female judges would also be required to decide a case.

---

[*] Ansar Burney v. Federation of Pakistan, *All Pakistan Legal Decisions* (1983), Federal Shariah Court 73.

The court rejected this argument and held that acceptance of the counsel's assertion would mean that no *qadi* sitting alone (since the minimum standard of proof is two male witnesses) could decide a civil or criminal case. The FSC then examined in detail all the relevant passages in the Qur'an and hadith and held that there was nothing in the sources that prohibited the appointment of women to judicial positions, and it was therefore permissible.

The court also reviewed a number of Qur'an commentaries on the precise meaning of *qawwamun* in the verse quoted. Various translations were recorded for this word, including 'rulers', 'masters', 'holders of sovereign power', 'persons holding authority', and so on, but the court held that many of them were inaccurate. 'Qawwam' in Arabic is a derivative of *qawama*, which means a provider, supporter, or furnisher for another with the means of subsistence. 'Abdullah Yusuf 'Ali's translation of the word 'qawwam' as 'protector' and that of A. J. Arberry as 'one who manages the affairs of women' were considered to accord with the subsequent segment of the verse to the effect that men utilise their property to support women. The superiority, if any, is not about the natural proficiency of one and the deficiency of the other, but is only on account of the responsibility for maintenance. It must follow then, the court added, that one who does not maintain his wife cannot be a *qawwam*. This explanation also holds for the meaning of the second verse and the rank men have been given, since this verse assigns this rank after a categorical statement of the reciprocal and equivalent rights that the spouses have over one another. 'To call a male sovereign,' the court concluded, 'or one who exercises full dominion over the life and property of a woman ... cannot be in accordance with the Qur'anic injunctions.'

Q121)   Does Islamic law permit polygamy?

A)   Yes there is a stipulated permission in the Qur'an, which is interpreted by commentators and lawmakers to also mean fulfilment of several conditions: the husband must be a just character, be financially able to maintain a separate household, provide his second wife a separate apartment, and divide his time equally among his co-wives, and there be a lawful benefit involved. Polygamy is also limited to the maximum of four. Lastly, that a judicial order is obtained to grant the request.

Historically, polygamy has been the practice of ancient societies long before the advent of Islam. Islam accepted it partly as a social necessity of the time and later due to its own predicament when frequent wars had brought about a population imbalance among Muslims and the presence, as a result, of large numbers of orphaned girls and widows who were in need of support. Polygamy was permitted but limited to the maximum of four wives under the said conditions. The stipulation that there should be a lawful benefit involved, may include the infertility of the existing wife and her illness, just character of the husband and his financial ability to maintain a second wife: for instance, when the existing wife is chronically ill and in need of help. The Qur'an strictly demands the equitable treatment and timesharing of the husband with his co-wives. Modern Islamic family law reforms of the post-colonial period have translated many of these conditions into the letter of the law, sometimes adding the requirement of obtaining the consent of the existing wife to the proposed polygamous marriage. This is based on the analysis that the husband's just and upright character, which is a Qur'anic requirement, will be difficult, even for the court, to ascertain, and the best person who would know that will be the existing wife. Her consent provides the assurance also over the involvement or otherwise of a lawful benefit in the proposed marriage.

Q122) Can Muslims marry non-Muslims?

A) There is no disagreement among the scholars that a Muslim man may marry a woman from the 'peoples of the book – the Ahl al-Kitab', that is Christians or Jews. The conversion of the wife to Islam is not a requirement, but the children will legally be regarded as Muslim. A Muslim woman, may not, on the other hand, marry a non-Muslim man. The reason given is that the husband is the head of the household and his religion influences the children of the marriage. Besides, Islam accepts Christianity and Judaism as valid religions, but Islam itself is not given the same recognition by these older religions. A Muslim husband of a Christian woman can thus be expected to respect her faith but the same is not expected of a non-Muslim man who marries a Muslim wife.

Q123) Does the Shariah encourage arranged marriages?

A) The fundamental principle of Shariah is that of the right of free will, freedom of choice and consent, which can only be expected when the parties to the marriage are adult and competent persons and are *also availed of the opportunity to express their consent.* Islam allows arranged marriages if the element of consent and freedom of choice are not compromised or suppressed. Both the adult parties must be allowed to enter the marriage contract based on their unhindered choice. But forced marriage is not allowed in Islam. This is because marriage is a civil contract concluded by mutual agreement, which consists of a valid offer and acceptance (*ijab* and a *qabul*). If an adult woman is married without her consent, the marriage contract is considered null and void.

Arranged marriage is not synonymous with the imposition and suppression of consent, especially when the parents and families encourage the prospective couple to make their own choices with the consultative input of their families. Arranged marriage which is conducted in this way can be beneficial and most likely introduce an element of stability and family support into the picture. The problem is, however, that this degree of sensitivity and care is often not shown, and in many societies, especially the male-dominated, economically underprivileged tribalist settings, arranged marriage is often tantamount to forced marriage, sometimes for ulterior motives and financial gain on the part of willful and greedy families and relatives, even the parents. Twentieth-century family law reforms have in many Muslim countries addressed this to some extent through the introduction of registration formalities and provisions over a legally stipulated marriageable age. Yet the problem of forced marriage, of which arranged marriage can be just a façade, has proven difficult to address through prescriptive legislation alone, and requires sustained persuasive, educational and policy measures and initiatives to address issues in their own context.

Q124)   Is child marriage permitted in Shariah?

A)   The Shariah provides the age of fifteen as the age of majority (*bulugh*), although support is also found for a lower age as at puberty and also the higher ages of eighteen and even above. The legal age of marriage is designed to ascertain legal competence and intellectual maturity (*rushd*) on the part of prospective spouses and their ability to manage their own affairs. There is no clear validation of child marriage in Shariah. Yet due to a certain lack of definitive ruling on the age of marriage in the Shariah texts, the position has remained somewhat flexible and open to interpretation, which is often taken to mean permissibility of child marriage.

Historically, child marriage was globally accepted and a widely practiced phenomenon. It still exists to a large extent in many parts of the Muslim world especially among tribal and rural populations of Asia and Africa. From the viewpoint of Islamic law, the father or grandfather of a boy or a girl is authorised to contract a minor person into marriage only if it is to the child's manifest interest – in cases, for instance, when the minor girl may not have a prospect of being looked after and the social environment may also be such that educational and employment opportunities for young persons are severely limited. But partly due to widespread abuses of this privilege, legislation in Muslim countries has generally stipulated a legal age and the ensuing registration formalities to conclude a valid marriage, which practically foreclose the door to child marriage. Marriage is a contract between a man and a woman; the Qur'an describes it as a 'strong and solemn covenant — *mithaqan ghalizan*' (al-Nisa', 4:21). This kind of covenant cannot be seen to exist in a child marriage or forced and arranged marriages. According to Islamic law, a child below the age of majority has no legal capacity to enter such a contract, or any contract for that matter, nor is he or she capable to create a firm bond of that kind.

The father, and by analogy also the grandfather, have been vested with the power of constraint (*ijbar*) in that their decision and choice for the marriage of their minor ward, boy or girl, is indisputable and binding. Yet here too the law makes a provision, known as the option of puberty (*khiyar al-bulugh*) which entitles the minor ward to refute the imposed marriage and declare his objection to it upon reaching the age of puberty/majority. Yet this provision of Islamic law has not gained sufficient visibility and support; not enough to overrule the power of *ijbar*, and the parent's choice often prevails as a result. Unless the law lays down a clear procedure for the option of puberty and gives it due visibility and significance, the parental power of constraint is likely to remain strong. Yet it is unfortunate that *ijbar* is often made into an instrument of imposition and abuse.

Q125)   How does the Shariah regulate divorce?

A)   The basic outlook of Shariah on divorce is embodied in a renowned *hadith* which has declared divorce as 'the worst of all permissible things in the sight of God'. Divorce should only be resorted to when there is no chance of reconciliation and a distinct possibility exists also of marital abuse and unhappiness. Traditionally, divorce was a prerogative of the husband, but which led to widespread abuse due largely to the oppressive exercise of the husband's unilateral power of *talaq*. Modern law reforms of Shariah law have opted for judicial separation and availability of divorce under court supervision, which means that a divorce, in order to be valid, must be approved by the court of justice. Legislation in most of the present-day Muslim countries has sought to restrict the husband's power of *talaq*, or transfer the power entirely to the court of justice. Yet instances of violation and oppressive exercise of *talaq* are still widespread. In many Muslim countries the traditional law of divorce, and the family law generally for that matter, have remained largely unchanged. Divorce law reform is still wanting in these countries.

Law reform on marriage and divorce has had an uphill struggle in the Muslim world in view of the fact that tribal forces and patriarchal custom have often resisted it. Governments in Muslim countries however, continued to introduce gradual reforms from time to time. Yet any hopes of progress that there might have been were negatively affected and slowed down due to the spread of terrorism, violence and foreign invasion in so many parts of the Muslim world in recent decades. Law reform cannot thrive under a tense socio-political environment which may well set a different order of priorities for the countries which suffer from incessant security problems. That said, marriage still remains strong in traditional Islamic societies and the Muslim world generally. One notes, to this effect, the prevalence of a solid sense of commitment to the sanctity of the family unit among the vast majority of present-day Muslim individuals and societies.

Q126)   Are women permitted to initiate a divorce? Is it more difficult for women to obtain a divorce than it is for men?

A)   Yes, it is more difficult for women to obtain a divorce in many Muslim countries and societies – though not all. Women are entitled, however, to seek annulment of the marriage contract, judicial separation or divorce in circumstances that are specified in Shariah law and statutory legislation, such as the husband's insanity, incurable disease, failure to maintain, cruelty, etc. In fact, the *fiqh* rules make provisions, in addition to unilateral divorce (*talaq*) by the husband, for divorce by mutual consent (*mubarat*), and also a form of divorce, known as *khul'*, in which the wife initiates the divorce proceedings and agrees to return any dower she might have received from her husband. Another and still related Islamic law provision is the permissibility of delegated divorce (*talaq al-tafwid*) in which the husband delegates his power of unilateral *talaq* to the wife, either at the time of drawing up the marriage contract or during the subsistence of marriage, which she may then be able exercise at her own initiative.

Q127) Are there rules pertaining to the custody of children in case of divorce?

A) According to Islamic law, the wife/mother has a superior right to the custody (*hadanah*) of the young child, whether boy or girl, below certain ages, unless she gets remarried or until the child, if a male, reaches seven years of age, and if female, nine years of age. If the mother of the child gets married and the father challenges her right to custody, then the court may transfer the custody right to the father or allow the mother to retain custody rights, whichever is deemed to be in the best interest of the child. If she is not fit, only then will the custody right be transferrable to the father. When the child reaches seven or nine years of age, the father is entitled to custody. The young boy or girl may, however, be offered the choice between staying with the mother or father. If the father cannot handle the responsibility, or he neglects the child or if he is a man of bad character, then the mother will most likely be given the right of custody. But financial assistance and support of children is the sole responsibility of the father until they reach the age of majority or as the court might decide.

Q128) Does the Shariah regulate domestic violence?

A) Violence, be it verbal, physical or sexual, including insulting and abusive language and aggressive behaviour are entirely forbidden by the Shariah. According to the Qur'an, the interaction between the spouses should be based on compassion and kindness. The wife is entitled to seek judicial relief and the husband, if proven guilty of abusive behaviour and violence, may be punished by the court of justice. Under normal circumstances, the husband is the head of the household and is entitled to discipline their young children. A certain amount of that is also true in the case of the wife, but only when she is recalcitrant (*nashizah*) and manifestly abusive, in which case the husband may discipline her. The purpose of this provision is to settle minor family issues internally and avoid adversarial processes and court litigations in domestic matters that can be resolved amicably without prejudice or abuse. Should the level of discord between the spouses become internally unmanageable, recourse may then be had to arbitration (*tahkim*), which is by appointment of one arbitrator from each side of the two families to settle the differences and enable the spouses to live in peace and harmony again. If all this fails, cases of domestic violence may be taken to the court of justice, by either the wife, the husband or both.

Q129) Is female genital mutilation allowed under Shariah?

A) Female genital mutilation (FGM), also known as female genital cutting and female circumcision, is the ritual removal of some or all of the external female genitalia. Typically carried out by a traditional circumciser using a blade, with or without anaesthesia, FGM is concentrated in twenty-seven African countries, Indonesia, Yemen and Iraqi Kurdistan, and found elsewhere in Asia, the Middle East and among diaspora communities around the world. It is conducted from days after birth to puberty and beyond. In half the countries for which national figures are available, most girls are cut before the age of five.

FGM was practiced among the pre-Islamic Arabs and has survived among some Arab communities after the advent of Islam. Its practice today is very widespread despite the generally negative opinion of Muslim scholars and intellectuals concerning it. FGM is seen as an injury and a violation of the physical integrity of a female person. Islamic law and religion only validates circumcision of the male child. Cliterodectomy and infibulation are in any case considered to be excessively invasive and forbidden — *haram*. The effects on health depend on the procedure, but can include recurrent infections, chronic pain, cysts, an inability to get pregnant, complications during childbirth, and bleeding. There are no known health benefits.

The procedures differ according to the ethnic group. They include removal of the clitoral hood and clitoral glans, removal of the inner labia and in the most severe form (known as infibulation) removal of the inner and outer labia. The practice is rooted in gender inequality, attempts to control women's sexuality and ideas about purity, modesty and aesthetics. It is usually initiated and carried out by women, who see it as a source of honour and fear that failing to have their daughters and granddaughters cut will expose the girls to social exclusion. At least 200 million women and girls in the key thirty countries have experienced FGM as of 2016.

FGM has been outlawed or restricted in most of the countries in which it occurs, but the laws are poorly enforced. There have been international efforts since the 1970s to persuade practitioners to abandon it, and in 2012 the United Nations General Assembly, recognising FGM as a human-rights violation, voted unanimously to intensify those efforts.

A minority opinion among Muslim scholars subscribe to the view that FGM was validated by the Prophetic hadith, and many have, as such, equated it with the male circumcision.

There is no reference to FGM in the Qur'an whatsoever. No ruling of a scholarly consensus (ijma') or of an analogy (qiyas) with the male circumcision has been recorded. The one hadith that is often quoted in support of FGM has also become highly controversial, as it is shown, by the researchers, to be unreliable and most likely a forgery.

According to the hadith at issue, a woman in Madinah by the name Umm 'Atiyyah used to practice FGM and other women used to go to her for the purpose. Then it is added that the Prophet told her one day: 'Oh Umm 'Atiyyah! Take the smallest amount [of the skin] so as not to weaken [the body]; for it gladens the face and is enjoyable for the husband.'*

Al-Bayhaqi has recorded this in his *Sunnan* and al-Hakim in his *Mustadrak*. Abu Dawud who has recorded a similar but a slightly different version of it in his *Sunnan Abu Dawud*, has followed it with the observation that the chain of transmission of the hadith is weak and broken in parts (*da'if, munqati'*). One of the narrators of this hadith is Muhammad ibn Hassan al-Kufi. Some

---

* Arabic version of the hadith reads: '*Ya Umm 'Atiyyah! Ashmi wa-la tanhiki, fa-innahu asra li'l-wajhi wa ahza li'l-zawj.*'

hadith scholars have identified this man to be the same as the one who was given the appellation, Muhammad b. Sa'id al-Maslub al-Kadhdhab. This was the person who had claimed to have fabricated 4,000 hadith, and was executed for it by the Abbasid caliph al-Mansur (d. 775 CE). Imam Ahmad ibn Hanbal has confirmed that Hassan al-Kufi aka Maslub al-Kadhdhab was a *Zindiq* (heretic) which was why he was executed.

The contemporary Egyptian scholar, Muhammd Salim al-'Awwa, author of several important works on Islamic criminal law, has discussed the evidence on FGM in detail and quoted a large number of prominent Muslim scholars, including Hafiz Zayn al-Din al-'Iraqi (d. 1403 CE), Muhammad b. 'Ali al-Shawkani (d. 1839 CE), Sayyid Sabiq (d. 2000 CE), Yusuf al-Qaradawi (b. 1926) and others to say that the hadith of Umm 'Atiyyah is unreliable and should be discarded. Al-'Awwa draws the conclusion that 'female genital mutilation is a violation of the physical safety of young girls by wounding and severing a part of their body. It is impermissible and a fallacy to call it *mubah* (permissible). Nay, it is forbidden both in Shariah and law (*al-mahzur wa'l-muharram shar'an wa qanunan*). The normative principle of Shariah in this regard is the prohibition of all acts of aggression on the lives, property and honour of people… it is absolutely harmful, injuring the body and dulling the senses of young innocent girls' (*al-Fiqh al-Islami fi-Tariq al-Tajdid*, 2nd edn by the Ministry of Culture — Wizarat al-Thaqafah — of Jordan, Amman, 2013, p. 195).

Salim al-'Awwa added that all of this notwithstanding, statistics in Egypt suggest that FGM is very widely practiced. It is estimated that ninety-five per cent of Egyptian females undergo FGM. He then recounts an episode when due partly to the campaign he personally spearheaded against FGM, the Minister of Health of Egypt issued an order to declare FGM prohibited. That was followed by an intervention by the Administrative Court of Egypt to revoke the ministerial order. A great deal of media controversy was generated and the saga did not come to a decisive end (ibid. pp. 196–205).

Q130) Do women and men enjoy equality under the Islamic inheritance law? Can Muslims and non-Muslims inherit from one another?

A) Inheritance law is very much embedded in the clear Qur'anic text and bears therefore an obligatory character for the most part. This is also the case largely with bequests, although some parts of the law of bequest are founded in the authority of hadith. The category of recipients and the quantum of their shares in the estate of their deceased relatives are stipulated in the Qur'an and make the whole schema of Qur'anic inheritance law internally self-contained. To try to change or adjust some parts of these entitlements is likely to affect the whole scheme and prove detrimental to the other relatives involved. This may explain why the jurists have resorted very little to *ijtihad* in this field and if they have done so it has been usually in a subsidiary, clarificatory and supportive capacity.

Broadly, the Qur'an improved the legal and financial status of the women of Arabia by assigning to them, especially the close relatives, specific portions in inheritance. Of the total of twelve Qur'anic sharers, known as *dhawil-furud* (the most important of the three classes of sharers: the other two being the agnatic and maternal relatives – *'asabah* and *dhawu al-arham* respectively), eight are women. This was a major improvement in the male-dominated tribalist setting of pre-Islamic Arabia. That said, the Shariah generally entitles the male to a double share of the female relative in the same degree of relationship to the deceased. Muslim jurists explain this aspect of the inheritance law by looking at Islamic law in its entirety, which makes it the responsibility of men to provide maintenance, shelter, and safe environment for women throughout their lives, that is, before marriage, during it, and afterwards. Women who get married are also entitled to a dower (*mahr*) from their would-be husbands. With regard to maintenance (*nafaqah*), it is an absolute duty of the husband to provide it to his wife regardless of her own financial status, and even if she happens to be affluent.

Difference of religion is a bar to inheritance on both sides in that Muslims and non-Muslims do not inherit from one another, as stipulated by the majority of Muslim jurists. Non-Muslims can be, however, beneficiaries of gifts (*hibah*) and bequests (*wasiyyah*) from Muslims. Gifts and bequests can also be used to rectify and adjust technical imbalances that may arise from the mandatory structure and share distribution of inheritance law in certain particular combinations as specified in the relevant *fiqh* manuals. The provisions of gift and bequest, if carefully utilised, can to a large extent compensate for the bar in inheritance between Muslims and non-Muslims. Modern developments and the pluralist make-up of most of the present-day Muslim societies also present compelling scenarios for adjustment. The religion-based bar here is not Qur'anic but founded in the authority of a solitary (*Ahad*) hadith, which may leave some room for innovative *ijtihad* so as to prevent situations of manifest injustice. This may be based either on a case-by-case solution by recourse to the principle of juristic preference (*istihsan*), or by general reform of the law through the exercise of independent reasoning and *ijtihad*.

Q131)   Are homosexuality and lesbianism considered violations of the sanctity of marriage?

A)   Yes they are. Homosexuality is not only a sin, but also a punishable offence under Islamic law, often said to be punishable by the same punishment as is provided for adultery or *zina*. Neither the Qur'an nor the hadith have stipulated a specified punishment for homosexuality, which means that it is most likely a *ta'zir* offence, not a *hadd* and it is, as such, punishable by a deterrent punishment that may be quantified by the court of Shariah. The leading Sunni and Shia schools of law differ, however, on the type and quantum of punishment for homosexuality. While some, like the Shafi'i and Shia Imamiyyah school, draw an analogy between adultery/*zina* and homosexuality/*liwat* and assign the same punishment for both, others, including the Hanafi school, have considered this to be a discrepant analogy and opt for a different approach yet still provide for severe punishments, even if it is treated as a *ta'zir* offence. The Shia Imamiyyah punish homosexuality even without penetration with 100 lashes of the whip. *Fiqh* scholars in all schools including the Shia on the enormity of lesbianism that it falls under the Qur'anic term *fahishah* (lewdness) (al-A'raf 7:80) but still hold that it is not a *hudud* offence. This is because there is no clear text on it and may therefore be punished by a deterrent *ta'zir* punishment. Homosexuality and lesbianism are objectionable for the following reasons:

(1) They are unnatural and clash with the moral principles of Islam; (2) They violate the integrity of the family unit and the institution of marriage; and (3) They are morally abhorrent and denigrate the moral fabric of the Muslim society.

Q132)   Does honour killing have any basis in Shariah?

A)   It is prohibited absolutely and considered as a great sin and a punishable crime under Shariah. There is no recognition whatsoever of the concept of honour in that sense in Islamic law. Islam waged a campaign against fanaticism and extreme revenge that was typical of the pre-Islamic Arab society. The Qur'an taught instead that if one chooses to punish (in the course of justice) then it must not exceed the pain that was inflicted on one in the first place, but if one decides to forgive, that is far better (Q al-Nahl, 16:126). The Prophet expressed strong aversion to tribalist fanaticism and warned anyone who acted in that way. Thus in a hadith, he said: 'He is not one of us who invites [others] to fanaticism (*'asabiyyah*), nor one who fights for fanaticism, nor one who dies for fanaticism.' Islam was an uprising for justice and a protest against lawlessness and all behaviour that violated human dignity, equity and fairness in personal and social relations. Moderation (*wasatiyyah*, *i'tidal*), dignified resistance to temptation (*al-hilm*), a certain inclination toward forgiveness and an easy-going encounter are integral to the ethos of Islam. Honour killing is a violation of Islamic teachings and its emphasis on moderation and law-abiding behaviour that is expected of everyone without exception or priviledge.

Q133) What does the Shariah say about domestic violence? Does it permit wife-beating?

A) There is a verse in the Qur'an which envisages situations of domestic tension and 'disobedience' by the wife and it provides: 'Good women are obedient, guarding in secret that which God has guarded. As for those from whom you fear disobedience, admonish them, then banish them to beds apart and strike them. Then if they obey, you have no right to harm them' (al-Nisa' 4:34). A gradual course of action is thus advised that begins with admonition or discussion between the husband and wife alone or with the assistance of arbiters. This practice, also recommended in (4:35) and (4:128), is to be used for couples considering divorce. If this fails, the second option is physical separation and sleeping in separate beds, to give the couple space for cooling off and reflection about the future of their marital relationship. The third and final method is striking, which takes grammatically the singular form, so that only a single strike is permissible.

The verse under review was revealed early in the Madinan period of the Prophet's mission, a time and place in which cruelty and violence against women remained rampant. Thus some contemporary commentators have argued that the single strike permitted in this verse was intended as a restriction on an existing practice, not as a recommended method for dealing with one's wife.

In the major hadith collections, al- Bukhari, Muslim, al-Tirmidhi, Abu Dawood and others – hadiths about striking emphasise that striking should be done in such a way that it does not inflict injury or harm. These sources stress that in cases where a single strike is used, it should be merely symbolic. The Shafii school and many other Muslim jurists have maintained that it is preferable to avoid striking altogether – especially in light of the added information to the effect that the Prophet, pbuh, has not resorted to it himself. In a hadith narrated by Aishah, the Prophet's widow, she went on record to say that the Prophet never raised his hand against her throughout their married life.

In recent years scholars have argued that 'obedience' refers to the woman's attitude towards God, not towards her husband. Furthermore, obedience in this verse is tied to the woman's guarding of her chastity, so that an obedient woman is one who does not commit sexual immorality. The word that is typically employed for 'disobedience' (nushuz) refers to a disruption of marital harmony when one spouse fails to fulfil the required duties of marriage. It is applied elsewhere in the Qur'an to both men and women. The end of the verse admonishes men not to mistreat women who obey them. Rather than granting men the right to strike their wives, reformers argue, this verse reminds men of their responsibility to treat women fairly.

Whenever the Prophet was informed of individual cases of a man striking his wife, he expressed his utter distaste for it. To take first recourse to striking and physical punishment would thus be a departure from the spirit of the Sunnah and also of the wider Qur'anic teachings on patience (sabr), dignified forbearance (hilm), kindness and compassion (rahmah), particularly with one's wife and family. God has bestowed 'dignity on the children of Adam' as the Qur'an declares in (al-Isra', 17:70), and it is not dignified for a man to abuse his wife and family. He is, on the contrary, strongly advised to honour her and be kind to her. In a renowned hadith, the Prophet is quoted saying that 'the best of you are those who are good to their families'.

More specifically, with reference to marriage, the Qur'an describes it as a way for the spouses to 'find peace therein', and it becomes for them a means of finding 'love and compassion (muwaddah wa rahmah)' (al-Rum, 30:21). In another verse the Qur'an describes the relationship of the spouses as a 'protective garment' to one another (al-Baqarah, 2:187). The ethos of Islam that emerges, therefore, is one of loyalty, dedication and protection within the family especially between the spouses. And, in a legal context, the Qur'an also provides that the wives have over their husbands rights equivalent to those that their husbands have over them (al-Baqarah, 2:229).

The basic notion of the three-step approach to overcoming minor marital irritations is that they should be dealt with quietly by the spouses between themselves, and should not be made the subject of outside intervention and court litigation. This positive purpose should be pursued in a constructive spirit. There is also a permission in Islam, for example, for parents who may administer light physical punishment to their children above a certain age, if they neglect their obligatory prayer (*salah*). The context is once again family leadership that conforms with the ethical teachings of kindness and compassion, one that protects the sanctity of marriage and family life with firm resolve and dedication, yet equipped also with a certain structure and role to address situations of disobedience and abuse.

Despite the fact that domestic violence continued to exist in male-dominated cultures and to be legitimated in the name of religion, neither the mainstream Qur'anic teachings, nor the hadith support or permit it.

Q134) Are women allowed to work under Shariah?

A) Yes, they are, but the matter calls for some elaboration.

Medieval society barred women from outside work that was unrelated to family business, farming, weaving, embroidery, etc. Some of the religious guidelines on modesty and self-control were also given exaggerated interpretations so as to ban women from working outside the home. Custom and culture, prevailing economic conditions, education and a host of other factors all played a role, as they still do, and need to be taken into account in presenting a holistic picture of women's right to work. The Qur'anic evidence on the right of work has no gender bias. Broadly, work is seen in the Qur'an as a dimension of the personal pride and honour of a Muslim, who must work to earn a living to support himself, his family and dependants:

'Tell the believers to work. Then soon will God, His Messenger and the believers see the work you have done.' (al-Tawbah, 9:105)

It is then provided in another verse:

'We shall not cause to waste the recompense of one who excels in work.' (al- Kahf, 18:30)

Work ('amal) can mean religious and charitable work as well as work in order to earn a living. These passages evidently show no gender bias and apply equally to all. The next verse we quote is explicitly on women's right to work and their exclusive entitlement to what they earn from it. Thus it is provided:

'Men are entitled to [the proceeds of] what they earn (iktasabu) and women are entitled to [the proceeds of] what they earn (iktasabna).' (al-Nisa', 4:32)

This verse is clear on its message and purpose, yet it has been given different interpretations that divert the reader's attention to other applications. Yet I shall only refer to how the renowned Qur'an commentator, al-Tabari (d. 923/310), understood this to be a clear authority on women's right of work. This conclusion is supported by the words used, as he pointed out, in particular, nasib (proceeds or result of work), and iktisab (acquisition), which means earning something through work. Al-Tabari disagrees with the view that iktisab in this verse refers to a share of inheritance. Al-Tabari explains that inheritance is not earned as such, but received without self-exertion and personal labour. Hence those who ignore the difference between iktisab and inheritance (mirath) are taking an unacceptable position. Other commentators have added that this verse also implies that women are entitled to take up all suitable occupations they might be capable of undertaking.

The Prophet has added his voice in a hadith that 'God loves it when a worker undertakes a work that he does it well', and declared in another hadith that 'No one has ever eaten food purer than what is earned by the toil of one's hands. For the Prophet (cum-King) David, pbuh, used to earn his living by the toil of his hands.' Historical records also show that during the Prophet's lifetime, women were a part of the social fabric of society and present in the public sphere, they worked and taught just as they also took part in military expeditions – although not in front-line positions, but in supportive roles. Thus it appears that a great deal of the subsequent restrictions on women's right to work is the product of medieval society's male-dominated culture and mindset.

Contemporary Muslim commentators have upheld these conclusions, yet have called attention in the meantime to the crucial services women render to society in their motherhood roles, which should be regarded as work and given due recognition. Then also that decisions over work and education should be made through consultation with the spouse and family. These latter are advised not to obstruct the choice of work and education of their women members.

Women should stay away in the meantime from works that compromise their personal and moral integrity, but otherwise make a contribution to society in all their creative endeavours and capacities.

Q135) Can women have an education?

> Yes. Women are entitled to have an education and no one, including her husband or family, should obstruct her wishes to gain educational qualifications.

There is much evidence in the hadith to the effect that the Prophet encouraged everyone, men and women, to increase their knowledge of Islam and of all beneficial disciplines that bring benefit to humanity. Thus according to a hadith, 'people are of two types: they are either the learned or the learners, and no good will come out of those who do not belong to either'. In another renowned hadith it is provided: 'Pursuit of knowledge is an obligation of every Muslim.'

Another version of this hadith actually adds the words '*wa muslimatin*' (and Muslim woman) thus making pursuit of knowledge a common obligation of the believers, men and women alike. Some commentators have noted, however, that this addition is a mere elaboration as the phrase 'every Muslim' includes women.

The Prophet took a decidedly affirmative stance on the dissemination of knowledge when he said: 'It is not becoming of a person gifted with knowledge to ruin himself (by abstaining from teaching it to others).' Those who attended the sermons of the Prophet were instructed to convey the basic message of his teachings to others who were unable to attend. Women were also encouraged to advance their knowledge of Islam and to this effect the Prophet responded positively to a request made by the women of Madinah 'to fix a day for us as the men were taking all of your time'. On (hearing) this he promised them one day in which to meet them and teach them.

According to a hadith al-Bukhari has recorded, on the authority of Mujahid: knowledge is not attained by one who is very shy or high-handed and arrogant. And 'Aishah, the Prophet's wife, is reported to have made the remark: 'How excellent the women of the Ansar are: they do not feel shy while learning religious knowledge.'

Among modern Muslim scholars, Subhi Mahmassani has observed that 'education from the Shariah viewpoint is not only a privilege, a right or liberty, but it is an obligation that is clearly conveyed in the Prophetic directive to 'seek knowledge even if it be in China', and that 'pursuit of knowledge is an obligation of every Muslim'. According to yet another observer, 'Islam recognises education as a natural right of every individual.' Mustafa al-Siba'i, and Sadiq 'Afifi have similarly held that everyone has a right to education in Islam and that includes men, women, rich and poor, ruler and ruled, rural dwellers and urban people all alike without any discrimination or preference. Islam stands by good reason and it is good common sense simply to say that educated women and mothers can make a tremendous contribution to the healthy upbringing of children in the family and society.

Q136) Are women free to travel under Shariah?

A) Traditional juristic rulings on this advised women to avoid travel without the company of a close male relative (*mahram*) and stressed that women should confine their movements outside the home, barring urgent circumstances such as emergencies, to visiting their parents, a doctor or jurisconsult. For these occasions she needed no permission of her husband or other relatives, but she was otherwise advised to obtain a permission. These positions were taken in the absence of a clear ruling in the Qur'an or hadith on the subject.

Twentieth-century legal opinions (*fatwas*) and *ijtihad* revised and changed the traditional positions and allowed women to travel unaccompanied by close relatives. The renowned Yusuf al-Qaradawi's initial *fatwa* validated air travel for women unaccompanied by male relatives. Al-Qaradawi explained that the prohibitory ruling of *fiqh* on this was intended to ensure women's physical and moral safety, but added that modern air travel fulfils this requirement. He further supported his view with an analysis of the relevant hadith on the subject, and arrived at a ruling better suited to contemporary conditions. The Darul Ifta (central *fatwa* authority) of Egypt has also issued a *fatwa* on this subject, which reads:

It is allowed for a woman to travel without *mahram* provided that she is sure about the safety of her trip, her residence and return and that she will not be interrupted in herself and her religion... The *fatwa* in our time is that a woman is allowed to travel on her own in the safe modes of travel, populated routes, ports, passages, harbours and airports, by public means of transport. This is permitted in Shariah without any objection, regardless as to whether the trip is obligatory, recommendable or permissible.*

One may also refer, perhaps, to the *fiqh* legal maxim which provides that 'the change of rules is undeniable with the change of times'. The maxim here is particularly relevant to the rules of *fiqh* that originate in customary practices and premodern *ijtihad*. When there is a change in the custom and culture of society, and the requirements of time, the relevant rules should also be changed and substituted with more suitable alternatives. Women in public service positions, such as members of parliament and ministers, often need to travel for important duties and it would be unreasonable to apply outdated *fiqh* rules to their position.

Q137)   Are women allowed to drive a car?

A)   Yes, they are allowed to drive a car and they do so in most Muslim countries except in Saudi Arabia, which is also beginning to change. There is no prohibitive ruling on this in the sources of Shariah, and our answer to the previous question regarding women's ability to travel also subsumes this question for the most part. If they are allowed to travel on their own unaccompanied by a close male relative, and also allowed to work outside the home, then by virtue of the same logic they are allowed to drive a car. This is once again a matter outside the category of religious observances (*'ibadat*) and a part clearly of customary and civilian activities of women. The Shariah normally refers such matters to the good judgment of people and general custom (*'urf*) of the society. A legal maxim of *fiqh* on this says that, 'The general practice of society is a valid basis of judgment – *al'adatu muhakkamatun*.' Another legal maxim that may be brought into the picture is that of the original position of permissibility (*ibahah*). The maxim thus has it: 'The normative position [of Shariah] in all matters [of concern to custom and civil transactions] is that of permissibility unless there be a prohibition to the contrary.' Driving a car by itself is not offensive, unless it is used as a means by which to commit an offence, or when a person drives so recklessly

---

* Fatwa no. 3684 dated 30.5.2011 available at http://www.daralifta.org/ViewFatwa.aspx?ID= 3684&LangID=1

that driving for him or her should be banned – there is no inherent objection to driving otherwise. There is no empirical evidence either to suggest that women are dangerous drivers and that banning them from driving will save lives. On the contrary women are seen as equal to men in this regard, and there is no reason why they should not be able to drive a car, or pilot an aeroplane, for that matter.

Q138)   What is *mahr*? Is it the price of purchasing a wife?

A)   Not at all. *Mahr* (dower) is a free gift that the husband gives to his wife as a gesture of goodwill and earnestness, not signifying any exchange. This is how the Qur'an characterises *mahr*: 'And give the women [you marry] their dower (*saduqatihinna*) as a free gift (*nihlah*)' (al-Nisa', 4:5). *Mahr* is actually a juristic term. The Qur'an does not even call it by that name, but refers to it as '*saduqat*' which is from '*sadaqah*', meaning 'charity', but then it is also characterised in the same verse as '*nihlah*' meaning a 'free gift' one gives as a gesture of goodwill *sadaqah* is also a derivative of *sidq*, meaning truth/sincerity, hence the Qur'anic use of it in that context. It is not the price of purchasing a wife. Sale and purchase is a contract of exchange, and it is void without an object of value and a price given in exchange of it. Dower in a marriage is not an essential requirement (*rukn*) of the contract, but a condition (*shart*). A marriage can be concluded even without it, but since it is also endorsed by the Sunnah of the Prophet it has become a subsidiary requirement, or a condition of completeness that partakes in an act of devotion, simply because the Qur'an refers to it as free gift and a charitable donation.

Marriage is a civil contract which is concluded with the consent of two competent parties, a man and a woman, provided there are no permanent or temporary impediments to the proposed union. The law treats dower as a gift and as such does not specify a maximum or minimum for it, although the minimum according to a hadith report can be an 'iron ring'. Interestingly, the reference to 'iron ring' occurs in a hadith which says that 'A woman came to the Prophet and said to him "O Messenger of God! I have gifted myself to you [in marriage]." The Prophet paused and after a few moments of delay, a man stood and asked the Prophet "O Messenger of God! Marry her to me." The Prophet asked the man if he had anything of value to give her as 'sadaq' (another name for dower – mahr). The man said he did not have anything other than the clothes he was wearing. The Prophet then said "Give her something even if it is an iron ring." The man said that he did not have even that. Then the Prophet asked if he knew anything of the Qur'an, to which the man replied in the affirmative and he specified the chapters that he knew. The Prophet then said to the man "I have married her to you; teach her what you know of the Qur'an." This is a widely reported hadith and has given rise to questions among jurist as to whether dower should be anything of monetary value.

So the manner of references to dower in the Qur'an and hadith makes it clear that it is not a price for the purchase of a wife, nor is it an essential requirement of the contract. An adult woman may omit the dower or exonerate the husband of it, or even gift it back to him. Since it is a free gift, there are no legal restrictions of the kind that would apply to an exchange contract.

Q139) Can women marry whom they wish?

A) Generally yes, in the sense that marriage is a contract and it requires two competent parties for its conclusion. An adult woman is fully competent to conclude her own marriage, just as she is also competent to conduct all her own property and financial affairs, without the involvement of a marriage guardian, or wali. This is the position, in fact, of the Hanafi school of law, whereas the other leading schools have given a greater role to the guardian in the marriage even of adult women. So it is this issue over the scope and authority of guardianship in marriage that has to some extent compromised the rights of women to conclude their own marriage contracts, as I will elaborate. But before I do so, it will be noted that the law prohibits marriage to one's close relatives, a restriction that applies to both men and women. Hence the freedom to marry whom one wishes is a qualified freedom.

Guardianship (wilayah) in Islamic law restricts a women's ability to marry whom she wishes. Guardianship is defined as the ability of a person to make decisions concerning another person, regardless of the wishes or agreement of the latter. Guardianship may be of persons or of property, and although the two mostly coincide, they are not always concurrent. There are arguably three grounds of guardianship under Shariah: minority, insanity, and within limits, feminine gender.

There is a legitimate need for guardianship that most legal traditions have recognised. A perusal of the relevant evidence in the sources suggests, however, that the guardian's power of constraint in marriage has little support in the Qur'an and Sunnah, and it is most likely to have originated in premodern social practices that were eventually adopted by the jurists. Juristic doctrine in the Maliki, Shafi'i, Hanbali and also the Shi'i schools has made the consent of the guardian a requirement for the solemnisation of marriage of all persons, except for divorcees, widows and male adults. The Hanafis do not require, as already noted, the consent of the guardian for adult persons, but it is required if the ward is a minor or insane.

Ibn Rushd al-Qurtubi (Aerroes d. 1198 CE) whose renowned work, *Bidayat al-Mujtahid*, on comparative *fiqh* is designed to explain and ascertain conflicts and concordances in scholastic jurisprudence, concludes his analysis on guardianship in marriage as follows:

> 'The cause of their disagreement is that there is no text in the Qur'an nor in the Sunnah of the Prophet which clearly validates guardianship as a prerequisite of marriage, let alone any clear text (*nass*) on the point. Rather the [Qur'an] verses and hadith that are cited by the proponents of guardianship are ambiguous, and so are the verses and hadith that are cited by their opponents. Although the hadith that are cited by the latter group are clear in respect of meaning, they are of questionable authenticity.'

Ibn Rushd has further observed that even the rational arguments advanced by both sides are less than satisfactory. The Prophet, himself has not practiced guardianship, nor has he given a clear mandate in its support, despite the frequent cases that were brought to his attention on this evidently important matter. Ibn Rushd then concludes that guardianship is not a legal requirement of a valid marriage but may be assigned an optional supervisory role to ensure due consideration and care of the interests of the ward.

Joseph Schacht (d. 1969) in his *Origins of Islamic Jurisprudence* (p. 183) has drawn the conclusion that in pre-Islamic Arabia, marriage without a guardian was the norm and that the requirement of a guardian was introduced during the Umayyads in the second century AH, probably no later than the reign of 'Umar ibn 'Abd al-'Aziz (d. 101/721).

While the validity of guardianship in Shariah law is based on the legitimate needs of persons who are insane or of impaired legal capacity, there is no such need on the part of an adult woman for marriage guardianship. On the contrary, the manner in which this power has been exercised in traditional societies down to the present has been oppressive for the most part. This is because marriage guardians are widely known to have imposed their own will on adult women and even men, and made child marriage a regular feature of those societies. These two instances of abuse of guardianship have virtually proven to be sources of widespread social mischief.

This was why when the Islamic family law reform gained momentum in the latter half of the twentieth century, many Muslim countries of the Middle East, Asia and Africa introduced provisions for marriageable age stipulating sixteen and eighteen years (many have stipulated eighteen years for both) for girls and boys respectively as a requirement of marriage registration and issuance of marriage certificates. The age provisions have thus practically proscribed child marriage, and also required expressed consent of the prospective spouses upon registration. Many laws, however, still permit marriage of a fifteen-year-old girl, with the consent of her guardian, should there be a special need for it.

In countries where the law enforcement agencies are effective and their laws have also adopted marriageable age provisions, such as Malaysia, Morocco, the Gulf countries, etc., the age provisions ensure that adult women conclude their own marriage contracts. For many other countries of the Muslim world that lack efficient enforcement mechanisms, legal provisions do not represent reality and the challenges of overcoming prejudicial custom and patriarchal society attitudes have unfortunately remained largely unmet. Prescriptive legislation has generally been less than effective, and are often wanting of adequate policy and public awareness campaign measures to upgrade their poor success records.

Q140) What are the consequences of violating Islamic law vis-à-vis the family?

A) It is considered a transgression and violation of what Islamic law seeks to defend, and may, in severe cases, call for judicial relief and punishment. Marriage is described in the Qur'an as a 'firm [unbreakable] bond – *mithaqan ghaliz*'. It is also described, as already noted, as 'friendship, protection and kindness'. Observance of the ties of kinship and family relations is similarly an integral part of the teachings of the Qur'an and hadith. These sources are emphatic on honouring one's parents and direct the latter, in turn, to teach their children and family members the ethics of moderation and self-restraint. The youth are instructed not to annoy their parents in words and in deeds. And then if instances of tension do arise, one should not let, according to clear instructions in the hadith, the rift/alienation extend beyond three days at the most. The young are advised to seek forgiveness of their parents for any shortcomings and the parents and elders to show kindness in return. Protection of the sanctity of marriage, which is the foundation stone of the family unit, is also one of the five over-riding objectives (*maqasid*) of Shariah. Preservation of lineage (*hifz al-nasab*) and safeguarding the purity of the parent-child relationship thus rank high in Shariah's order of priorities. Adultery (*zina*) is a grave violation of those values and a punishable crime for which the Qur'an has imposed a prescribed punishment (see for details Chapter VII). It is instructive to read in a hadith that 'the best of you is one who treats his wife and family well'.

SUPPORTIVE EVIDENCE

▢ Qur'an and Hadith

+ 'Among His signs is that He created for you spouses from among yourselves, that you might dwell in tranquility with them, and God has placed between you love and compassion. Surely in that there are signs for people who reflect.' (Q al-Rum, 30:21)[3]
+ 'They [your wives] are your garment and you are their garment [for protection, comfort, confidentiality].' (Q al-Baqarah, 2:187)[4]
+ 'Whoever does good, whether male or female, and is a believer, We shall certainly make them live a good life, and We shall give them their reward for the best of what they have done.' (Q al-Nahl, 16:97).[5]
+ 'Muslim men and Muslim women, believing men and believing women, obedient men and obedient women, patient men and patient women, humble men and humble women, men who give alms and women who give alms, men who fast and women who fast, women and men who guard their modesty, women and men who remember God abundantly – God has prepared for them forgiveness and great rewards.' (Q al-Ahzab, 33:35)[6]

+ 'And the recompense of evil is an evil like it, but one who forgives and makes amends, his reward will be with God, and He loves not the oppressors.' (Q al-Shura, 42:40)[7]
+ 'Good morals are the weightiest of all things that are weighed (on the Day of Judgment).' (Hadith).[8]
+ 'The best part of faith (iman) is (to have) beautiful manners.' (Hadith)[9]
+ 'I was sent in order to perfect the virtues of morality.' (Hadith)[10]
+ 'Every religion has its ethos, and the ethos of Islam is modesty (al-haya').' (Hadith)[11]
+ 'Gentleness fails not to create beauty in all things, and it is not taken away from anything without causing ugliness.' (Hadith)[12]
+ 'Do not underestimate the value of decency and good manners, even if it be by facing your brother with a smile, or by giving water to the thirsty.' (Hadith)[13]
+ 'If you spend a dinar in the way of God, and another with which to support your servant, and another that you give in charity to the poor, and yet another by which you support your family, the dinar that you spend on your family earns you the greatest reward.' (Hadith)[14]

[] **Legal Maxims**

+ 'The rules [of shariah] are objectively understood regardless of gender specification.'[15]
+ 'All conditions [inserted in a marriage contract] that benefit the woman and do not violate the purpose of marriage are valid and binding.'[16]
+ 'The wealthy of the family are to support its needy ones.'[17]
+ 'Testimony of women is credible generally in all [judicial] rulings unless it has been restricted based on reason/evidence.'[18]
+ 'A woman is like a man in respect of legal capacity.'[19]
+ 'A woman is like a man in respect of her property.'[20]
+ 'A woman is like a man in regard to ownership.'[21]
+ 'A woman is subject to no guardianship in respect of her property.'[22]
+ 'Credibility in the wording of a marriage contract is attached to the purpose and meaning.'[23]

+ 'An explicit divorce occurs independently of intention.'[24]
+ 'No divorce [is valid] in a state of unconsciousness.'[25]
+ 'Every condition that contravenes the requirements of marriage is void but the marriage survives with a proper dower.'[26]
+ 'Maintenance that is determined by adjudication or consent is not omitted without either payment or waiver.'[27]
+ 'Divorce can only occur over a subsisting marriage.'[28]
+ 'Marriage is not terminated by a revocable divorce but it is terminated by a final one.'[29]
+ 'That which establishes a permanent prohibition and [subsequently] befalls a marriage terminates the latter.'[30] (For example, if the couple later discover that they were related by blood tie.)
+ 'There is no limit to a dower, minimum or maximum.'[31]
+ 'Incurrence of debt by the wife [for her maintenance, for example] based on a judicial order is tantamount to her husband's incurring of that debt for himself.'[32]
+ 'All that is forbidden to Muslims in regards to marriage is also forbidden to the non-Muslims.'[33]
+ 'A blood tie that entails inheritance also constitutes the basis of maintenance.'[34]
+ 'The child belongs to the marital bed.'*[35]
+ 'Khul' [divorce] is an exchange contract and requires due payment of its countervalue.'[36]
+ 'Allusive pronouncements of divorce require proof of intention or its equivalent.'[37]
+ 'The norm in regards to divorce is that it is revocable.'[38]
+ 'Divorce depends on the intention when it is implicit but not so when it is explicit.'[39]
+ 'Divorce is indivisible.'[40]
+ 'Khul' [divorce] incurs a final rupture [of the marital tie].'[41]
+ 'Every marriage that is valid among Muslims is also valid among non-Muslims.'[42]

---

* A child's paternity and relationship to its mother is, in other words, proven by the valid cohabitation of its parents without recourse to other means of proof such as proving of the facts of conception, etc.

XII

Islamic Banking and Finance

Q141) What are the principles that govern or influence Muslims' economic transactions?

A) The core principles of Shariah that govern economic life of Muslims include the following. First, human beings are considered to be trustees and custodians of the wealth they own, while God Most High is the true owner of all wealth. In their capacity as God's vicegerents on earth, humankind must manage wealth according to a set of principles laid down in Shariah, which seek to promote social justice and forbid activities that violate other people's rights or which may harm society, including waste and mismanagement of resources. Muslims have rights to enjoy whatever wealth they have lawfully earned and spend in ways that benefit them, their families and the general public. They are within their rights to spend as they wish provided it is not for unlawful and destructive purposes that inflict harm on others. They must observe the following five principles: First, Muslims are forbidden from wrongful appropriation of the property of others, engagement in fraudulent and usurious activities and businesses. Second, material pursuits should be balanced with an individual's spiritual needs. Third, an individual's material needs must be balanced with society's needs, all of which are manifested in a set of moral and religious principles in Islam. The wealthy are required, for instance, to spend a certain percentage of their wealth on helping the poor and the deprived in their midst through obligatory and voluntary charity. Fourth, economic transactions should be conducted within a just, responsible free-market economy where individual enterprise is encouraged and so is the free and unhindered flow of market transactions. Last, in support of these principles, Islamic law prohibits business transactions based on usury, excessive speculation and risk-taking, hoarding, gambling and trading in a certain number of prohibited substances.

Q142) Does Islamic law support free market capitalism? Does it support socialism?

A) Islam allows a free-market economy where the supply and demand of goods and services are determined through the natural flow of market operations, but it directs the functioning of the market mechanism through a set of rules and guidelines. Islam itself emerged in a free-market environment. Prior to his apostolic mission, the Prophet Muhammad was involved in commercial activities and consequently showed considerable interest in market regulations. Profit-making and free enterprise are acceptable but hoarding, profiteering and cornering the market through manipulation of supply and demand by powerful individuals and syndicates are not. Whereas in capitalism, the profit motive and private ownership do not admit of any restrictions based on religion, the Shariah regulates Muslims' economic transactions by certain principles, both legal and moral, with the main purpose of promoting social justice and equitable distribution of wealth and opportunities. These must not be concentrated in the hands only of a few while most others suffer in deprivation and poverty. These guidelines also ensure that the basic norms of law and morality are not violated.

The sympathy and support that socialist principles exhibit towards the underprivileged resonate well with the Islamic outlook and rules on social justice. Yet Islam protects individual's rights to property, free enterprise and the accumulation of wealth through lawful means. It also maintains economic justice and social equilibrium by encouraging circulation and distribution of wealth among diverse social strata through both obligatory levies (such as *zakah, fitr* charity, tithes, and inheritance laws) and supererogatory donations (such as voluntary charities, *waqf* charitable endowments and bequests).

Q143) How does the Shariah regard economic development?

A) Shariah law encourages economic development through productive labour and exploitation of the natural resources that proceed over the real economy and contribute to human welfare and comfort. This is the principal motif of the Qur'anic assignment of Muslims to build the earth (*i'mar al-ard*, or what ibn Khaldun calls '*umran*) and a just social order therein where people's needs are met and no one suffers from penury and lack of the essentials of life. Earning one's living through lawful work is an obligation of all able-bodied individuals, just as they have obligations also to support their families and dependants. The ruler and ruled have shared responsibilities for the establishment of a fair and stable economic environment. Economic development and increase of wealth are encouraged through all lawful means and ways that contribute to the well-being of others in the society, and to the safety also of the natural environment. Shariah's concept of economic development is also premised in the mobilisation of labour and capital together, and not the latter alone where usurious applications of capital generate wealth at the expense often of the user of capital or those in debt.

Market activities in a Shariah-compliant environment should also relate to the real economy and proceed over goods and services that benefit the people. This conception of development and finance discourages market financialisation of the kind where transactions are often reduced to paper exchanges and the money generated tends to enrich the wealthy corporate entities and persons the most. For debt-based operations and money generated through highly financialised market operations burden the real economy and lead to the so-called asset bubbles and financial crises of globalised proportions, as the world has been seeing in recent years. The European debt crisis and huge bailouts of the major banking institutions invoked the often-cited expression 'privatisation of profits and socialisation of losses'. In the build-up to 2007–2008 crisis, there was a rapid increase in debt in developed economies.

Debt was used to drive economic growth, allowing immediate consumption or investment beyond the repayment capacity of borrowers. Spending that would have taken place over a period of years was accelerated because of the availability of debt. In many countries, debt reached three to four times GDP levels not normally reached other than in wartime. Debt that is not matched by proportionate growth in income and production is not sustainable. This is precisely what the Islamic regulatory system and conception of economic development will not entertain.

Q144)   How does Shariah law view banking? How are Islamic banks different from Western banks?

A)   Islamic banks began to emerge in the early 1970s. A number of contracts and recognised modes of transaction in *fiqh*, such as partnership (*musharakah*), commenda partnership (*mudarabah*), deferred payment sale (*bay' al-mu'ajjal* – also known as *bay' bi-thaman aajil*), profit added sale (*murabahah*), leasing (*ijarah*) and a few other nominate contracts lie at the centre of the bulk of Islamic banking transactions. Islamic banks distinguished themselves from Western banks by their commitment to interest-free banking and the promotion of equity financing and partnership models by way of profit and loss sharing. The bulk of Islamic banking transactions proceed over trade financing that is tied to the exchange of goods and services, and not so much over debt and credit-based financing. Transaction over pure debts, which is known to cause formation of the notorious 'asset bubbles', is not accepted in Islamic banking and finance. This is ascertained, in a sale contract, for instance, by the rule that at least one of the countervalues must be present, if not both, at the time of contracting, a restrictive measure that comes in the way of paper transactions and financialisation of the economy, as we have been increasingly witnessing of late.

The Shariah also relies very little on pure debts and debt-based transactions, hence the ruling in contemporary Islamic banking and finance that debt and debt-based transactions must not exceed the limit of one-third (in some cases one-half) of the available tangible assets of an Islamic financial institution. Restrictions of this kind also help to reduce and slow down development of asset bubbles, debt and paper transactions in the economy.

The main principles of Islamic finance include equity participation, risk sharing and trade financing, the prohibition of usury (*riba*) and avoidance of excessive risk-taking (*gharar*) in contractual agreements. Added to these is the prohibition of hoarding, profiteering and gambling, and avoidance of transactions that proceed over certain prohibited substances, such as pork, alcohol, narcotics, pornography and weapons.

Q145) How do Muslims living outside Muslim-majority countries handle their banking?

A) Muslim minorities living in the West face the challenges of a secular consumerist culture as well as issues of identity and citizenship that took a turning for the worse in the aftermath of the September 2001 attacks and the ensuing upsurge of extremism and violence, the so-called 'war on terror', military intervention and forced regime change.

Muslims living outside Muslim-majority countries who do not have access to Islamic banking may continue banking with conventional banking institutions but make an effort to avoid interest-based financing. In countries and localities where Islamic banks do exist and banking through them does not involve hardship, they should go to Islamic banks. Yet, the present day non-Muslim democracies do provide space for their Muslim citizens to practice their religion and follow the Shariah in their personal lives as they may wish, but also expect them to be law abiding citizens. They are granted the rights to form private societies and associations to find appropriate ways and solutions for their challenges in accordance with their own beliefs.

The *fiqh* tradition is elaborate on the position of non-Muslim minorities living in Muslim majority countries but not so well-developed with regard to Muslim minorities living in non-Muslim majority countries. This has prompted twentieth-century Muslim scholarship to mark the beginning of a new branch of *fiqh*, the so-called *fiqh al-aqaliyyat*, or jurisprudence of minorities, and it is as such, a work in progress. Broadly speaking, Muslim minorities are expected to observe the religious and ethical guidelines of Qur'an and hadith concerning their religion and moral conduct especially in their relations with people of other faiths, and nurture good relations with all people regardless of race, colour and creed. They must accordingly cultivate mutual respect and friendship with their host communities. The same holds true with regard to the treatment of religious minorities living in Muslim majority coun-tries. It is important, however, that text and scripture is read and interpreted in the light of historical and contemporary realities and developments as well as the respective laws and constitutions of the present-day Muslim countries. To this may be added observance of the international treaty obligations that Muslim countries may have in their relations with other states and communi-ties. The Shariah is generally supportive of all this with the proviso, however, that the basic principles of Islam are not violated although compromise on certain subsidiary rules may need to be determined in their own context, espe-cially in situations of necessity or hardship.

Q146)   Are there differences between the Sunni and Shia schools of thought on banking and finance?

A)   Islamic banking and finance do not show much variation in their Sunni and Shi'i applications. The basic outlines of contracts and transac-tions as well as the relevant prohibitions that apply to them are about the same on both sides. Islamic banking and finance (IBF) proceed over a range of nominate contracts, and there is basically no variation here. The Shi'i law of contracts, similar to that of its Sunni counter-part, articulate about nineteen nominate contracts (exactly the same as under Sunni law) and they include virtually every one of the half dozen or so contracts that are currently in vogue in the IBF practices on both sides. The position is similar with regard to the main head-ings of prohibitions, such as usury (*riba*), gambling (*maysir, qimar*), uncertainty and exorbitant risk-taking (*gharar*), and the ban on a range of prohibited substances, such as pork and porcine products, alcohol, narcotics, firearms, etc. There may be some variation in the detailed procedures of the IBF products and practices from country to coun-try and between different regions, but this is not due only to differ-ences on scholastic lines as such. For there are such differences among the Sunni countries and jurisdictions themselves, and the general tendency here is that disparity and variation should be reduced and minimised for the sake not only of market preference, but also if IBF were to inspire greater market credibility and confidence in its global reaches as it has actually been progressing in recent years. Uniformity and standardisation in IBF practices and procedures are desirable yet much work remains to be done to achieve them.

SUPPORTIVE EVIDENCE

☐ Qur'an and Hadith

+ 'And to God belongs the ownership/kingdom of all that the heavens and the earth contain.' (Q al-Ma'idah, 4:131)[1]
+ 'Say to whom belongs all that is in the heavens and the earth? Say: To God. He has prescribed mercy upon Himself.' (Q al-Hadid, 6:12)[2]
+ 'God commands justice and the doing of good.' (Q al-Nahl, 16:90)[3]
+ 'So that wealth does not circulate only among the wealthy.' (Q al-Hashr, 59:7)[4]
+ 'God has explained to you in detail what is forbidden to you unless you are compelled into it [acting under duress is thus exonerated].' (Q al-An'am, 6:119)[5]
+ 'O believers! Do not forbid the good things which have been made lawful to you [unnecessary rigour is thus inadvisable].' (Q 5:87)[6]
+ 'And if [the debtor] is in straightened conditions, let there be respite until [he is in] ease.' (Q al-Baqarah, 2:280)[7]
+ 'God intends every facility for you, and He does not want to put you in hardship.' (Q 2:185)[8]
+ 'O Believers! Eat not up your property among yourselves wrongfully, but let there be among you traffic and trade by mutual consent.' (Q al-Nisa' 4: 29)[9]
+ 'God has permitted sale and forbidden usury.' (Q 2:275)[10]
+ 'God commands you to render the trusts to whom they are due, and when you judge among people you judge with justice.' (Q 4:58)[11]
+ 'One who engages in hoarding is a transgressor.' (Hadith)[12]
+ 'Muslims are bound by their stipulations, unless it be a stipulation which declares unlawful what is permissible or permits what is unlawful.' (Hadith)[13]
+ 'One who interferes with market prices in order to push them up reserves for himself God's punishment of Hell-fire in the heareafter.' (Hadith)[14]
+ 'One who buys something he has not seen shall have the option [of cancellation] when he sees it.' (Hadith)[15]
+ 'Sell not that which is not with you.' (Hadith)[16]
+ 'It is not permissible to combine *salam* [forward sale] with a [spot] sale, nor two transactions in the same sale [such as the one is made contingent on the other], nor to gain profit over something which is

not guaranteed [in terms of liability for loss and damage] nor a sale of what is not with you [that you neither own nor possess and may be unable to deliver].' (Hadith)[17]

+ 'He who sells foodstuffs should not sell until he has taken possession of it [thus ensuring physical availability of food supplies in the market].' (Hadith)[18]

+ 'The parties to a sale are free to revoke their agreement before they part company, except in a sale that is subjected to option.' (Hadith)[19]

+ '[The Companions reported that] The Prophet, pbuh, prohibited the sale of *gharar* [sale that involves excessive uncertainty and risk in terms of availability of countervalues, timing, deliverability, etc.].' (Hadith)[20]

+ 'Procrastination [in repayment] by a solvent debtor is injustice.' (Hadith)[21]

+ 'Harm may not be inflicted nor reciprocated in [the name of] Islam.' (Hadith)[22]

[] **Legal Maxims**

+ 'Profit [must be] commensurate with liability.'[23]
+ 'Whoever owns an object also owns that which is indispensable to it.'[24]
+ 'Promises made contingent upon conditions become binding when the conditions materialise.'[25]
+ 'Liability for loss commensurates with (prospective) gain.'[26]
+ 'When prohibition and permissibility co-exist, prohibition prevails.'[27]
+ 'What is forbidden to take is also forbidden to give.'[28]
+ 'What is permissible due to an excuse ceases to be permissible with its cessation.'[29]
+ 'Retention of all that which harms the general public amounts to hoarding, be it gold, silver, or clothes.'[30]
+ 'It is obligatory to remove and do away with all that harms the Muslims.'[31]
+ 'A contract is observed with a disbeliever in the same way as it is observed with a Muslim.'[32]
+ 'In contracts credibility is attached to purposes and meanings and not to words and forms.'[33]
+ 'Every contract which does not serve its purpose is nullified.'[34]

+ 'All [instances of] ignorance which lead to conflict vitiate the contract.'[35]

+ 'Every stipulation/condition that serves the interest of the contract or its requirement is permissible.'[36]

+ ' A contract that secures something good and is founded on beneficence is not obstructed by uncertainty/*gharar*.'[37]

+ 'The norm in contracts and [contractual] stipulations is permissibility and validity unless there be a juridical reason to the contrary.'[38]

+ 'Fraud in exchange transactions is the basis of liability for compensation.'[39]

+ 'Every condition that contravenes the purpose of contract is null and void.'[40]

+ 'What is unknown may not be owned by means of contracts.'[41]

+ 'The purpose of [entering] a contract is [to incur] commitment.'[42]

+ 'Contracts follow their purposes.'[43]

+ 'All that which is permissible to sell can also be mortgaged, and if it cannot be sold may not be mortgaged either.'[44]

+ 'One who commits himself to a condition willingly without any duress must observe it.'[45]

XIII

Shariah and Private Property

Q147) How does Shariah law look upon property rights?

A) Shariah law protects private ownership and ownership rights, and opposes aggression and unwarranted interference in the property of others in much the same way as in Western law and other legal traditions. It is also a shared concern, for the most part, of both Islamic and Western laws that the owner's uses of ownership rights do not involve inflicting harm on others. Most of the limitations on property rights, such as usurpation, trespass and property offences such as fraud, embezzlement and theft, and so on, are also in common between the major world traditions. Certain varieties of ownership, such as collective ownership, communal property and state ownership of public places and facilities are also recognised in Shariah. The latter similarly makes provisions for expropriation in some cases of private property for public benefit purposes against payment of fair compensation by the authorities. Thus, the provisions concerning the building of roads, parks, bridges and places of worship, for example, are not very different in the Islamic and Western legal systems. Islamic law prohibits hoarding and profiteering, aggressive monopolies as well as gambling, perhaps more strictly than some other legal systems do.

Q148)   Does the Shariah regulate commerce and contracts? How does it affect commerce in Muslim-majority countries?

A)   Shariah law recognises the freedom of contract and actively seeks to facilitate the smooth flow of transactions in the market place. Shariah law also specifies a number of nominate contracts, such as sale, leasing, partnership, agency, marriage, and so on – about nineteen in number; according to some twenty-five – which serve different purposes and are regulated in accordance with their own characteristics.* These are classified under several categories and clusters. The basic contours of contract law tends to be common to all the major legal traditions. The essential feature, for instance, that all contracts are based on the mutual agreement of contracting parties, runs through all of them. Recognition of the basic freedom of contract also means that the contracting parties may create new contract varieties that may serve their interests provided they do not violate the basic principles of equivalence in the exchange of values, morality and justice.

Apart from the element of consent that consists of a valid offer and acceptance of two competent parties, the subject matter of contract in the Islamic law of contract should also be in principle lawful, existing at the time of contract, valuable, usable, capable of ownership, capable also of delivery/possession, specified and quantified, and the seller must have a valid ownership title over it although there may be exceptions to some of these requirements in respect of certain contracts, or new varieties thereof. The contract must also be free of any prohibited activities and substances over which they flow, such as usury, gambling, giving and taking of prohibited substances, and not contradict public interest and morals. Islamic laws of contract and commerce may generally be said to advocate ethical and responsible investment and trading activity which observe the basic norms of equivalence and fair exchange. Ethical investment also shuns promotion and support of harmful trades, such as production and sale of arms, narcotics and lethal drugs, indeed all that which endangers public safety and due observance of legal norms.

---

* Some new contract varieties such as the futures contract, lease ending in ownership (*ijarah muntahiyah bi-tamlik*), diminishing partnership (*musharakah mutanaiqisah*) and a few others have been added in recent decades to the existing range of nominate contracts known to the classical *fiqh*.

Q149) How does the Shariah view affluence and acquisition of wealth?

A) Acquisition of wealth is viewed positively in Shariah provided it is acquired through lawful means and is free of exploitation and injustice. No quantitative limits are imposed, although there are restrictions that will presently be reviewed. This is understood from the numerous verses in the Qur'an which refer to property and wealth by such expressions as God's bounty and His favour (fadl Allah), blessing/benefit, bounty (khayr, ni'mah) and means of creating beauty (zinah) in life, and also encourages the faithful to exert themselves, explore the earth and its resources, in earning it. The Qur'an and Sunnah also encourage personal effort and labour in the quest for lawful earning by one who supports oneself and family so much so that if done with good intention they partake in service to God and an act of devotion ('ibadah). By the testimony of clear hadith, it is also far better if a person leaves behind assets for his family than leaving his family in penury and need. There are also instances, in hadith reports, where the Prophet Muhammad prayed for some of his Companions, including Anas bin Malik, in such terms as, 'O my Lord, increase his wealth and offspring.' The Prophet also did that for himself in a supplication on record where he said: 'O my Lord, grant me guidance, piety, purity and affluence.' In yet another hadith the Prophet has advised the faithful not to leave their wealth idle so that it is eaten up by zakah and other taxes. All of this is indicative of an affirmative outlook that Islam maintains on the acquisition of wealth.

Q150) Are there any restrictions on wealth and property ownership?

A) Yes there are restrictions, some legal and others by way of advice and recommendation. Legally in the sense that the Shariah makes ownership liable to certain rights, such as support for one's immediate family and dependants, one's wife, children and parents. The wife and minor children are entitled to support absolutely, but one's parents and certain other relatives only when they have no assets of their own and are in need of support. The Shariah also subjects personal wealth beyond certain quantitative limits to both obligatory and supererogatory charities. Government is similarly authorised to impose taxes on the wealthy if it has no other means for fulfilment of its basic functions, such as maintenance of law and order, justice and defence of the homeland. It is also indicative of Islam's concern for social justice that usury (*riba*), which consists of earning money on money without labour or trading in goods and services, is forbidden (*haram*). The list of prohibitions extends to a number of other activities, such as gambling, hoarding, and immoral and oppressive activities, as already mentioned.

Then there are moral concerns over the exploitative and excessive uses of personal wealth. The Qur'an speaks very strongly against the evils of materialistic indulgence, amassment of gold and silver, profiteering and monopolistic trading practices, oppressive and indolent use of property, which is often referred to as transgression, lawlessness and indecency (*ithm, baghy* and *fawahish* respectively). These must be avoided, not just outwardly but sincerely and truthfully if it were to gain God Almighty's pleasure. The Qur'anic guidelines, and those of the hadith, on the uses of property are supportive of moderation (*tawassut, i'tidal*) that avoids prodigality, greed and arrogance, on the one hand, and meanness and misery, on the other.

Q151) How much should Muslims give to charity? How is charitable giving organised?

A) Charity (*sadaqah*) in Islam includes both obligatory and voluntary varieties. As already indicated, *zakah* (poor-due) is an obligatory charity, payable by every Muslim who has enjoyed for one complete year full ownership of assets above the minimum quorum (*nisab* – for silver, 200 grams, and for gold, 85 grams or equivalents thereof). The amount of *zakah* to be paid on income and certain varieties of capital assets is 2.5 per cent (1/40). It is considered a religious duty and ranks as one of the five pillars of Islam. Obligatory alms also include a variety of religious taxes such as *sadaqat al-fitr*, a religious poll tax of certain specified amounts payable at the end of the fasting month of Ramadan by every Muslim to the poor and the tithe ('*ushr*), which is levied at ten per cent on (non-irrigated) agricultural land and its produce, treasure troves and minerals, etc.

Muslims used to pay the *zakah*, and may still do so, directly to the poor at their own initiative without any official demand by the state authorities. Yet, during the early years of Islam, the state took the responsibility for *zakah* collection and administration. The government may thus appoint collectors and administrators for that purpose. *Zakah* revenues are to be spent on welfare assistance, preferably on the poor and needy of the same locality where the *zakah* revenues originate, and should not be mixed with the general state budget. The Qur'an has identified eight groups of recipients wherein the poor and needy top the list, but they also include insolvent debtors, freeing of slaves, helping the beggars, travellers and wayfarers, and even the *zakah* collectors who may be paid a salary out of the *zakah* revenues (al-Tawbah, 9:60).

Q152) What is a charitable endowment (*waqf*)? Who can establish one and how does one do so?

A) *Waqf* is a voluntary charity and a religious endowment in perpetuity. The owner relinquishes his ownership and transfers it in perpetuity nominally to 'God's ownership'. People may thus donate buildings, plots of land, books, plants and equipment or even cash for the benefit of society and in support of welfare objectives. The donated and accumulated assets are held by a charitable trust. The person founding the *waqf* is called *waqif*, who must be an adult of sound mind, capable of handling financial affairs and not under legal interdiction or bankruptcy. Being Muslim is not a requirement for the beneficiary of *waqf*. Non-Muslims can also be recipients or even the founders of *waqf* endowments. Historically *waqf* endowments supported education and mosque-related activities, animal welfare, health facilities ranging from hospitals to homes for the disabled, the provision of drinking water, welfare of prisoners, rest rooms for travellers and caravans, helping young people to get married and the like, all on a voluntary basis by pious individuals throughout the Muslim world.

Since *waqf* is an endowment in perpetuity, vast amounts of *waqf* assets have been accumulated throughout the ages in all parts of the Muslim world – and they still exist in vast amounts but are not very well managed. However, this is beginning to change as *waqf* assets are drawing the attention of the finance and corporate sectors in Muslim countries, the assets being increasingly seen as another area of wealth generation, next to, for instance, Islamic banking and finance products, or even an extension thereof, with due recognition of the distinctive characteristics of *waqf*. New ideas, formulas, institutions, laws and guidelines are being drawn up and developed at a fairly rapid pace in many Muslim countries, including Malaysia, Indonesia and the Arab world, to tap the vast resources of *waqf* in beneficial and income-generating ways. All this is geared toward overcoming the historical legacy of mismanagement and neglect of the *waqf* properties due partly also to legal constraints, specifications of the *waqf* deeds and the expressed wishes of the *waqif*, that is, the *waqf* founder.

Q153) Is slavery accepted under Islamic law? Is slavery still practiced in Muslim countries?

A) Generally, the Shariah forbids all types of forced labour and entitles every worker to full and fair payment for the work accomplished. Slavery existed for many centuries before Islam. Islam addressed the reality of slavery by bringing new legislation on fair treatment of slaves that aimed at raising their status and laid down rules that looked toward their eventual freedom and the termination of slavery. The slaves are accordingly entitled to marry, divorce, study as well as be witnesses in court litigations, regardless as to whether the litigants are freemen or slaves. Shariah also encouraged the freeing of slaves and established certain rules to compel the owners to free them; it has articulated many ways on how the slaves can earn their freedom. In fact, the Qur'an specifies securing freedom for slaves as one of the eight heads of expenditure on which the *zakah* revenue may be expended (cf. al-Tawbah, 9:60). Other opportunities and avenues for the termination of slavery have also been opened. Slaves were to be freed in situations, for instance, when they were able to pay their master through labour or other assets. Similarly, when a slave girl gave birth to the child of her master, the child automatically became a free person. Also when a slave was owned by two persons and only one of them decided to free him to the extent of his portion, it became the responsibility of the state to pay the balance and secure his freedom. Freeing a slave is also a most meritorious act of charity, and the Shariah has made many provisions for freeing of slaves in the context of expiations (*kaffarat*) and atonements for certain offences and religious sins, such as taking a false oath in jest, breaking of fast in Ramadan without a valid excuse, and certain instances of errone- ous or unintended manslaughter and bodily injury. Releasing a slave is sometimes added as a supplementary penalty to legal punishments as may be the case.

SUPPORTIVE EVIDENCE

☐ Qur'an and Hadith

+ 'O you who believe! Do not devour your wealth among yourselves wrongfully, but let there be amongst you traffic and trade by mutual consent.' (Q al-Nisa', 4:29)[1]
+ 'God permitted sale but prohibited usury.' (Q 2:276)[2]
+ 'O believers! Fear God and give up of what remains of your demand for usury. Your capital sums belong to you. Deal not unjustly, nor be the victims of injustice.' (Q al-Baqarah, 2:278–79)[3]
+ 'And tie not your hand to your neck, nor stretch it forth to its utmost reach, so that you are then left with destitution and regret.' (Q al-Isra', 17:29)[4]
+ 'And [blessed are] those who spend and they are neither extravagant nor mean, but hold a just balance between those (two extremes).' (Q al-Furqan, 25:67)[5]
+ 'If the debtor is in hardship, grant him time until it is easy for him to repay.' (Q 2:280)[6]
+ 'And those in whose wealth there is an appointed right for the needy (who asks for help) and the deprived (who does not even ask).' (Q al-Maʿarij, 70:24)[7]
+ 'Every person is entitled to his own property more than his father, his son and the whole of mankind.' (Hadith)[8]
+ 'It is unlawful to take the property of a Muslim without his consent.' (Hadith)[9]
+ 'No-one has ever eaten food purer than that which is eaten from the labour of one's hands.' (Hadith)[10]

☐ Legal Maxims

+ 'Everything that is useful and permissible may also be the subject of an exchange [transaction].'[11]

- 'It is unlawful to take another's property except for a valid legal cause.'[12]
- 'An oppressor has no right to make a claim for his effort.'[13]
- 'Harm does not establish a precedent.'[14]
- 'An order given in respect of dealing with the property of others is void.'[15]
- 'It is not permissible to expropriate anyone's property that is validly owned without there being incontrovertible evidence to the contrary.'[16]
- 'All lost property whose owner is not found is to be spent by the ruler on public interest expenditures.'[17]
- 'The purpose of sale is transfer of ownership.'[18]
- 'The judge takes possession of the lost properties to keep them for their owners.'[19]
- 'Conditions that do not contravene the requirement of *waqf* are to be acted upon.'[20]
- 'One who pays the debt of another without the latter's instruction has no right of recourse against him.'*[21]
- 'Actual control only proves possession but not necessarily ownership.'[22]
- 'One who receives assets due to an error/doubt without knowing who is entitled to it should give it to charity.'[23]
- 'All that which is the subject of an absolute Shariah ruling with nothing further to regulate it in law or language, may be referred to the prevailing custom.'†[24]
- 'All that which perishes in the hands of a trustee with no transgression on his part incurs no liability.'[25]

---

* This is called 'unauthorised agent' (*fuduli*) and there are differences of opinion among the jurists on whether or not he should be entitled to repayment by the owner.

† Most of the general (*'aam*) and absolute (*mutlaq*) in the Qur'an have been specified either by the Qur'an itself, by hadith or by *ijtihad*. Should there be none of these available, then the matter is to be referred to custom.

XIV

Modern Bioethical and Environmental Questions

Q154) How does Islamic law view contraception and birth control?

A) Islamic law permits contraception used in order to preserve the health of the mother and the well-being of the family. In the event where the family is poor and has a second infant below two years of age that is in need of breastfeeding/nursing, his/her needs take priority and may justify use of contraception by the mother. Family planning is also in principle acceptable. Pregnancy is strongly discouraged in the event where an illness of one or both parents is likely to affect normal growth of the offspring. Contraception with the aim of having a permanently child-free marriage (sterilisation) is, however, not acceptable. This is because procreation of the human species is the primary purpose (*maqsad asli*) of marriage in Shariah and may not therefore be obstructed. This would not, however, hinder the marriage of elderly persons who may be unable to be parents. Yet insertion of an explicit condition in the marriage contract for fit persons to preclude childbirth will be deemed as invalid and unenforceable.

Marriage is referred to as one of God's favours on humankind as we read in the Qur'an: 'God has made for you mates (and companions) of your own nature, and made for you, out of them, sons, daughters and grandchildren' (al-Nahl, 16:72).[1] One also reads in the hadith the address to the faithful: '[you should] Get married and procreate – *Tanakahu tanasalu.'*

As a Sunnah and exemplary practice of the Prophet, marriage is encouraged for all able-bodied persons, just as the Prophet has also said that he takes pride with increase in the number of his followers. Population increase is thus seen as a source of strength and pride for the Ummah. Yet if a particular country is highly over-populated and faced with scarcity of land and resources, it may well discourage expansion of the nuclear family beyond a certain number – although a total ban will not be acceptable.

Procreation being the primary Shariah purpose of marriage would also signify that the Shariah takes a negative view of the same-sex-marriage, which has been gaining recognition in some Western countries as of late; it frustrates the normative purpose of marriage, it is unnatural and also amounts to a violation of the ethical norms of the religion. Contraception may be used, however, for reasons of health based on medical advice, and there may also be situations that justify recourse to the rules of necessity (*darurah*), which the Shariah has regulated separately. Necessity, according to a legal maxim, makes the unlawful lawful. The spouses are advised, however, to consult one another in all family matters and make appropriate decisions through mutual understanding and agreement.

As for the commencement of legal capacity/personality (*ahliyyah*) in the foetus, the Prophet has taught that complete humanity does not begin at conception, but during the first forty days of pregnancy. This is the time when an angel breathes the soul into the unborn foetus, although a receptive legal capacity (*ahliyyat al-wujub*) is endowed in the foetus as of the moment of conception. Receptive legal capacity means that the foetus can receive a gift or inheritance, but cannot have any obligations at that time. The foetus at this stage cannot owe debt nor can anyone inherit from it. This differs from the view of some other traditional cultures, which hold that the soul enters the womb of the mother with the husband's seed. Thus it appears that, in Islam's view, contraception is not curtailing or obstructing a human's life. For this reason, most forms of contraception are permitted. Reports indicate that some of the Prophet's Companions were practicing sexual withdrawal (*al-'azl*) so as to prevent unwanted pregnancy, and the Prophet who had knowledge of this had not objected to it.

Q155)   Is abortion permissible under Islamic law? Under what circumstances?

A)   Abortion (*isqat al-haml*, also *ijhad*) means the deliberate termination of pregnancy, which may be before it has reached the state of viability or after that stage. Science identifies four stages in the pre-natal develop-ment of a human being. The first is in the fallopian tube where the ferti-lised ovum remains for about three days. Cell division begins during this time. The next stage begins with implantation in the uterus, where rapid cell division continues. The embryo stage begins two weeks after conception. At this time, there is organ differentiation. All the internal organs one will ever have are present in rudimentary form by the end of the sixth week. The foetus stage begins from eight weeks to birth, in which there is continuous growth but nothing new is added. A foetus is thus in possession of all necessary human characteristics.

Yusuf al-Qaradawi wrote in his renowned book *The Lawful and the Unlawful in Islam* (Eng. Tr. of *Al-Halal wa'l-Haram fi'l-Islam*), that 'all Muslim jurists hold abortion after the ensoulment of the foetus to be forbidden (*haram*) and a crime against a living and fully formed human being'. A certain ambiguity has remained, however, about the precise time of ensoulment into the foetus. In a long hadith that Imam Muslim has recorded, it is stated: 'After the lapse of forty-two nights of *nutfah* (drop of sperm) in the womb, God sends an angel that shapes it into human form and equips it with the faculties of hearing and sight.' The hadith continues to point out that the gender of the foetus and its course of destiny in life are also determined from that time. The implication is that ensoulment occurs after six weeks. This hadith has been differently interpreted, however, by some commentators based on their understanding that the hadith identifies three stages and then mentions six weeks, thus implying that each stage lasts six weeks; a total of what Muslim jurists often put at 120 days, although strictly it would be 126. Yet an alternative, and probably preferable, interpretation has it that all the three stages are completed in forty days.

The Shafi'i school has allowed abortion in the first forty days of preg-nancy provided that the spouses are in agreement, and it is not harmful to the mother. Abortion is forbidden after forty days, which is believed to be the starting point of life in the foetus. Abu Hamid al-Ghazali (d. 1111 CE), himself a Shafi'i, and some other jurists have held, on the contrary, that abor-tion is forbidden absolutely even at the early stages of pregnancy. The Hanafi and Hanbali schools are less rigorous and have held abortion to be permissible prior to the inception of life in the foetus within the first 120 days, which to them marks the point of ensoulment, but it is generally considered reprehensible and sinful if it is without a valid ground. The Shia Imamiyyah have held similar views and add that the perpetrator of abortion is liable to an expiation (*kaffarah*) even if it be prior to ensoulment.

In a 1996 resolution of the Fiqh Academy of India, it was decided: if a woman suffering from AIDS becomes pregnant and a qualified doctor confirms that, in all likelihood, the foetus will also develop AIDS, then prior to the inception of life into the foetus, which the Muslim jurists have determined at 120 days, permission for abortion can be given.

In sum, Muslim jurists have generally viewed abortion as a grave matter, although most classical Muslim scholars regarded it as lawful if it is done at the early stages of pregnancy, and on condition that the mother's life is not put at risk. Abortion is thus permissible with the agreement of the spouses before the completion of 40 days of conception that signifies according to Islamic beliefs the event of ensoulment, or the beginning of life. Abortion is not permissible between forty and 120 days of pregnancy, except in two situations: first, when continued pregnancy would endanger or substantially harm the mother's life and health and, second, when it is established that the foetus would be an invalid or permanently deficient and the deficiency is incurable. After the expiry of 120 days, abortion is held to be *haram* and equivalent to a crime committed in respect of a living person. Abortion is in all cases permitted in situations of necessity (*darurah*) subject to expert medical advice. In severely distorted and stressful situations where the mother cannot decide and needs advice and guidance, there may be room for a *fatwa* and juristic advice by qualified medical and duly accredited Shariah experts.

Q156) How does Islamic law view artificial insemination? Surrogate motherhood?

A) Resorting to artificial insemination and surrogate motherhood is permissible, in principle, if they would achieve a valid and beneficial purpose and when only the husband and wife are involved. All biotechnological manipulations involving human procreation in which a third party is introduced, be that in the form of a womb, egg, sperm or cell, are therefore unlawful from the Shariah perspective. This is due to the importance Shariah attaches to the preservation of lineage and identity of the child. If the sperm of a man is inserted into his own wife, or the wife's egg is artificially inseminated with the husband's sperm outside her body at a time when there is a valid marriage subsisting, it is permissible, and it is immaterial whether this procedure is through sexual intercourse or medical means. The other type of artificial insemination, in which a stranger's sperm is inserted into the womb of someone else's wife or another woman, is illegal and deemed unacceptable as will presently be explained.

A surrogate mother is a woman who carries a child usually for an infertile couple. A contract is made with the surrogate mother to hand over the baby after delivery to the couple. This is deemed unlawful from the Shariah viewpoint.

Other types of surrogacy may briefly be mentioned as follows:

a) When the wife cannot conceive or generate eggs and hires another woman to donate her eggs, which are fertilised through the semen of her husband and then implanted in the donor's body. This is basically artificial insemination with an element of surrogacy.
b) Cases where a woman fears pregnancy complications and hires a surrogate mother in order to avoid risk.
c) When a perfectly normal woman prefers the technique to avoid the inconveniences of conception and pregnancy and wishes to preserve her figure.

All these forms of surrogate motherhood are deemed prohibited from the Shariah perspective. One possible situation when surrogate motherhood can be permitted is of a person married to two women, one of whom suffers from problems with her eggs or uterus. In this case the other wife might serve as a surrogate mother.

Surrogate motherhood which introduces a third party into the family equation is most likely to throw into confusion the issue of the identity of the child and raises questions also as to who is the child's mother. The Qur'an mentions that, 'Their mothers are only those who gave them birth' (al-Mujadilah, 58:2).[2] So the surrogate mother who carries the child to its full term and then gives birth to it will be considered the real mother. It may be relevant to mention in this connection that the Shariah recognises fosterage, and the foster mother who breastfeeds a child below two years of age is treated like a real mother in some respects. She is regarded as a family member and a relative in that the child is not permitted to marry her nor her close relatives.

She is to be honoured and respected by the child and family. That said, foster-age only involves suckling of the breast of another woman by an infant below two years of age and does not, as such, involve interference in the reproduction processes. One might argue that if suckling or nourishment of the infant is the criterion of a foster relationship between the child and foster mother in Shariah, then one can extend the same logic to a surrogate mother who nourishes the embryo internally prior to birth. The surrogate mother herself and her close relatives would be unlawful in marriage to the offspring of surrogate motherhood.

Q157) Does the Shariah take any position on pre-conception gender selection?

A) Pre-conception gender selection (PGS) has been debated by Muslim scholars and many have considered it permissible based on the principle of genuine benefit, or *maslahah*, and the happiness it could bring to the concerned parents. Yet it is recommended that PGS applications should be selective and need-based as it can give rise to moral issues of discrimination that privilege the affluent and those who have access to means. For example, a couple with five daughters or sons might wish to have a son or a daughter and may select PGS provided they give assurance that they will not mistreat the child of the opposite gender. Sheikh Yusuf al-Qaradawi has maintained, in a *fatwa* dated 17 May 2003, that although PGS does not constitute a usurpation of the divine will and prerogative, and it is allowed, it is better, nevertheless, not to opt for it and leave the matter in God's hands.

Q158) How does Islamic law view organ donation? Blood donation?

A) The human body, dead or alive, is sacrosanct and immune against aggression and manipulation that violate its God-ordained dignity and integrity. Mutilation of human body parts is normally forbidden, but is permitted on medical grounds if it will save life. There are two opinions regarding organ donation. The majority of Indo/Pakistan scholars are of the view that organ donation and transplant are not permissible, while the Arab scholars and some scholars of the Indian subcontinent permit them under certain conditions. It is unlawful (*haram*) to transplant or use an organ on which life depends, such as taking a heart from a living person to be transplanted into another person. It is permitted to transplant an organ from a dead person, or one who is in his last moments and certain to die, to a living person when his life depends on receiving that organ, or when vital functions of his body are otherwise impaired, on condition that permission is given either by the person before his death or by his legal heir or guardian. The sanctity of life and its protection is one of the higher purposes (*maqasid*) of Shariah and strongly emphasised in the Qur'an. Giving one person, or causing to do so, the gift of life is like doing the same to the whole of humankind. Organ donation that saves life would thus qualify as an act of great merit when a qualified physician carries it out in accordance with proper medical advice and espoused with consent of the donor and the intention on his part to save life or help reduce the suffering of another human being. It is generally permitted to transplant an organ from one person's body to another if it is an organ that can regenerate itself, such as skin, liver and blood, provided that the donor is mature and fully understands what he is doing, grants his consent and that all the relevant Shariah conditions are met.

Q159)   Is euthanasia permissible under Shariah law?

A)   The destruction of life in all of its forms is forbidden in Shariah, and this also applies to euthanasia (Arabic *qatl al-marhamah* or mercy killing). In the event, however, where medical evidence conclusively declares a patient's condition to be beyond recovery and there remains no prospect of survival, euthanasia may be permissible strictly on a case by case basis given reliable medical evidence in situations especially of intolerable suffering. The basic position is that God Most High only is the Creator of life, and it may be taken by His will and command alone. Since we do not create our own life, we are not authorised to put an end to it either. It is often difficult also to draw a clear distinction between what is known as voluntary or active euthanasia, which involves taking active steps to procure death such as by administering lethal drugs, and involuntary or passive euthanasia that involves no active intervention by the patient or doctor, for example by not providing or discontinuing the life support system

as may be the case. These factors plus the moral and jurisprudential questions that euthanasia evokes make it difficult to determine
objectively and precisely what is intolerable suffering, or indeed what
is the right course to take. This would explain why a case-by-case
approach is recommended, hence the evidence in each case would
need to be examined and careful conclusions drawn while assuming
that every case is governed by the general principle of the sanctity
of human life. Despite what has just been said, however, it is often
difficult to draw a clear line of distinction that would determine the
doctor's act as active or passive. These are some of the unanswered
questions about euthanasia, and the same may be said regarding the
patient's state of mind and disposition.

A clear recognition of the right to die would logically seem to give the patient
the sense of autonomy in regard to his own life and death. From a philosophical viewpoint, the right to life may be incomplete unless it is accompanied also
by the right to die. Euthanasia has not been addressed in such terms by a clear
text in the scriptural sources of Islam, nor has it been separately treated by
classical Muslim jurists. Yet the fact that the Shariah forbids suicide implies
that the right to life cannot be claimed negatively, and the right to die is clearly
not recognised. This same argument also makes duelling unlawful, which
means that two or more persons are not within their rights to make an agreement to kill one another.

Suppose that a terminal cancer patient or one with severe head injuries
will certainly die if his treatment is discontinued. To discontinue treatment
may also mean putting an end to the suffering of the patient and his family. It
also means that natural causes are left unmediated and the law of causation
is left to take its course. Provided the physician does not actively engage in
putting an end to a patient's life, his inaction to 'let nature take its course' is
arguably neither reprehensible nor forbidden, which probably means that it
is permissible. The physician may abandon medication or discontinue a life
support system to a greatly suffering patient who may have also been classified as brain dead. This is the view also taken by Yusuf al-Qaradawi, who
recounts that he has discussed this matter with experts in both medicine and
fiqh in conferences and that those whom he consulted generally concurred
with his view.

As for the active euthanasia where the physician takes measures, such as
administering a greater quantity of a dangerous drug with the intention to

kill a patient who is not in an absolutely hopeless situation, this is forbidden beyond question and may even qualify as murder, regardless as to whether or not the physician acted compassionately in order to put an end to the patient's suffering.

In sum, only when the continuation of a vegetative life of great suffering amounts to what may be deemed as decidedly harmful and tantamount to intolerable *darar*, may one be able to make a carefully considered decision to end intolerable suffering in the case of passive euthanasia. Consider the example of keeping alive a terminally ill patient who is in a vegetative state, against the wishes of the patient's family, and at great expense when precious medical resources would be better targeted at those with a decent chance of recovery. Such a scenario may induce the experts to comply with the request of a euthanasia patient to end his or her life. But no one, including the experts, legal guardian, the *ulama* or the state has the authority under Shariah to impose a decision to end the life of a patient in the name of mercy killing.

Q160)   How does Islamic law view human genetic engineering and human cloning?

A)   Broadly, Islam urges people to study and conduct scientific experiments as long as this is for the benefit of humanity and in keeping also with the basic principles of morality and religion. It should be noted at the outset, however, that general answers to questions that arose due only to recent developments in technology and science are often unprecedented, and answering complex and unprecedented genetic engineering questions would be more likely to mean indulgence in a measure of speculation, or *zann*. The jurist and *mufti* are, in principle, allowed, for practical purposes, to give considered responses, even if speculative, but also to say that this is indeed so. There is no direct evidence in the sources of Shariah on genetic engineering issues and cloning due to their non-existence during the lifetime of the Prophet or even for centuries thereafter. One may be able to refer to certain Islamic positions and pass a tentative judgment over relevant issues, as are also attempted here, but no definitive responses can be given to many of the leading questions. Further developments in scientific knowledge and juristic opinion concerning them may enable clearer responses to such issues.

That said, genetic engineering applications on plants and animals are permitted in Shariah if they aim to bring or increase benefit to humankind and their safety is scientifically ascertained. Genetic engineering applications, which are used to fundamentally alter human nature and God-ordained design and make-up of the human constitution, are broadly considered a violation and thus prohibited. Should there be a specific application of genetic engineering that seeks to offer a definitive cure for an incurable disease, this will most likely be acceptable on grounds of necessity (*darurah*) and considerations of public interest (*maslahah*), provided it is well-defined and geared specifically towards that purpose. The Qur'an enjoins Muslims to 'Take not a position over that of which you have no knowledge' (al-Isra', 17:36). Definitive knowledge of the nature and consequences of any particular application of genetic engineering is a prerequisite of Shariah so that human safety and existence is not subjected to doubtful experimentation. Careful scientific assessment of each application should also stand in harmony with the higher purposes (*maqasid*) of Shariah and reason, and the consequences of such applications to the individual and the society at large must be scientifically verified. In the event of a direct conflict between the interests of the individual and that of society at large, then according to legal maxim of Islamic law 'a private harm may be tolerated if it would avert harm to the general public'. According to yet another legal maxim, 'A lesser harm may be tolerated if it averts a greater harm.'

The OIC (Organisation of Islamic Conference – now Cooperation) Fiqh Academy of Mecca resolved in its fifteenth session in 1998 that it is permissible to utilise genetic technology for therapeutic purposes, provided that a bigger harm is not caused as a result of it. It is also permissible, subject to safety considerations, to apply genetic engineering for agricultural and animal breeding purposes. However, GE applications to manipulate human genetic make-up, or eugenics, is deemed forbidden. The basic concerns expressed here relate closely to human hereditary characteristics and the possibility also of science becoming an instrument of discrimination whereby those who have access to means can eventually select their genealogies. There is also the concern about human dignity and security, and one's right and desire to be genetically connected with one's genealogical line of descent. And last, considerations of safety and environmental care and the fear of causing uncontrollable injury and destruction that speculative manipulations in GE applications can lead to, are paramount in the whole gamut of GE on humans, animals and plants.

In the early 1970s, the geneticists themselves expressed the fear that GE could cause uncontrollable spread of serious diseases. They asked, for example, whether the laboratory bacterium carrying a cancer virus (SV40), if released or accidentally escaped from the laboratory environment and which rapidly increase, might cause a human cancer epidemic. Such concerns prompted in turn public debates that the activities in question should be carefully regulated. In the mid-1970s, several bills were consequently introduced in the US Congress but none was approved. Some communities introduced local ordinances restricting GE. But soon all these fears were found to be exaggerated and no physical injuries were found to have resulted from the new organisms created with GE. Eventually the restrictions were also relaxed.

Another concern is that the release of genetically engineered organisms might play havoc with the ecosystem, as these are not naturally occurring life forms but artificial agents introduced into a complex environment. It is feared that if modified microbes escaped the constraints of the laboratory environment, they might upset the balance of nature. It has been further pointed out that the loss of 'genetic diversity' among animals and plants might also result from GE.

What may be a decisive answer even in this context has to be weighed in light of new scientific breakthroughs, in specific cases at least, that may elucidate the Shariah questions concerning the principle of necessity (*darurah*) and the degree of certainty or doubt over its prospective benefits and harms. One can say this as there is no scriptural prohibition in the sources of Shariah on GE as such. It is not possible to pass sweeping ethical judgments on areas of science and the multifarious and complex questions they generate at their early stages of development.

It is even suggested by some commentators that the Qur'anic invitation for us to study and investigate God's creation and His signs both 'in the horizons and within themselves [our human selves]' (Fussilat, 41:53), may suggest a basic permissibility of GE from the Islamic viewpoint. Islam's generally affirmative stance on discursive knowledge and investigative endeavour on all aspects of God's creation may also be cited in support. One can even add perhaps the *fiqh* legal maxim that declared the normative position in Shariah regarding all things as being that of permissibility (*ibahah*) unless there be clear evidence to the contrary. A cautious acceptance of GE in the light of stronger affirmative evidence for human benefit may be considered in specific cases as and when supportive evidence becomes available. Yet it must be added that the whole range of questions we have touched upon is a matter for the expert, not the layman. The Shariah also gives weight to credible expert opinion in the passing of judgment on matters of expert knowledge. Consultation (*shura*) is also highly recommended between the various strata of society and their leaders as well as the scientific community for decisions that exceed the boundaries of science. Yet textbook data record only a limited role for consultation over precise questions of expert knowledge. This is the prerogative only of those who are in the know.

Q161) What of genetic testing. Is it permissible in Shariah?

A) Genetic testing can assist detection of serious disease and the determination of exposure to risk well before the appearance of symptoms. But it gives rise to sensitive issues of causing harm, and violation of the consent and confidentiality concerns of the persons involved. Genetic testing of the foetus and foetal cells has given rise to greater reservations and should be confined to cases strictly of necessity (*darurah*), as a liberal approach to this may raise the likelihood of higher rates of abortion on questionable grounds.

Genetic testing is allowed in respect only of ordinary somatic cells, which does not involve manipulation of genetic cells and eggs. For these last are responsible for the genetic transfer of heredity to future generations. The testing procedure must similarly not involve any risk of personal injury or harm to the person tested, nor even violation of the privacy of the patient. To do otherwise is likely to go against the spirit of the Shariah principle which requires the prevention and removal of harm (*darar*) as far as possible. Testing may be done only when there is a reasonable promise of benefit, and it is strongly recommended to obtain consent of the person being tested or of his/her legal guardian.

Q162) What is the nature of the concerns over the non-permissibility of human cloning?

A) The main difference between a normal child and a cloned child is in the genes. Whereas the normal child has twenty-three chromosomes from the mother and twenty-three from the father, a cloned child has twenty-three pairs of chromosomes from just one person. The Qur'an refers on more than one occasion to the natural way of human creation from a male and a female, and it is seen as one of the signs of God in creation. Any interference or manipulation that amounts to altering this God-ordained creation for eugenic purposes in order to produce human beings with better physical and intellectual features is tantamount to deviation from the basic Islamic vision of creation and therefore unacceptable. Human cloning clearly manifests an instance of drastic alteration and interference in the divinely ordained reproductive process.

A point has also been made about the nature of the human soul in the cloned child. It is argued that the product of cloning may have all the biological properties but not necessarily have that spiritual aspect of human creation when ensoulment takes place, as the religious sources maintain (as mentioned), by divine inspiration and command. A human being combines both body and soul, and the spiritual constitution of the cloned child may or may not fit into the vision of the Qur'anic narrative of creation and endowment of the human soul with a spark of the divine. Yet this is a point we cannot fathom, as we have no knowledge of the human soul in the first place; hence we have no clear answer to its related questions either, and the issue remains inconclusive.

Cloning of animals is allowed when it serves manifest human welfare interests generally and not of a particular group, class or profession, provided also that it does not involve futile infliction of harm on the animals, and the nature of the intervention is also observant of the Shariah advice on *ihsan*, or being good to others, including the animals.

Q163) How would you assess the Shariah position regarding genetically modified crops?

A) Issues of biotechnology and biomedical ethics are often not amenable to straightforward answers nor to clear judgments of the lawful and unlawful (*halal* and *haram*) over them, just as they also give rise to profound philosophical, intellectual and spiritual questions. Subject to the relevant principles of Shariah, it is permissible to resort to the cloning of microbes, plants and animals so as to prevent a manifest harm, such as eliminating a harm that may be due to a fatal disease. Cloning of this kind may also be allowed for the manifest benefit of humankind, the environment and, to acquire, for instance, beneficial proteins and hormones to fight hunger and malnourishment.

It has been argued, however, that GE on animals and plants can give human beings too much power over them, and that it is based on a very exploitative view of nature. Some religious observers have consequently advised greater caution regarding GE based on the fear that the technology may blur the dividing lines between humans and the rest of the created order.

The product of biotechnology or genetic engineering is referred to as Genetically Modified Organisms (GMO), which refers to any organism that has been manipulated by molecular genetic techniques to exhibit new traits. Most of the established regulations internationally and in developed countries agree that modern biotechnology or genetic engineering differ from the classical techniques such as traditional breeding and mutagenesis. Modern biotechnology involves selective and deliberate alteration of an organism's DNA through human intervention, by way of introducing, modifying or eliminating specific genes through molecular biology or recombined DNA techniques. It is a matter of concern to some extent also to mention that current biotechnology products are mostly focusing on the commercialisation of biopharmaceuticals, followed by genetically modified crops.

The Islamic perspective on genetically modified food is complex and goes deeper than simply a determination of whether a certain food is *halal* or not. Whether Islam approves or disapproves of genetically modified foods does not have a straightforward answer, and many jurists and commentators continue debating this issue. The Qur'anic position is that any attempts to modify living things that seek to alter the God-ordained nature thereof would be considered circumspect, even sinful, until a time when modification as such becomes a matter of certain knowledge and the benefit in it is also established to be predominant. However, if the purpose behind the modification is to secure an essentially beneficial result or is carried out in order to prevent an intolerable harm and promote the welfare of all, then such a modification would presumably be permissible. This may not be so much of a religious issue but one of rationality and scientific evidence to be determined by reference to expert opinion and knowledge. Definitive knowledge is once again a requirement both of the Shariah and science. Altering the genome of plants and (staple) foods for commercial purposes while not knowing the long-term consequences to human safety and health and their environmental impact would also go against the purport of the *fiqh* maxim, which provides that 'certainty may not be overruled by doubt'. The state of certainty here is the natural goodness of wholesome food and agricultural produce that should not be overruled in favour of some material gain or doubtful long-term benefits that are, however, not a matter of certainty and definitive knowledge, and even more so when the purpose is to create microbes and organisms that may imperil human safety and health and that of the ecosystem as a whole – sometimes for commercial gain disguised in the name of public interest and scientific advance.

As already mentioned, the permissible areas of GE applications refer mainly to the cloning of microbes, plants and animals to avoid harm, such as the prospects of a fatal disease, or for a manifest benefit to humankind, to acquire, for instance, beneficial materials such as proteins and hormones that fight hunger, poverty and disease.

Q164)   Does the Shariah take any position on the environment?

A)   The Qur'an contains numerous guidelines about the human treatment of the earth and the rest of God's creation while highlighting the sacredness of nature and the divinely ordained balance in the created world. A closer look at the Qur'an and prophetic hadith reveals a set of principles that point to a rich reservoir of environmental ethics with far-reaching socio-economic and political ramifications. The Qur'anic notions of the vicegerency (*khilafah*) and trusteeship (*amanah*) designate humankind, individually and collectively, as God's custodians of the earth, and place upon them the responsibility to safeguard not only the rights of their fellow humans but of nature and other inhabitants of the earth, make humankind the guardians and gatekeepers of the earth and responsible for the preservation of the divinely ordained balance of its resources.

Scientific evidence shows that the harmful effects of industrial pollution have reached alarmingly dangerous levels that threaten dire consequences for humans and other life forms on planet earth. The ever-increasing production of fossil fuels, carbon emissions, and other pollutants, careless and persistent deforestation, expanding desertification and wasteful consumerist behaviour have accelerated resource depletion, climate change and water supply problems. The results are alarming for human health and safety especially of the poor countries and economies which are unable to protect and defend themselves against them. There is incontrovertible evidence to show that disturbance of the natural balance envisaged in the scriptural sources of Islam has become a reality. Remedial action and protective measures are therefore necessary and urgent. The renowned hadith-cum-legal maxim which stipulates that, 'Harm may neither be inflicted nor reciprocated in [the name of] Islam – *la darar wa la dirar fi'l-Islam*', would authorise legal action against the violators, be they individuals, corporate bodies, multinationals or national states. They can be held responsible under Shariah to compensate for the harm they have inflicted provided there is evidence of deliberate violation.

Q165) How would you describe the Shariah's stance on scientific discoveries?

A) Shariah is supportive of exploratory scientific research and discovery that bring benefit to humankind and may also help advance the purposes of spirituality and God-consciousness. But knowledge of science and technology that is predominantly harmful and destructive is discouraged. The Islamic view of scientific knowledge and research is thus geared towards the purposes which they advance. If scientific discovery can be used to facilitate better methods of truth-discovery and involve no violaton of the rule of law and Shariah, there is no question over its acceptability. For instance, if new methods of fact-finding, such as the DNA analysis, can resolve confusion over paternity or identification of the war dead or those who died in a plane crash, for example, this will serve the Shariah objective regarding the preservation of lineage (*nasab*), which is one of the higher purposes (*maqasid*) of Shariah, in a better way. Similarly, if technological tools can determine the precise time and location in unknown places and in outer space for purposes of prayer and fasting, this will be seen as an instance of harmony between religion and science. If science can help find cures for incurable diseases, this will be conducive to the preservation of life, which is also one of the higher purposes or *maqasid* of Shariah. Yet if science and technology research is pursued only to produce weapons of mass destruction for hegemonic purposes that also exacerbate hostility and conflict among people, this would violate the same Islamic principles in respect of the preservation of life and building of a safe and peaceful order and cannot therefore be supported in the name of Islam or Shariah. The harm to the people would be even greater if a country with meagre resources allocated vastly disproportionate amounts of its national wealth to warlike purposes when peaceful approaches and policies would offer preferable options.

SUPPORTIVE EVIDENCE

▢ Qur'an and Hadith

+ 'And take not a position on that over which you have no knowledge. For [your] hearing, seeing and intellect are all accountable (on the Day of Reckoning).' (Q al-Isra', 17:36)[3]
+ 'Say! O my Lord! Increase my knowledge.' (Q Taha, 20:114)[4]
+ 'Above everyone endowed in knowledge, there is one, the All-Knowing.' (Q Yusuf, 12:76)[5]
+ 'Say! Observe [and investigate] what is there in the heavens and the earth.' (Q Yunus, 10:101)[6]
+ 'God will elevate in ranks those of you who have been granted knowledge.' (Q al-Mujadilah, 58:16)[7]
+ 'We have bestowed dignity on the children of Adam.' (Q al-Isra', 17:70)[8]
+ 'Indeed We created humankind in the best of moulds.' (Q Tin, 95:4)[9]
+ 'And I breathed into him (Adam) of My Spirit.' (Q Saad, 38:72)[10]
+ 'Cooperate in good work and righteousness, and cooperate not in transgression and hostility.' (Q al-Ma'idah, 5:2)[11]
+ 'We created man from a quintessence of clay. Then We placed him as (a drop of) sperm in a place of rest, firmly fixed. Then We made the sperm into a clot of congealed blood; then of that clot We made a (foetus) lump; then We made out of that lump bones and clothed the bones with flesh; then We developed out of it another creature.' (Q al- Mu'minun, 23:12–15)[12]
+ 'O humankind! Keep your duty to your Lord who created you from a single soul and created its mate of the same [kind] and created from them countless numbers of men and women.' (Q al-Nisa', 4:1)[13]
+ 'Say! Travel in the earth and see how God originated the creation.' (Q al-'Ankabut, 29:20)[14]
+ 'Ask those who know if you know yourselves not.' (Q al-Nahl, 16:43)[15]
+ 'Soon We will show them Our signs in (furthest) regions (of the earth), and within themselves.' (Q Fussilat, 41:53)[16]

+ 'People are equal like the teeth of a comb.' (Hadith)[17]
+ 'People are God's children. Those dearest to God are the ones who are kind to His children.' (Hadith)[18]
+ 'None of you is a [true] believer unless you like for your brother that which you like for yourself.' (Hadith)[19]
+ 'Pursuit of knowledge acts as an expiation (*kaffarah*) to what has taken place (of wrongdoing) preceding it.' (Hadith)[20]
+ 'Wisdom is the lost property of the believer. He is entitled to it wherever he finds it. (Hadith)[21]
+ 'Seek knowledge from the cradle to the grave.' (Hadith)[22]
+ 'Seek knowledge even if it be in China.' (Hadith)[23]
+ 'People are of two types. They are either the learned or the learners, and no good comes of them if they belong to neither.' (Hadith)[24]

[] Legal Maxims

+ 'The norm [of shariah] in all things is that of permissibility.'[25]
+ 'Harm must be eliminated.'[26]
+ 'Hardship begets facility.'[27]
+ 'Harm may neither be inflicted nor reciprocated in [the name of] Islam.'[28]
+ 'Necessities make the unlawful lawful.'[29]
+ 'Necessity is measured in accordance with its true proportions.'[30]
+ 'The norm [of Shariah] in matters of worship is that of prohibition.'[31]
+ 'The lesser of the two evils is to be preferred.'[32]
+ 'Harm may not be eliminated by its equivalent.'[33]
+ 'Harm to an individual is tolerated if it prevents harm to the general public.'[34]
+ 'Prevention of harms [or corruption] takes priority over the attraction of benefits.'[35]
+ 'When rigidity sets in, a way out of it must be found.'[36]
+ 'Custom is a [valid] basis of judgment.'[37]
+ 'Certainty may not be overruled by doubt.'[38]

XV

Freedom of Religion and the Rights of Minorities

Q166) Is Islamic law tolerant of non-Muslims?

A) Yes. The Qur'an and Sunnah are supportive of equality and justice for all and protection also of their human dignity and fundamental rights, including their lives and properties. Justice in Islam is not only for Muslims but for everyone without discrimination. Muslims are advised to treat non-Muslims who have not been aggressive towards them well, be good to them and nurture good relations with them. The Qur'an clearly permits Muslims to eat food prepared by non-Muslims, and animals slaughtered by Jews and Christians, thus contributing to an atmosphere of conviviality and amicable social relations. Islam also upholds the validity in principle of all mono-theistic religions and beliefs, and takes further steps to recognise the personal laws and customs of non-Muslim minorities living in Muslim countries. They may practice their personal laws and cultural traditions so long as they observe peace and order in society. The Qur'an also recognises freedom of religion explicitly by declaring that 'there shall be no compulsion in religion' (al-Baqarah, 2:256). Furthermore, Islamic history compares favourably with that of other religious traditions over the treatment of non-Muslims who lived in Islamic lands and in their midst. In the multi-religious societies in which we live today, it is not only good religion but good advice generally to treat people of all faiths well and nurture good relations with them in the true spirit of the human fraternity (*ukhuwwah insaniyyah*) which Islam advocates for the whole of humanity.

Q167) What is a *dhimmi*? Are *dhimmis* second-class citizens?

A) *Dhimmi* is derived from the word 'dhimmah', which means 'commitment' in the sense that the state is from the Shariah viewpoint committed to the protection of its non-Muslim citizens. *Dhimmah* also signifies a legal contract that is concluded between two parties: the individual and the state. It is a permanent contract and once concluded not even the state is authorised to dissolve and terminate it save for specific and pressing reasons, such as treason or when the non-Muslim citizen joins enemy forces. *Dhimmis* are permanent non-Muslim residents and citizens of Muslim-majority countries. They are not second-class citizens, but citizens with their own identity who also enjoy the liberty to practice their own religion and cultural traditions and be treated with equality. Equality is an aspect of justice and subsumes all citizens, Muslims and non-Muslims alike. Non-Muslim citizens may hold the post of ministers and be elected to parliament to represent their communities. The *dhimmis* may also be consulted in public affairs and matters especially of concern to them. Only the head of state in a Muslim majority state is to be a Muslim by convention, but even on this point there is no clear text to say so in the Qur'an or hadith. The general view is that the state in Islam is civilian and its affairs are determined on the basis of public interest (*maslahah*), consultation (*shura*) and independent reasoning (*ijtihad*). Only the last of these may be said to be for Muslims since the carrier of *ijtihad*, namely the *mujtahid*, must be a Muslim whereas *maslahah* and *shura* are inclusive of non-Muslims and *dhimmis*. The fourth caliph of Islam, 'Ali b. Abu Talib (d. 661 CE) is often quoted for the statement he made with regard to the *dhimmis* that they 'have the same rights as us and bear the same obligations as we do'.

The historical context has evidently changed due to new political realities. The modern nation state has effectively removed the earlier distinctions among citizens based on religion. The laws of citizenship and constitutional guarantees of basic rights and equality before the law have, on the whole, departed from the earlier positions of differentiation based on religion in favour of citizens' equality in rights and obligations. Many Muslim scholars of the post-colonial period have gone on record to say that non-Muslim minorities have the same rights and obligations as other citizens – they pay tax and participate in military service and the police force just like everyone else. It is further suggested that the *fiqhi* expression *dhimmi* (non-Muslim citizens) should be replaced now by the more egalitarian expression *muwatinun* (compatriots) for they are citizens and compatriots in the full sense, entitled to be treated equally before the law, as will be explained.

As already noted, *dhimmah* is a contract that is concluded between two parties. It is not a ruling or *hukm* of Shariah of permanent standing and has no independent existence unless it is created by the contracting parties. *Dhimmah* exists when the parties to it are in existence. In historical terms, *dhimmah* came to an end with the onset of colonial rule in Muslim lands, because the parties to it no longer existed, hence neither the *dhimmah* nor its bearer *dhimmi*, nor an independent Islamic polity, existed any longer. This was because the Western colonial state did not apply the regime of *dhimmah* and no *dhimmis* could therefore be said to exist as of that time. The whole concept of *dhimmah* has therefore effectively given way to *muwatanah* (citizenship). For purposes of equality and social harmony, *muwatanah* and its active participle and carriers, *muwatinun*, should be considered both as citizens and compatriots.

Q168) In the past, were non-Muslim residents of countries ruled by Muslims forced to pay a special tax? Does this practice continue today?

A) Yes, they were required to pay the polltax (*jizyah*), which is at about the same rate as that of the poor-due, or *zakah*, that is payable by the Muslims themselves. But since *zakah* is a religious duty in Islam, non-Muslims are not required to pay it; they pay *jizyah* instead as a contribution to the cost of protection and security that the state incurs for them. Non-Muslims were exempted from military service as it also partook in *jihad*, again a religious duty only for Muslims. But if non-Muslims themselves wished to serve in the army, they were entitled to be exempted from the payment of *jizyah*. Furthermore, the sick and disabled, the elderly, children, women and monks among them were not required to pay the *jizyah*. This practice does not continue today due to the general accept-ance and prevalence of the nation-state and the nature also of its taxation laws that no longer proceed on the basis of the religious identity of its citizens. Yusuf al-Qaradawi has also held the view, as already mentioned, that if non-Muslim citizens are exempted from *jizyah* but the Muslims continue to pay the *zakah*, then there should be no objection against non-Muslim citizens also paying the *zakah*, not as a religious duty, but as their contribution to the larger community.

Q169) Are non-Muslims living under Shariah forced to obey it?

A) Broadly, only in the sphere of public law, such as constitutional and criminal laws, economic activity and commerce, the Shariah applies equally to both Muslim and non-Muslim citizens. But non-Muslims are free to follow their own laws and traditions in religious, customary and personal law matters, such as marriage, divorce and inheritance, that may be said to be closely associated with the religion. Non-Muslims are not subject to the jurisdiction of Shariah courts, and may only refer to the civil courts, unless they request to seek judicial relief through the Shariah courts, in which case the Shariah court may adjudicate their cases based on Islamic law – although limited recognition may be given to the religious and customary traditions of the litigant even in the Shariah courts. But this is a matter that may be regulated by the head of state largely under the principle of *siyasah shar'iyyah*. Most of the present-day Muslim countries have a variety of other specialised courts, such as criminal courts, administrative courts, industrial and commercial courts, and so on, which operate side by side with the Shariah courts. Only in Saudi Arabia are the Shariah courts the courts of general jurisdiction. In most other present-day Muslim countries that have separate Shariah courts, their jurisdictions tend to be confined to matrimonial law, inher-itance matters and religious offences, with the overall result that non-Muslims are not likely to go to Shariah courts but mainly to the civil courts.

Q170) What are the consequences for non-Muslims who break the Shariah?

A) Non-Muslims are free to practice their own religion and customary traditions, which may even contravene the Shariah such as wine-drinking or the consumption of pork, provided that they do not promote these practices among Muslims. They are free to follow their own rules on these matters, and also in respect of their own personal laws such as marriage, divorce and inheritance, for example. They are not treated differently, however, when they commit crimes of violence and property or harm others without a just cause. As a matter of principle, public law applies equally to all citizens. Most of the present-day Muslim national states have introduced written constitutions, penal codes, civil codes and sometimes even commercial laws and codes, which are usually not based on religion and would normally apply to all citizens alike. One would expect that under such circumstances, and because they are allowed to follow their own traditions, the situation of non-Muslims breaking the Shariah would not be a major issue.

Q171) What is the origin of blasphemy law? What constitutes blasphemy? Which countries have blasphemy laws and how are they enforced?

A) Insulting and reviling God and the Prophet Muhammad, as well as the Qur'an, is generally considered as blasphemy. It is a blatant violation of the Right of God (*haqq* Allah). Historically, blasphemy and apostasy were predominantly political offences which had religious overtones. In the early years of Islam, blasphemy was also equivalent to high treason and posed a serious threat to both the religious and political foundations of the new community and state in Madinah. Today, blasphemy consists mainly of violation of the religious sensitivities of Muslims. It continues to be a dangerous offence, which can incite violence and loss of life and pose a threat to law and order in society, as was seen in the aftermath of Salman Rushdie's misguided venture, the Danish cartoons, and so on. There is no prescribed punishment for blasphemy, hence it falls under the category *ta'zir* offences and its punishment is open to a measure of discretion and the influence of circumstantial factors. The court of Shariah or the general courts of justice, as the case may be, are thus authorised to dispense a discretionary and deterrent punishment under *ta'zir* for those convicted of the offence of blasphemy. It may be added in passing, however, that the *fiqh* literature on the subject tends to subsume blasphemy, when committed by Muslims, under apostasy (*riddah*) and has not drawn a clear distinction between the two. The reader may be interested to know, however, I have made an attempt to draw this distinction in my book, *Freedom of Expression in Islam*, especially in its chapter on apostasy (pp. 212–50).

Q172) What does Shariah say about apostasy? Is it an offence for a Muslim to leave Islam?

A) The Qur'an does not explicitly provide any temporal punishment for apostasy. The most widely quoted Qur'anic verse and principle on this is: 'there is to be no compulsion in religion' (al-Baqarah, 2:256). The substance of this declaration is also confirmed in a number of other verses in the Qur'an as mentioned in Chapter 15. The basic position in Islamic law is supportive of the freedom of the individual to profess the religion of his or her choice without compulsion. Neither the Prophet Muhammad, nor any of his Companions, compelled anyone to embrace Islam. They did not sentence anyone to any punishment solely for renunciation of Islam, and there is evidence also in the Qur'an to that effect. The handful of cases of apostasy reported during the Prophet's lifetime are in effect offences of treason: the individual would renounce Islam, leave Madinah, join the pagans of Quraish and fight the Muslims – all in rapid succession. This was the scenario at a time when the two communities, the pagans of Mecca and the nascent Muslim community in Madinah, were actively at war. There were no neutral grounds under those circumstances. Bearing in mind also that there were over twenty-six military engagements (and many more smaller skirmishes) between Muslims and non-Muslims in the space of about ten years, there was an active but extended state of war. This was the context in which the Prophet uttered the hadith where he said: 'One who changes his religion shall be killed.' Although it was most likely, in my opinion, a temporary legislation (*tashri' zamani*) designed for those particular situations to begin with, in time it became standard law to the extent even of suppressing the Qur'anic position, due most probably to the outbreak of religious wars, the so-called 'wars of apostasy' (*hurub al-riddah*) during the time of the first caliph Abu Bakr. They were, in reality, tribal rebellions staged mainly to reject the payment of *zakah* tax to the new state, but they were fought in the name of apostasy nevertheless. Such was the hold of the idea of religion and Muslim vulnerability over the success or possible collapse of Islam at that sensitive juncture of history that political upheavals were also subsumed under religion – which was why the wars over refusal of *zakah* were labelled 'wars of apostasy'.

The hadith just quoted is also in need of interpretation as its standard wording would otherwise fail to convey its purpose. For the literal wording of the hadith would penalise say a Jew or Hindu who becomes a Muslim – which would be contrary to the intent of that hadith. According to the rules of Islamic jurisprudence, when a text becomes open to one level of interpretation, it is automatically reduced from the level of the definitive (*qat'i*) to that of speculative (*zanni*) and may henceforth be subjected to further levels of interpretation, which would, in this case, most likely be that this hadith had envisaged treason as a capital offence and not apostasy as such.

Q173)   How does Islamic law view non-Muslims who proselytise Muslims?

A)   Islamic law prohibits non-Muslims who are living under the Muslim authority from proselytising Muslims with the intention of inciting them to renounce Islam. Christian missionary activity in the Muslim lands became widespread in colonial times and continues to this day. The issue also touched on Muslim sensitivities in multi-religious societies such as Malaysia, with about forty per cent of its population being non-Muslim. Hence many of the Islamic by-laws or Enactments in the various states of Malaysia do not permit non-Muslims to proselytise Muslims. Even the Muslims themselves are not allowed to propagate Islamic doctrines among their fellow Muslims, due to the sensitivity of the matter and the incidence, whether intentionally or otherwise, of 'propagation of false doctrine'. On a comparative note, this may not be a major issue in some other Muslim countries, such as Turkey, Afghanistan and even Indonesia, for different reasons in each case, but also due to the fact they have homogenous Muslim populations close to 100 per cent.

Q174)   How does Islamic law view Muslims who proselytise?

A)   The Qur'anic guidelines on disputation and dialogue in religious matters, including the call to religion (for instance *da'wah*), is that they must be conducted in the most courteous and reasonable manner possible. It should be only in the form of persuasive engagement and advice, but Islam forbids Muslims from the use of coercive methods in propagating their faith. The basic principle of Islam is that there shall be no compulsion in religion.

SUPPORTIVE EVIDENCE

[] **Qur'an and Hadith**

+ 'Let him who will, believe, and let him who will, disbelieve.' (Q al-Kahf, 18:29)[1]
+ 'If God had willed, everyone on the face of the earth would have been believers. Are you [O Muhammad] then compelling the people to become believers?' (Q Yunus, 10:99)[2]
+ 'Say to the unbelievers! "Unto you, your religion, and unto me, my religion."' (Q al-Kafirun, 109:6)[3]
+ 'And call to the way of your Lord with wisdom and good advice.' (Q al-Nahl, 16:125)[4]
+ 'And argue not with the People of the Book except in the best of forms.' (Q al-'Ankabut, 29:46)[5]
+ 'Those who accept the faith and then disbelieve, then accept the faith, and then [renounce it and] disbelieve again, and then increase in their disbelief – God will not forgive them nor guide them to His path.' (Q al-Nisa', 4:137)[*6]
+ 'O humankind! We have created you from a male and a female, and made you into tribes and nations that you may know each other. Surely, the noblest of you in the eyes of God is the most pious among you.' (Q al-Hujurat, 49:13)[7]

---

[*] Had apostasy been subject to a temporal punishment, it would have been mentioned here. For this Qur'anic verse clearly visualises instances of renunciation of Islam more than once without actually mentioning a punishment for it.

+ 'God forbids you not to be good and just to those [of other faiths] who have not fought you over your religion, nor evicted you from your homeland. For God loves those who are just.' (Q al-Mumtahanah, 60:8)[8]
+ 'I have been sent in order to perfect the virtues of morality.' (Hadith)[9]
+ 'Whoever annoys a *dhimmi*, I shall be a litigant against him on the Day of Judgment.' (Hadith)[10]
+ 'O people! Your Creator is one, and you are all descendants of the same ancestor. There is no superiority of an Arab over a non-Arab, nor of the black over the red, except on the basis of righteous conduct.' (Hadith from the Prophet's Farewell Sermon)[11]

[] **Legal Maxims**

+ The normative position [of Shariah] in regards to people is their freedom.'[12]
+ 'People are free of (financial) liability unless the opposite is proven by evidence.'[13]
+ 'Plays and games fall under original permissibility unless there be evidence on their prohibition.'[14]
+ 'Islam is the religion of [harmony with pristine] human nature.'[15]
+ 'The unbeliever does not inherit from a Muslim nor does a Muslim inherit from an unbeliever.'[16]
+ 'When a Muslim takes by force the property of another Muslim he is not entitled to own it.'[17]
+ 'Muslims are bound by their stipulations [commitments].'[18]
+ 'The contracts of non-Muslims are held valid even if they oppose Islam but when they convert to Islam they are subject to the rules that apply to Muslims.'[19]

XVI

Goals and Purposes (*Maqasid*) of Shariah

Q175) What Are the *maqasid* of Shariah and how important are they in understanding the Shariah itself?

A) The *maqasid* (plural of *maqsad* – goals and purposes) of Shariah, or the higher purposes of Islamic law (henceforth *maqasid*) refer to the meaning, purpose and wisdom that the Lawgiver has contemplated in the enactment of Shariah laws. *Maqasid* thus refer to the higher purposes of the law, which are meant to be secured through the implementation of that law, and they give the law a sense of direction and purpose. It also means that the rules of Shariah, especially in the spheres of human relations and *mu'amalat*, are not meant for their own sake but to secure and realise certain objectives. When the dry letter of the law is applied in such a way that it does not secure its intended purpose and fails, for instance, to secure the justice and benefit it is meant to secure, or when it leads, on the contrary, to harm and prejudice, the law is most likely reduced to a purposeless exercise, which must be avoided. The laws of Shariah are generally meant to secure justice and the interests and prosperity of the people both in this world and the hereafter. But the detailed rules, commands and prohibitions of Shariah also have their specific purposes, which are often identified in the text of the law, or by recourse to interpretation and *ijtihad*.

Q176) Is *maqasid* another name for the rationale or *ratio legis* of the law?

A) *Maqasid* bear similarity with the notions of *ratio legis* and *ratio decidendi* in Western jurisprudence, but differ with them in some respects. Broadly, the goals and purposes of Shariah law cannot be separated from the twin notions of rationality and revelation, whereas Western law precludes the latter and makes rationality the sole basis and indicator of the purposes of law. What this means is that the law and its purposes are both grounded in rationality and are detectable by rational means alone. The *maqasid* of Shariah also strike a close note with the Islamic jurisprudence notions of rationale and effective cause (*hikmah, 'illah*) of the law and they also come close to the Western law concepts of *ratio legis* and *ratio decidendi* (both grounded in ratio or rationale), but differ with them in certain respects. The *maqasid* constitute the test often of the validity of the law especially in the sphere of civil transactions (*mu'amalat*), which regulate human relations, whereas devotional matters (*'ibadat*) may not be so testable. Devotional matters do have their purposes but since they are not always known to us, and we also do not know the *'illah* (effective cause) or *ratio legis*, of devotional matters, we cannot make them the subject of rational enquiry, the search for *ratio legis*, or *ijtihad*.

Q177) What is the benefit of knowing the *maqasid* of Shariah?

A) One often hears of a clever lawyer who may be bent on the prospect of winning a case and on working his way through the law at the expense even of twisting it to suit his or his client's purposes, regardless of what the law might have intended. This is why the Shariah penalises what is called in the *fiqh* jargon al-Mufti al-Majin, that is, a trickster or fraudulent jurisconsult who does just that, either to please his client, follow self-seeking interests, or obtain a specific answer at any cost. This is a violation of the Shariah, which is in principle a divine law, and twisting it in such ways is reprehensible. Ibrahim al-Shatibi (d. 1388 CE) of Andalus who wrote extensively on the *maqasid* stressed the importance of this area of Shariah by saying that a clear understanding of *maqasid* equips one with the knowledge of enabling one to identify instances of distortion and abuse. Also, that anyone who manipulates the Shariah by isolating its letter from its intent and purpose, through recourse to legal stratagem (*hilah*), is guilty of violating the purpose of the Lawgiver. Knowledge of the *maqasid* thus helps keep the letter of the law and its spirit in harmony with each other.

To illustrate more specifically how the letter of the law can sometimes move in a different direction from its proper intention and purpose, one may look at some of the Shariah contracts. The proper purpose, or *maqsad* of sale, for instance, is transfer of ownership of the object of sale for the seller and acquisition of ownership for the buyer; the *maqsad* of lease on the other hand is transfer of the usufruct of the object of sale; the *maqsad* of marriage is procreation of the human species, and that of giving a gift is charity and donation (*tabarru'*) – just as another *maqsad* of giving a gift is transfer of ownership by the owner to another party without a consideration. If any of these contracts are applied and manipulated such that they fail to secure their valid Shariah purpose or *maqsad*, a distortion in the application of the law is likely to have occurred.

Q178) Are there any conditions the *maqasid* must fulfil in order to be valid?

A) The renowned Tunisian scholar, Ibn 'Ashur (d. 1973) who wrote an important book, *Maqasid al-Shariah al-Islamiyyah*, on the subject also specified certain conditions: for a *maqsad* or purpose to be valid, it must qualify four conditions. These are: to be proven, to be evident, to be general, and to be exclusive (*thabit, zahir, 'amm* and *tard* respectively). For a *maqsad* to be proven means that it is supported by clear laws and is not subject to disagreement and dispute. A *maqsad* must also be evident, not a hidden factor, so that it can be identified and proven by admissible evidence. Furthermore, *maqsad* must be general and objective in that it applies to all of its intended applications – and generally to all people, not a group or class of people, and does not promote partisan interests. And a *maqsad* is exclusive when it is clearly defined in that it includes all which properly belongs to it and excludes all that which falls outside its scope.

Q179)   How are the *maqasid* known and identified?

A)   Briefly, *maqasid* are identified in the clear text (*nass* – Qur'an or hadith) or by general consensus (*ijma'*), failing which they may be identified by recourse to independent reasoning and *ijtihad*. The language of the Qur'an or hadith may either be explicit on the identification of a certain purpose, or it may be implicit and require a degree of scrutiny to identify a certain *maqsad*. For instance, when the text of the Qur'an or hadith refers to the benefit, rationale, purpose and the consequences of its rulings, the judge and jurist are given a certain guidance and insight into the *maqsad* or purpose of that law, which they should strive to secure in their decisions. Al-Shatibi (d. 1388 CE), who is known as the master architect of *maqasid* (Shaykh al-Maqasid), due to the unique contribution he has made to this subject, also added inductive reasoning, or *istiqra'* (being essentially a form of *ijtihad*), as a reliable method by which to identify the *maqasid* of Shariah.

Ibn 'Ashur also added, in line with the writings of 'Izz al-Din 'Abd al-Salam al-Sulami (d. 1262/660) and others, that human intellect (*'aql*), enlightened human nature (*fitrah*) and unrestricted reasoning (*istidlal*) are also capable of identifying the *maqasid* of Shariah, although these last two are not unanimously agreed upon by Muslim scholars. Most of these methods can actually be subsumed under *ijtihad*. To say that *maqasid* can be identified by way of induction looks basically to the data of the Qur'an and hadith generally. The text may have made numerous references to a *maqsad*, or purpose, of the Lawgiver without explicitly declaring it as such. When all such references are read and put together, their collective weight or meaning emerges and leaves little doubt on the identification of a certain purpose as the valid objective of Shariah.

Q180)   Has the methodology of *maqsid* remained relatively underdeveloped?

A)   Yes, it has remained underdeveloped. The methodology of *maqasid* (identification, classification, conditions of validity, and even definition, etc.) is not as well-developed as that of the legal theory of *usul al-fiqh*. For the *maqasid* are generally subsumed by the *usul al-fiqh* discourse. This underdeveloped status of the *maqasid* is explained by reference to a variety of factors, one of which is a certain textualist orientation of the legal theory of *usul al-fiqh*, which means that Muslim jurists exercised restraint and did not encourage enquiry into the purposes and intents of the Lawgiver. This is because the *maqasid* tend to have a philosophical bent and engaging into an inquisitive philosophical enquiry into the intents and purposes of the Lawgiver was not encouraged.

The *usul al-fiqh* often subsumed the *maqasid* under the rubrics of the effective cause and rationale of the law (*'illah, hikmah, manat*), which was less than accurate, and was certainly another reason for the relative underdevelopment of the methodology of *maqasid*. But the latter part of the twentieth century witnessed a revival of interest in the *maqasid* and scholarly writings have also steadily increased in developing the various aspects of the methodology of *maqasid*.

Q181) One often hears of the different types of *maqasid*, such as essential *maqasid*, or necessities, complementary *maqasid* and the embellishments (*daruriyyat, hajiyyat, tahsiniyyat* respectively). Are there other classifications of *maqasid*?

A) Yes, there are. *Maqasid* have been classified into several types, depending on the viewpoint and purpose of classification. From the viewpoints of their importance, scope, proof, and the party or person who apply and pursue them, the *maqasid* have been classified into three types that may be summarised as follows.

From the viewpoint of their importance, the *maqasid* have been classified into three types – as already mentioned, of essential *maqasid*, complementary *maqasid*, and the embellishments (*daruriyyat, hajiyyat, tahsiniyyat* respectively). Essential *maqasid* include the protection of life, faith, intellect, property and lineage (a minority opinion also adds protection of honour to this list). Protection and preservation of these is a top priority of the entire Shariah as their destruction and collapse is certain to lead to chaos and disturbance of normal law and order in the community. Complementary *maqasid* have not been specified into the five or six subheadings as such, but include those without which one would be faced with hardship. They complement, on the whole, the essential purposes or *maqasid* of Shariah. The embellishments are also an open category and virtually unlimited in number and scope. One may give cleanliness and hygiene as an example perhaps: a basic amount of cleanliness is essential and necessary for normal life and also for performance of certain religious rituals and so on. To wear clean clothes to congregational prayers, or when visiting a doctor or clinic may be complementary, but any enhancement in cleanliness that brings beauty and elegance suitable to the occasion or when it beautifies one's living environment and that of the community becomes desirable enhancement, or embellishment.

Without delving into details, the other classifications of *maqasid* are: general *maqasid* and particular *maqasid* (*maqasid 'ammah, maqasid khassah*), primary and secondary *maqasid* (*maqsid asliyyah, maqasid tab'iyyah*), definitive and speculative *maqasid* (*maqsid qat'iyyah, maqasid zanniyyah*); *maqasid* of the Lawgiver and those of the individual (*maqasid al-shari', maqasid al-mukallaf*).

The reader can find fuller details on these in my book *Shariah Law: An Introduction* (Chapter 5) and some of my other publications on the subject.[*]

The general purposes of Shariah are ones that characterise Islam and its Shariah generally, and they apply to all areas and subjects they can conceivably apply to. They are on the whole broad and comprehensive. For instance, realisation of benefit (*maslahah*), prevention of harm and corruption (*darar, mafsadah*), building the earth (*i'mar al-ard*), administration of justice, and removal of hardship (*raf al-haraj*) are among the general purposes of Shariah. They differ from particular purposes in that the latter contemplate specific areas and subjects of the Shariah, such as commercial transactions, crimes and punishments, matrimonial law, acts of charity and so forth. Each of these have their particular purposes which are often, but not always identified in the *fiqh* manuals. The general and the particular *maqasid* are not totally separate in that the particular *maqasid* should comply with the broader objectives of Shariah or should at least not go against them. Other classifications of the *maqasid* are addressed under separate questions below.

Q182)   Are God's purposes, or the purposes of the Lawgiver, about the same as those of human beings?

A)   They should be but they are not always the same. This is the subject of a separate classification of *maqasid* into the Lawgiver's purposes (*maqasid al-shari'*) and the human purposes (*maqasid al-mukallaf*).

---

[*] Mohammad Hashim Kamali, *Shari'ah Law: An Introduction*, Oxford: Oneworld, 2008.

To say that human welfare and benefit, or knowledge of the religion, are God's illustrious purposes of the pursuit of knowledge illustrate the former, whereas seeking employment or a university qualification may represent the human purposes of seeking knowledge. It is recommended that all competent persons should bring, as far as possible, their own purposes into conformity with the purposes or *maqasid* of the Lawgiver. People may pursue different purposes and that is not an issue provided they do not contravene the expressed purposes of the Lawgiver.

Q183) Does the Qur'an always speak with clarity regarding the Lawgiver's purposes?

A) It does sometimes but not always. The Qur'anic language is diverse. Sometimes a purpose is identified in a clear text (*nass*) but this is not always the case. This is the subject of another classification of *maqasid* into the two classes of definitive (*qati*) and speculative (*zanni*). The definitive *maqasid* signify purposes that are conveyed in a clear text of the Qur'an, hadith, or are determined by general consensus (*ijma'*), whereas the speculative *maqasid* may be conveyed in a text that is not clear and categorical in its message and may need to be clarified by means of interpretation and *ijtihad*. In the event that a conflict arises between them, the definitive purposes of Shariah take priority over the speculative ones.

Q184) What are the primary as opposed to secondary purposes of Shariah?

A) The primary purposes (*al-maqasid al-asliyyah*) and subsidiary purposes (*al-maqasid al-tabbiyyah* or *far'iyyah*) refer to the originally intended purposes as opposed to those which may be secondary and additional. The former are the ones which the Lawgiver, or a human agent, for that matter, have originally intended, whereas the latter are those which support and complement the primary *maqasid*. For instance, the primary Shariah purpose of marriage is procreation of the human species, which may or may not materialise in a marriage among elderly persons contracted with the purpose mainly of companionship, which is a secondary purpose of marriage in their case. Similarly, the primary purpose of sale and purchase is transfer of ownership from seller to buyer. Yet the seller or buyer may also be following additional purposes, which may vary from case to case, and it is not an issue provided that the secondary purposes do not contradict or frustrate the primary ones.

⬜ Legal Maxims:*

+ 'Acts are judged by their intentions.' (Hadith-cum-legal maxim)[1]
+ '[People's] Affairs are determined by reference to their purposes.' (Hadith-cum-legal maxim)[2]
+ 'All dispositions that deviate from their [proper] purposes are null and void.'[3]
+ 'Observance of purposes is always given priority over the observance of means.'[4]
+ 'The whole of the Shariah is meant to subjugate whimsical desires of the individual to the purposes of the Lawgiver.'[5]
+ 'Hindrances [and obstacles] are not desired by the Lawgiver.'[6]
+ 'Facilitation is one of the objectives of Shariah.'[7]
+ 'The means are subsumed by the value of their ends and purposes.'[8]
+ 'Building the earth and continuity of its benefits for the good of its inhabitants is a general objective of Shariah.'[9]
+ 'A transaction that contradicts its [proper] purpose is void.'[10]
+ 'The purposes of Shariah are known by reference to the Qur'an, the Sunnah, and general consensus.'[11]
+ 'Knowledge of the original context and occasions of revelation cast light on the purpose of the Lawgiver.'[12]
+ 'The purposes of Shariah and its benefits are known by reference to enlightened human nature.'[13]
+ 'When there is no purpose to something, it is invalid.'[14]
+ 'The purpose of Shariah behind legislation is validation/enactment and change.'[15]

---

* Almost all of the legal maxims quoted here and throughout this volume have been taken from *Mu'allimah Zayid li'l-Qawa'id al-Fiqhiyyah wa'l-Usuliyyah*, Abu Dhabi: Mu'assasah Zayid b. Sultan Aal-Nahyan and Majma' al-Fiqh al-Islami al-Duwali, 41 vols, 2013/1434. All entries are alphabetical in this extensive Arabic encyclopaedia of legal maxims.

+ 'Enactment of laws are always to secure both the immediate and future benefits of [God's] servants/people.'[16]
+ 'Looking into the consequences of acts is a valid purpose of the Shariah.'[17]
+ 'The Lawgiver's purpose concerning the competent person is for the latter to align his action with the purpose of His law.'[18]
+ 'The Lawgiver's purpose is not established except through certainty or strong probability.'[19]
+ 'Credibility in speech and acts is attached to their purposes and meanings.'[20]
+ '*Maqasid* (goals and purposes) of Shariah are the permanent sources of reference for protection of the basics of legislation and adjudication in Islamic jurisprudence.'[21]
+ 'The purposes of Shariah are founded in pristine human nature.'[22]
+ 'Primary and explicit prohibitions are indicative of the purposes of the Lawgiver.'[23]
+ 'The general principles of *maqasid* can be established through inductive reasoning (*istiqra'*).'[24]
+ 'All aspects of *ijtihad* require knowledge of the purposes [of Shariah].'[25]
+ 'The purposes of contracts affect determination of their validity and vitiation.'[26]
+ 'Should the issue revolve around observance either of the literal meaning or the purpose of a word, the latter prevails.'[27]
+ 'Forbearance and ease are among the purposes of religion.'[28]
+ 'Protection of religion is a primary purpose of Shariah.'[29]
+ 'Protection of life is a primary purpose of Shariah.'[30]
+ 'Protection of reason is a primary purpose of Shariah.'[31]
+ 'Protection of lineage is a primary purpose of Shariah.'[32]
+ 'In the event of conflict among benefits/purposes, that which is certain takes priority over the uncertain and doubtful.'[33]

XVII

Legal Maxims of *Fiqh* (*Qawaʿid kulliyyah fiqhiyyah*)

Q185) What are the legal maxims?

A) Legal maxims of *fiqh* were briefly introduced in the Introduction, and I will now extend that discussion a little further. A legal maxim (Ar. *qaʿidah kulliyyah fiqhiyyah*) is a theoretical abstraction in the form usually of a short epithetic statement that is expressive, often in a few words, of a general principle of law that applies to all or most of its detailed applications. Legal maxims are derived from the detailed reading of the rules and provisions of *fiqh* on its various themes and subjects. Some maxims are broad and panoramic in scope applying to the whole gamut of the Shariah whereas others are more specific and confined to certain themes or topics. The former are legal maxims proper whereas the latter are often known as controlling rules, or *dawabit* (sing. *dabitah*). A more specific definition of a legal maxim may be given as 'a general rule which applies to all or most of its related particulars'. It is due partly to the abstract and generalised terms of their language that legal maxims are hardly without some exceptions or situations to which they may not apply.

Q186)   Do the legal maxims relate in any way to the general purposes, or *maqasid*, of Shariah?

A)   Yes, they do indeed. The legal maxims are often expressive of the general principles but also of the goals and purposes of Shariah: the one can hardly deliver an integrated message without the other. It is due to their versatility and comprehensive language that legal maxims tend to encapsulate the broader purposes and characteristics of Shariah. Historically the legal maxims and *maqasid* of Shariah were not separate as they were thematically interrelated and were seen as extensions of one another, often appearing under one and the same heading. But they were separated later at a time when legal maxims became diverse and covered not only the purposes of Islamic law but also its thematic rules and principles derived from the detailed reading of *fiqh*. This can perhaps be more clearly seen with regard to a sub-variety of legal maxims, known as the *dawabit*, which are, as earlier mentioned, often specific and substantive rules rather than statements of objectives. So, for example: 'when the water reaches two feet (*qullatayn*) in depth, it does not carry dirt', and with reference to the tanning of hides, 'when the skin of an animal is tanned, it becomes clean'. Both of these are controlling rules, or *dabitahs*, which have, incidentally, been derived from the exact wordings of hadith; both are related to cleanliness, but they do not provide statement of purposes as such. These are different, for instance, to a legal maxim proper that provides, for instance, 'hardship begets facility', or one that reads 'forbearance and ease are the objectives of Shariah'.

Q187)   Do the legal maxims differ from the *usul al-fiqh*, the roots and sources of Islamic law?

A)   Yes, they do differ from the *usul al-fiqh*, notwithstanding the fact that in their Arabic rendering *qawa'id kulliyyah fiqhiyyah* and *usul al-fiqh* they bear a striking resemblance to one another, so much so that sound about the same in their Arabic nomenclatures. The main difference is that *usul al-fiqh* refers to the sources of law, methodology of legal reasoning, the rules of interpretation and so forth. The sources of law in Islam are the Qur'an, the Sunnah, general consensus, analogical reasoning and so on; these are neither specific rules nor general maxims as such, although the legal maxims are also, in the final analysis, derived from these same sources. In their early stages of development, both the legal maxims and the *maqasid* were subsumed under the *usul al-fiqh*. The legal maxims were separated from the latter on the analysis that legal maxims were derived from the *fiqh* itself and thus belonged to the branches rather than the sources of Islamic law. The *maqasid* were gradually developed into a distinctive discipline of its own. Though still not entirely separate from the *usul al-fiqh*, the *maqasid* were seen to provide a different and more purposive reading of the Shariah that was focused on values and objectives, and not so much on the deduction of rules from their sources and methodologies that was the main preoccupation of *usul al-fiqh*.

Q188)   Do the legal maxims carry a binding force?

A)   No, they are not binding. Unless they affirm and reiterate an injunction of the Qur'an or hadith, the legal maxims as such do not bind the judge and jurist, but they do provide a persuasive source of influence in the formulation of judicial decisions, *fatwa* (legal opinion) and *ijtihad* (independent reasoning). Legal maxims are primarily designed for a better understanding of their subject matter rather than enforcement. Some of the broader legal maxims are similar in this respect to the legal theories (*al-nazariyyat*), such as the theory of contract, constitutional theory and the like – although most of the legal maxims are not as broad and comprehensive. Yet the legal theories are also constructed for better understanding of their subject matter and are generally not binding. This is further elaborated in the next question.

Q189)   How do a legal maxim and a legal theory (*al-nazariyyah*) differ from one another?

A)   As already mentioned, legal maxims are limited in scope and do not seek to establish a theoretically self-contained framework over an entire discipline of learning, whereas a legal theory does just that. Another difference is that a legal maxim usually incorporates a ruling (*hukm*) which is applicable to its relevant subject matter. Thus, the maxim 'custom is the basis of judgment' conveys a certain ruling with identifiable applications. A legal theory, such as the theory of ownership, is different in that it does not incorporate any ruling as such. The theory of ownership is expected to offer a broad, coherent and comprehensive entry into its theme. One may have, on the other hand, numerous legal maxims on the subject of ownership.

Q190) Do legal maxims differ in the various schools, or *madhhabs*, of Islamic law?

A) Legal maxims are, on the whole, inter-scholastic in that the bulk of legal maxims seem to be accepted by almost all the leading schools of Islamic law. This is partly due to the fact that legal maxims are devoid of specific details and focus on the statement of principle at the level of brevity and abstraction. The leading legal maxims, which are relatively small in number (most would say only five), are common between the leading schools of Islamic law. That said, differences of perspective and position do exist and it is not unusual, although rare perhaps, to see divergent even conflicting statements of the same principle between different schools. Such differences are more noticeable, however, with regard to controlling rules (*dawabit*), which are more specific and may reflect scholastic differences over details. One may even add to this that such differences over details do arise sometimes between the leading scholars of the same school or *madhhab*, and are not confined therefore to the leading schools of Islamic law. The Shia school of law subscribes to certain legal maxims that originate in the principle of Imamate, or uphold some such positions that may be peculiar to their scholastic orientation which may not be shared by their Sunni counterparts, and such differences are, in turn, reflected in their related maxims.

Qur'anic Verses, Hadith and Legal Maxims
(in Original Arabic)

I. SHARIAH AND *FIQH* – MEANING, DEFINITION, SOURCES, SALIENT FEATURES AND COMPARISONS WITH OTHER LEGAL SYSTEMS

Quran

1   يَرْفَعِ اللَّهُ الَّذِينَ آمَنُوا مِنكُمْ وَالَّذِينَ أُوتُوا الْعِلْمَ دَرَجَاتٍ.

2   وَلَا تَقْفُ مَا لَيْسَ لَكَ بِهِ عِلْمٌ إِنَّ السَّمْعَ وَالْبَصَرَ وَالْفُؤَادَ كُلُّ أُولَئِكَ كَانَ عَنْهُ مَسْئُولًا.

3   وَمَا آتَاكُمُ الرَّسُولُ فَخُذُوهُ وَمَا نَهَاكُمْ عَنْهُ فَانْتَهُوا.

Hadith

4   أن رسول الله صلى الله عليه وسلم لما أراد أن يبعث معاذ إلى اليمن, قال: كيف تقضي إذا عرض لك قضاء؟ قال: أقضي بكتاب الله, قال: فإن لم تجد في كتاب الله؟ قال: فبسنة رسول الله صلى الله عليه وسلم, قال: فإن لم تجد في سنة رسول الله ولافي كتاب الله؟ قال أجتهد رأيي.

5   إني قد تركت فيكم شيئين إن تمسكتم بهما لن تضلوا بعدهما, كتاب الله وسنتي.

6   طلب العلم فريضة على كل مسلم ومسلمة.

7   طلب العلم كان كفارةً لما مضى.

8   الحكمة ضالة المؤمن حيث وجدها فهو أحق بها.

9   لاينبغي لأحد عنده شيء من العلم أن يضيع نفسه.

10   الناس رجلان: عالم ومتعلم و لاخير في سواهما.

Legal Maxims

11   الشريعة جاء ت بتحصيل المصالح وتكميلها وتعطيل المفاسد وتقليلها.

12   القرآن كله كالكلمة الواحدة في وجوب بناء بعضه على بعض.

13   الشريعة داعية إلى تقويم الفطرة والمحافظة عليها.

14   الشريعة الإسلا مية أباحت كل طيب و حرمت كل خبيث.

15   لا ثواب ولا عقاب إلا بنية.

16   المباحات تختلف صفتها بإعتبار ما قصد ت لأجله, فإن قصد بها التقوى على الطاعة والتوصل إليها, كانت عبادة.

17   الشريعة أجملت المتغيرات و فصلت الثوابت.

18   الشريعة جارية على الوسط العدل.

19   الخبر المتواتر يجب العلم القطعي.

20   السنة المطهرة مستقلة بتشريع الحكم.

21   ما يعاف في العادات يكره في العبادات.

22   يمنع القياس في الإثبات أصول العبادات.

23   القياس يترك بالعرف.

24   ألعرف لايعتبر إذا خالف أحكام الشرع.

25   الأصل بقاء ماكان على ماكا ن حتى يقوم الدليل على خلافه.

26 الأصل أن تزول الأحكام بزوال عللها.

27 قد يظهر الشئ بسببين فلا يرتفع بإرتفاع أحدهما مع بقاء السبب الأخر.

28 لايقطع على تحر يم شيئي إلابيقين.

29 البا طل مفسوخ, لايحتاج إلى فسخ حاكم ولاغيره.

30 الأصل في الأشياء إباحة حتى يد ل الد ليل على التحر يم.

31 الأصل براءة الذ مة.

II. LEGAL OPINION (*FATWA*) AND INDEPENDENT REASONING (*IJTIHAD*)

Qur'an

1 أَفَلَا يَتَدَبَّرُونَ الْقُرْآنَ أَمْ عَلَى قُلُوبٍ أَقْفَالُهَا.

2 فَاسْأَلُوا أَهْلَ الذِّكْرِ إِنْ كُنْتُمْ لَا تَعْلَمُونَ.

3 وَالَّذِينَ جَاهَدُوا فِينَا لَنَهْدِيَنَّهُمْ سُبُلَنَا.

4 يُرِيدُ اللَّهُ بِكُمُ الْيُسْرَ وَلَا يُرِيدُ بِكُمُ الْعُسْرَ.

Hadith

5 إذا أراد لله بعبده خيرا يفقهه في الد ين.

6 إذا حكم الحا كم فاجتهد ثم أصاب فله أجران و إذا حكم فاجتهد ثم أخطأ فله أجر.

7 اعملوا فكل ميسر لما خلق له.

Legal Maxims

8 إذا أفتى أهل للفتوى بإتلاف ثم تبين خطاؤه فالضمان على المفتي.

9 الإجتهاد لاينقض بالإجتهاد. الإجتهاد لاينقض بمثله.

10 لا إجتهاد في قطعيات.

11 إذا اختلف على المقلد إجتهاد مجتهدين فإنه يقلد من شاء منهما.

12 لا يحل للمجتهد أن يتقلد مجتهد آخر فيما يخالف إجتهاده.

13 إذا تعادلت الامارتان فالمجتهد يخير بينهما.

14 المجتهد مكلف بما أضاحه إليه إجتهاده.

15 الفتوى تدور مع المصالح حيثما دارت.

16 لاينكر تغير الفتوى بتغير الأزمان.

17 المفتي مخبر عن الحكم والقاضي ملزم به.

18 العدالة شرط الفتوى.

19 يفتى في كل بلد بحسب عرف أهله.

20 لا إلزام في الفتيا.

21 إذا اختلف على المقلد فتيا المفتيين تخيير في الأخذ.

22 الفتوى دائرة على مقتضى الحال.

23 الفتوى على خلاف النص أو الإجماع باطلة.

24 التوصل بالأحكام الشرعية إلى ما يخالف مراداله ومقاصده الشريعة باطل.

25 إنما يبتني الحكم على المقصود لاعلى ظاهر اللفظ.

26 جميع وجوه الإجتهاد تحتاج إلى معرفة المقاصد.

27 الإجتهاد إن تعلق بالمعاني من المصالح والمفاسد فيلزم العلم بمقاصد الشرع.

28 من شروط المجتهد الممارسة والتتبع لمقاصد الشريعة.

29 لامساغ للاجتهاد في مورد النص.

30 رأي المجتهد حجة من حجج الشرع.

31 المجتهد إذا رجع من قول لايجوز الأخذ به.

32 اليقن لا يزول بالشك.

33 المشقة تجلب التيسير.

34 لاضرورة في الأثقل مع إمكان تحصيل المقصود بالأسهل.

35 الشارع لا يقصد التكليف بالشاق والإعنات فيه.

36 المباح يتقييد بالسلامة.

37 السماحة واليسر من مقاصد الدين

38 العبرة للغالب الشائع لا للقليل النادر.

39 درء المفاسد أولى من جلب المنافع.

40 يختار أهون الشرين.

41 الضرر يزال بقدر الإمكان.

42 الضرر لا يزال بمثله.

43 إذا زال المانع عادالممنوع.

44 لا ينكر تغير الأحكام بتغير الأزمان.

45 الحكم يدور مع علته وجودا وعدما.

46 الأصل أن تزول الأحكام بزوال علله.

47 الإجتهاد إن تعلق بالمعاني من المصالح والمفاسد فيلزم العلم بالمقاصد الشرع.

48 الأصل في الكلام حقيقة.

49 لاعبرة بالدلالة في المقابلة التصريح.

50 كل ما دعت الحاجة إلية في الشريعة مما فيه منفعة ولم يعارضه محظور فإنه جائز وواجب بحسب حاله.

III. SHARIAH AND ACTS OF WORSHIP (*'IBADAT*)

Qur'an

1 وَأَقِيمُوا الصَّلَاةَ وَآتُوا الزَّكَاةَ وَارْكَعُوا مَعَ الرَّاكِعِينَ.

2 ولله على الناس حج البيت لمن استطاع اليه سبيلا.

3 إِنَّ الَّذِينَ آمَنُوا وَعَمِلُوا الصَّالِحَاتِ وَأَقَامُوا الصَّلَاةَ وَآتَوُا الزَّكَاةَ لَهُمْ أَجْرُهُمْ عِنْدَ رَبِّهِمْ وَلَا خَوْفٌ عَلَيْهِمْ ولاهم يحزنون.

4 فَمَنِ اضْطُرَّ غَيْرَ بَاغٍ وَلَا عَادٍ فَلَا إِثْمَ عَلَيْهِ.

5 لَيْسَ الْبِرَّ أَنْ تُوَلُّوا وُجُوهَكُمْ قِبَلَ الْمَشْرِقِ وَالْمَغْرِبِ وَلَكِنَّ الْبِرَّ مَنْ آمَنَ بِاللَّهِ وَالْيَوْمِ الْآخِرِ ... وَآتَى الْمَالَ عَلَى حُبِّهِ ذَوِي الْقُرْبَى وَالْيَتَامَى وَالْمَسَاكِينَ .

6 قُلْ يَا عِبَادِيَ الَّذِينَ أَسْرَفُوا عَلَى أَنْفُسِهِمْ لَا تَقْنَطُوا مِنْ رَحْمَةِ اللَّهِ إِنَّ اللَّهَ يَغْفِرُ الذُّنُوبَ جَمِيعًا إِنَّهُ هُوَ الْغَفُورُ الرَّحِيمُ.

7 لَا يُكَلِّفُ اللَّهُ نَفْسًا إِلَّا وُسْعَهَا.

Hadith

8 ألطهارة شطر الإيمان.

9 إنما الأعمال بالنيات.

10 عليكم برخصة الله الذي رخص لكم.

11 ليس من البر الصوم في السفر.

12 رفع عن أمتي الخطأ والنسيان وما استكرهوا عليه.

Legal Maxims

13 الميسور لا يسقط بالميسور.

14 لا ثواب إلا بالنية.

15 الإسلام يجب ما قبله في حقوق الله دون ما تعلق به حق الآدمي.

16 ليس للمكلف أن يقصد المشقة في التكليف نظرا إلى عظم اجرها.

17 البناء على المقاصد الأصلية يصير تصرفات المكلف كلها عبادات.

18 المباح إذا قصد به وجه الله تعالى صار طاعة.

19 القضاء لا يدخل في العبادات.

20 في العبادة قبل وقتها لا يقع أداء ولا قضاءا.

21 من فاته شئ من العبادات فعليه القضاء.

22 النافلة لا تقضى.

23 العبادة كلها لها معان فإن الشرع لا يأمر بالعبث.

24 العزم في العبادات مع العجز يقوم مقام الإداء في عدم الإثم.

25 العادة تنقلب عبادات بالنيات الصالحات.

26 ما أحل للضرورة أو حاجة يقدر بقدرها و يزول بزوالها.

IV. SCHOOLS OF ISLAMIC LAW, THE *MADHHABS*

Legal Maxims

1 الفتوى بالتخريج من مذهب المفتي لا تصح.

2 نص إما مه في حقه كنص الشرعي في حق المجتهد المستقل.

3 يلزم كل مقلد أن يلتز م بمذهب معين.

4 كل ما حكم به القاضي العد ل من مذهب من رأه صوابا مما إختلف النص فيه فهو نا فذ.

5 يستحب الخروج من الخلا ف.

V. THE SCALE OF FIVE VALUES (*AL-AHKAM AL-KHAMSAH*)

Qur'an

1 وَقَدْ فَصَّلَ لَكُمْ مَا حَرَّمَ عَلَيْكُمْ إِلَّا مَا اضْطُرِرْتُمْ.

2 وَلَا تَقُولُوا لِمَا تَصِفُ أَلْسِنَتُكُمُ الْكَذِبَ هُذَا حَلَالٌ وَهُذَا حَرَامٌ لِتَفْتَرُوا عَلَى اللَّهِ الْكَذِبَ.

3 وَيُحِلُّ لَهُمُ الطَّيِّبَا تِ وَيُحَرِّمُ عَلَيْهِمُ الْخَبَائِثَ.

Hadith

4 إن الله يحب أن تؤتي رخصة كما يحب أن تؤتي عزائمه.

Legal Maxims

5 مالايتم الواجب إلا به فهو واجب.

6 الأصل في المضار التحريم.

7 الحكم إنما يجري على الظاهر وإن السرائر موكولة إلى الله سبحا نه وتعالى.

8 كل أمر يتذرع به إلى محظور فهو محظور.

9 الحكم إذا كان وجوبه معلقا بشيئين لم يجب إلا بورودهما معا.

10 التكليف وضعت على التوسط وإسقاط الحرج.

11 مسلك الاعتدال أصل يرجع إليه.

12 الرخص لا تناط بالمعاصي.

13 المباح يتقييد بالسلامة.

14 إذا إجتمع الحلال والحرام غلب الحرام.

15 علل الأحكام تدل على قصد الشارع فيها فحيثما وجدت اتبعت.

16 السلامة من المكروه أولى من تحصيل المستحب.

17 إذا تعارض جمع الواجبين, قدم أرجحهما و سقط الآخر بالوجه الشرعي.

18 الإحتياط في الخروج من الحرمة إلى الإباحة أشد منه في العكس.

19 قواعد الشرع تتقاضى أنه لا يعاقب من لم يقصد المفسدة.

20 أفضل عمل كل رجل ما هو أكثر نفعا لغيره و اجود ثمرة و اتم فائدة.

21 لا يرتكب المكروه لأجل المندوب.

22 مالا يتم المندوب إلا به فهو مندوب.

23 المندوب لايترك له الواجب.

VI. SHARIAH COURT PROCEEDINGS, EVIDENCE AND PROOF

Qur'an

1 إِذَا تَدَايَنْتُمْ بِدَيْنٍ إِلَى أَجَلٍ مُسَمًّى فَاكْتُبُوهُ وَلْيَكْتُبْ بَيْنَكُمْ كَاتِبٌ بِالْعَدْلِ... وَاسْتَشْهِدُوا شَهِيدَيْنِ مِنْ رِجَالِكُمْ فَإِنْ لَمْ يَكُونَا رَجُلَيْنِ فَرَجُلٌ وَامْرَأَتَانِ مِمَّنْ تَرْضَوْنَ مِنَ الشُّهَدَاءِ أَنْ تَضِلَّ إِحْدَاهُمَا فَتُذَكِّرَ إِحْدَاهُمَا الْأُخْرَى.

2 إِنَّ اللَّهَ يَأْمُرُ بِالْعَدْلِ وَالْإِحْسَانِ وَإِيتَاءِ ذِي الْقُرْبَى وَيَنْهَى عَنِ الْفَحْشَاءِ وَالْمُنْكَرِ وَالْبَغْيِ.

3 إِنَّ اللَّهَ يَأْمُرُكُمْ أَنْ تُؤَدُّوا الْأَمَانَاتِ إِلَى أَهْلِهَا وَإِذَا حَكَمْتُمْ بَيْنَ النَّاسِ أَنْ تَحْكُمُوا بِالْعَدْلِ.

4 يَا أَيُّهَا الَّذِينَ آمَنُوا كُونُوا قَوَّامِينَ بِالْقِسْطِ شُهَدَاءَ لِلَّهِ وَلَوْ عَلَى أَنْفُسِكُمْ أَوِ الْوَالِدَيْنِ وَالْأَقْرَبِينَ إِنْ يَكُنْ غَنِيًّا أَوْ فَقِيرًا.

5 وَلَا يَجْرِمَنَّكُمْ شَنَآنُ قَوْمٍ عَلَى أَلَّا تَعْدِلُوا اعْدِلُوا هُوَ أَقْرَبُ لِلتَّقْوَى.

6 وَتَمَّتْ كَلِمَتُ رَبِّكَ صِدْقًا وَعَدْلًا لَا مُبَدِّلَ لِكَلِمَاتِهِ.

Hadith

7 إذا جلس إليك الخصمان فلا تقض بينهما حتى تسمع من الآخر كما سمعت من الأول، فإنك إذا فعلت ذلك تبين لك القضاء.

8 لو يعطى الناس بدعواهم لادعى ناس دماء رجال وأموالهم ولكن اليمين على المدعي عليه.

9 إنما أنا بشر وإنكم تختصمون إلي فلعل بعضكم أن يكون ألحن بحجته من بعض فأقضي نحو ما أسمع منه فمن قضيت له بحق أخيه بشيء فلا يأخذ منه شيئا فإنما أقطع له قطعة من النار.

10 ولصاحب الحق مقال.

Legal Maxims

11 الأصل مراعاة التسوية بين الخصمين في المجلس القضاء.

12 البينة لاتصير حجة إلا بقضاء القاضي.

13 لا قضاء إلا بعد السماع من الخصمين.

14 لا يجوزلقاضي أن يحكم بالتسمع.

15 لا يقضى على الغائب.

16 لا يملك القاضي العفو والإسقاط في الحدود ويملك في التعازير.

17 ما حكم به القاضي لا يجوز نقضه ما لم يخالف كتاب أو سنة أو إجماع.

18 مبنى القضاء على الإلزام.

19 إذا تعذر إيجاب القود وجبت الدية.

20 العقل شرط التكليف.

21 الإكراه الملجئ يمنع التكليف.

22 لا تكليف دون العلم.

23 لا تكليف إلا في حدود الوسع.

24 لا تكليف على الصبي.

25 الجنون سبب لزوال التكليف.

26 العذر السماوي مسقط للتكليف.

27 إذا تعارض القول والفعل, فالقول أولى.

28 حصانة القاضي مكفولة.

29 حكم القاضي لايبطل بموته ولا بعزله.

30 حكم القاضي نافذ إلى حين علمه بعزله.

31 المدعي أولى بالقول والطالب أحق أن يتقدم بالكلام و إن بدأ المطلوب.

32 إقامة الحدود ورفع التنازع في الحقوق يختص بالحكام.

33 كل ما حكم به القاضي العدل من مذهب من رأه صوابا مما إختلف النص فيه فهو نافذ.

34 إقامة الحدود ورفع التنازع في الحقوق ونحو ذلك يختص بالحكام.

35 خطأ القاضي في بيت المال غير مضمون عليه.

36 لايجوز نقض حكم الحاكم بعد الحكم.

37 كل معصية ليس فيها حد مقدر ففيها التعزير.

38 من جهل حرمة شيئي مما يجب فيه الحد أو العقوبة وفعله لم يحد, وإن علم الحرمة وجهل الحد والعقوبة حد.

39 الذمة والأموال لا تستحق بالدعاوي دون البينات.

40 القضاء بالظواهر لا بالمقاصد والسرائر.

41 المقصود من القضاء وصول الحقوق إلى أهلها وقطع المخاصمة.

42 الرجوع عن الشهادة لا يصح بعد قضاء القاضي ويصح قبله.

43 قول الخبرة طريق معتمدة يرجع إليه في الأقضية وفصل الخصومات.

44 قضاء القاضي في محل الإجتهاد يرفع الخلاف.

45 اليقين مقدم على الظن والظن مقدم على الشك و المظنة لايعتبر مع وجود الحقيقة.

46 الحقوق لايعتبر فيها الحرمة والمنزلة إلا الوالد في حق الولد.

47 يكتفي بشهادة المرأة الواحدة فيما لايطلع عليه الرجال.

VII. SHARIAH, CRIMINAL LAW AND THE PRESCRIBED *HUDUD* PUNISHMENTS

Qur'an

1   وَجَزَاءُ سَيِّئَةٍ سَيِّئَةٌ مِثْلُها فَمَنْ عَفَا وَأَصْلَحَ فَأَجْرُهُ عَلَى اللَّهِ إِنَّهُ لَا يُحِبُّ الظَّالِمِينَ.

2   وَإِنْ عَاقَبْتُمْ فَعَاقِبُوا بِمِثْلِ مَا عُوقِبْتُمْ بِهِ وَلَئِنْ صَبَرْتُمْ لَهُوَ خَيْرٌ لِلصَّابِرِينَ.

3   فَمَنْ تَابَ مِنْ بَعْدِ ظُلْمِهِ وَأَصْلَحَ فَإِنَّ اللَّهَ يَتُوبُ عَلَيْهِ إِنَّ اللَّهَ غَفُورٌ رَحِيمٌ.

Hadith

4   ادرؤوا الحدود بالشبها ت.

5   التائب من الذنب كمن لا ذ نب له.

Legal Maxims

6   إذا رفعت الحدود للإ ما م و القاضي فلا شفاعة ووجب الحد.

7   لا تقام الحد ود إلا بأ مر الأما م.

8   حقوق الله مبنية على المسا محة بخلا ف حقوق الآد ميين.

9   حق العبد لايسقط إلا بالعفو والإبراء.

10   يسمح الإنسان في حقوق نفسه وليس له المسا محه في حق غيره.

11   يتدخل الحد قبل إقا مته لابعد.

12   القصاص لا يتجزأ.

13   القصا ص لا يسقط بالتقا د م وفي الحد ود خلا ف.

14   من قتل ولا وارث له إقتص له الإما م.

15 إذا اجتمع المباشر و المتسبب يضاف الحكم للمباشر.

16 الاصل براءة الذمة.

17 الحدود تسقط بالشبها ت.

18 من شرب خمرا جاهلا به فلا حد و لا تعزير.

19 من شك هل فعل شيئا أو لا؟ فالأصل أنه لم يفعل.

20 من تيقن الفعل وشك في القليل أو الكثير, حمل على القليل.

21 الشبهة لا تسقط التعزير وتسقط الكفارة.

22 لا يضاف الفعل إلى الآمر ما لم يكن مجبرا.

23 من استعجل شيئ قبل اوانه عوقب بحرما نه.

24 الحدود المقصود بها الزجر.

25 ما لايقبل التعو يض يكون اختيار بعضه كإختيار كله و إسقاط بعضه كإسقا ط كله.

26 الد فع أقوى من الرفع.

27 إذا إجتمع أمرا ن من جنس واحد, ولم يختلف مقصودهما, دخل احد هما في الأخر.

28 قطع الخصومة والمنا زعة واجب.

29 الأصل أ ن من ساعده الظاهر فا لقول قوله والبينة على من يدعي خلا ف الظاهر.

30 الأصل أن يسمع بقول دافع ما له.

31 إقامة الحد للإ مام.

IX. SHARIAH, CONSTITUTIONAL LAW AND CIVIL LIBERTIES

Qur'an

1   لَا إِكْرَاهَ فِي الدِّينِ.

2   وَلَوْ شَاءَ رَبُّكَ لَآمَنَ مَنْ فِي الْأَرْضِ كُلُّهُمْ جَمِيعًا أَفَأَنْتَ تُكْرِهُ النَّاسَ حَتَّىٰ يَكُونُوا مُؤْمِنِينَ.

3   فَمَنْ شَاءَ فَلْيُؤْمِنْ وَمَنْ شَاءَ فَلْيَكْفُرْ.

4   وَمَا أَنْتَ عَلَيْهِمْ بِجَبَّارٍ فَذَكِّرْ بِالْقُرْآنِ مَنْ يَخَافُ وَعِيدِ.

5   قُلْ يَا أَيُّهَا الْكَافِرُونَ... لَكُمْ دِينُكُمْ وَلِيَ دِينِ.

6   يَا أَيُّهَا النَّاسُ إِنَّا خَلَقْنَاكُمْ مِنْ ذَكَرٍ وَأُنْثَىٰ وَجَعَلْنَاكُمْ شُعُوبًا وَقَبَائِلَ لِتَعَارَفُوا إِنَّ أَكْرَمَكُمْ عِنْدَ اللَّهِ أَتْقَاكُمْ.

7   إِنَّ اللَّهَ يَأْمُرُكُمْ أَنْ تُؤَدُّوا الْأَمَانَاتِ إِلَىٰ أَهْلِهَا وَإِذَا حَكَمْتُمْ بَيْنَ النَّاسِ أَنْ تَحْكُمُوا بِالعدل.

8   وَالَّذِينَ هُمْ لِأَمَانَاتِهِمْ وَعَهْدِهِمْ رَاعُونَ.

9   يَا أَيُّهَا الَّذِينَ آمَنُوا لَا تَخُونُوا اللَّهَ وَالرَّسُولَ وَتَخُونُوا أَمَانَاتِكُمْ وَأَنْتُمْ تَعْلَمُونَ.

10   وَلَا تُطِيعُوا أَمْرَ الْمُسْرِفِينَ الَّذِينَ يُفْسِدُونَ فِي الْأَرْضِ وَلَا يُصْلِحُونَ.

11   وَلَا تُطِعْ مَنْ أَغْفَلْنَا قَلْبَهُ عَنْ ذِكْرِنَا وَاتَّبَعَ هَوَاهُ وَكَانَ أَمْرُهُ فُرُطًا.

12   وَلَمَنِ انْتَصَرَ بَعْدَ ظُلْمِهِ فَأُولَٰئِكَ مَا عَلَيْهِمْ مِنْ سَبِيلٍ.

13   وَلَا تَأْكُلُوا أَمْوَالَكُمْ بَيْنَكُمْ بِالْبَاطِلِ وَتُدْلُوا بِهَا إِلَى الْحُكَّامِ لِتَأْكُلُوا فَرِيقًا مِنْ أَمْوَالِ النَّاسِ بِالْإِثْمِ وَأَنْتُمْ تَعْلَمُونَ.

Hadith

14   على المرء السمع والطاعة فيما أحب أو كره إلا أن يؤمر بمعصية فلا سمع ولا طاعة.

15 من ولاه شيئا من أمور المسلمين فاحتجب دون حاجتهم وخلتهم وفقرهم احتجب الله دون حاجته وخلته وفقره يوم القيامة.

16 أفضل الجهاد كلمة حق عند سلطان جائر.

17 كلكم راع و مسئول عن رعيته فالإمام راع ومسئول عن رعيته والرجل في أهله وهو مسئول عن رعيته.
والمراءة في بيت زوجها راعية وهي مسئولة عن رعيتها والخادم في مال سيده راع وهو مسئول عن رعيته.

18 السلطان ولي من لاولي له.

19 من خلف مالا أو حقا فلورثته ومن خلف كلا أو دينا فكله إلي و دينه علي.

20 لعن الرسول صلى الله عليه وسلم الراشي والمرتشي.

21 الراشي والمرتشي والرائش في النار.

22 هدايا العمال غلول.

Legal Maxims

23 ليس للإمام أن يخرج شيئا من يد أحد إلا بحق ثابت معروف.

24 ليس للإمام أن يقطع ما لاغنى للمسلمين عنه.

25 كل من له حق فهو على حاله حتى يأتيه اليقين على خلاف ذلك.

26 جماعة المسلمين العدول يقومون مقام الحاكم عند تعذره.

27 تصرف الامام على الرعية منوط بالمصلحة.

28 حكم الحاكم لا يدخل العبادات استقلالا ويدخلها تبعا.

29 لا يقتصر الولاة على الصلاح مع قدرة على الأصلح.

30 يقدم في كل ولاية من هو أقوم بمصالحها.

31 ليس للإمام ولاية النظر في الملك الخاص للإنسان.

32 العدالة معتبرة في جميع الولايات.

33 إذا تعذرت العدالة في الإمامة والحكم قدم أقلهم فسقا.

34 كل متصرف عن الغير فعليه أن يتصرف بالمصلحة.

35 ولاية خاصة أقوى من ولاية عامة.

36 الأمانة لاتضمن إلا بالتعدي.

37 تصرف الراعى على الرعية منوط بالمصلحة.

38 الأصل أن الشورى ملزمة للحاكم.

39 الشورى لا تجوز فيما يكون فيه نص.

40 ما صرف إلى بيت المال فسبيله أن يسرف في مصالحه.

41 كل تصرف جر فسادا أو دفع صلاحا فهو منهي عنه.

42 اصل اللباس الإباحة.

43 الاصل في الأفعال والعادات الاباحة وعدم الحظر.

44 أفعال المباح إنما تجوز بشرط عدم إيذاء أحد.

45 الأصل السلامه حتى يعلم غيرها.

46 الأصل السلامة من العيوب.

47 الأصل في تصرفات المسلمين الصحة.

48 الأصل في المسلم العدالة.

49 حق العبد مقدم عند التعارض.

50 حق الحي مقدم على حق الميت عند التعارض.

51 إذا تعارض هتك الحرمة وبراءة الذمة قدم براءة الذمة.

52 أمور المسلمين محمولة على الصحاح والجواز ولا يجوز حملها على إفساد والبطلان مع
وجود لها مساغ في الصحاح.

53 الحق الثابت في الذمة لا يسقط بالإسلام.

54 يتسامح في أنكحة الكفار مالا يتسامح في أنكحة المسلمين.

55 يحرم على الكافرين نكاح ما يحرم على المسلمين.

56 يدخل الكافرين تحت خطاب النص وكل لفظ عام.

57 الكف عن الظلم واجب.

X.   JIHAD, VIOLENCE AND WAR

Qur'an

1 وَقَاتِلُوا فِي سَبِيلِ اللَّهِ الَّذِينَ يُقَاتِلُونَكُمْ وَلَا تَعْتَدُوا إِنَّ اللَّهَ لَا يُحِبُّ الْمُعْتَدِينَ.

2 أُذِنَ لِلَّذِينَ يُقَاتَلُونَ بِأَنَّهُمْ ظُلِمُوا وَإِنَّ اللَّهَ عَلَىٰ نَصْرِهِمْ لَقَدِيرٌ. الَّذِينَ أُخْرِجُوا مِنْ دِيَارِهِمْ
بِغَيْرِ حَقٍّ إِلَّا أَنْ يَقُولُوا رَبُّنَا اللَّهُ.

3   As in note (1) above.

4 وَمَنْ أَحْيَاهَا فَكَأَنَّمَا أَحْيَا النَّاسَ جَمِيعًا.

5 وَلَا تَقْتُلُوا النَّفْسَ الَّتِي حَرَّمَ اللَّهُ إِلَّا بِالْحَقِّ.

6 من حمل علينا السيف فليس منا.

7 من سل علينا السيف فليس منا.

8 كل المسلم على المسلم حرام
دمه وماله وعرضه.

9 وَلَقَدْ كَرَّمْنَا بَنِي آدَمَ.

10 لَقَدْ خَلَقْنَا الْإِنْسَانَ فِي أَحْسَنِ تَقْوِيمٍ.

11 وَعِبَادُ الرَّحْمَنِ الَّذِينَ يَمْشُونَ عَلَى الْأَرْضِ هَوْنًا وَإِذَا خَاطَبَهُمُ الْجَاهِلُونَ قَالُوا سَلَامًا.

12 وَلَا تَسْتَوِي الْحَسَنَةُ وَلَا السَّيِّئَةُ ادْفَعْ بِالَّتِي هِيَ أَحْسَنُ فَإِذَا الَّذِي بَيْنَكَ وَبَيْنَهُ عَدَاوَةٌ كَأَنَّهُ وَلِيٌّ حَمِيمٌ.

13 وَلْتَكُنْ مِنْكُمْ أُمَّةٌ يَدْعُونَ إِلَى الْخَيْرِ وَيَأْمُرُونَ بِالْمَعْرُوفِ وَيَنْهَوْنَ عَنِ الْمُنْكَرِ وَأُولَئِكَ هُمُ الْمُفْلِحُونَ.

14 إِنَّ اللَّهَ يَأْمُرُ بِالْعَدْلِ وَالْإِحْسَانِ وَإِيتَاءِ ذِي الْقُرْبَى وَيَنْهَى عَنِ الْفَحْشَاءِ وَالْمُنْكَرِ وَالْبَغْيِ.

15 كُلَّمَا أَوْقَدُوا نَارًا لِلْحَرْبِ أَطْفَأَهَا اللَّهُ وَيَسْعَوْنَ فِي الْأَرْضِ فَسَادًا وَاللَّهُ لَا يُحِبُّ الْمُفْسِدِينَ.

16 وَإِنْ جَنَحُوا لِلسَّلْمِ فَاجْنَحْ لَهَا وَتَوَكَّلْ عَلَى اللَّهِ.

17 يَا أَيُّهَا الَّذِينَ آمَنُوا اسْتَعِينُوا بِالصَّبْرِ وَالصَّلَاةِ إِنَّ اللَّهَ مَعَ الصَّابِرِينَ.

18 وَإِنْ تَصْبِرُوا وَتَتَّقُوا فَإِنَّ ذَلِكَ مِنْ عَزْمِ الْأُمُورِ.

19 يَا أَيُّهَا الَّذِينَ آمَنُوا اصْبِرُوا وَصَابِرُوا وَرَابِطُوا وَاتَّقُوا اللَّهَ لَعَلَّكُمْ تُفْلِحُونَ.

20 كُتِبَ عَلَيْكُمُ الْقِتَالُ وَهُوَ كُرْهٌ لَكُمْ وَعَسَى أَنْ تَكْرَهُوا شَيْئًا وَهُوَ خَيْرٌ لَكُمْ وَعَسَى أَنْ تُحِبُّوا شَيْئًا وَهُوَ شَرٌّ لَكُمْ وَاللَّهُ يَعْلَمُ وَأَنْتُمْ لَا تَعْلَمُونَ.

21 خُذِ الْعَفْوَ وَأْمُرْ بِالْعُرْفِ وَأَعْرِضْ عَنِ الْجَاهِلِينَ.

22 إِدْفَعْ بِالَّتِي هِيَ أَحْسَنُ.

Hadith

23 إني لم أبعث لعانا و إنما بعثت رحمة.

24 إنما يرحم الله من عباده الرحماء.

Legal Maxims

25 تكريم بني ا د م مقصد شرعي أساس.

26 كل ما كان سببا للفتنة فإنه لايجوز.

27 مبدأ التعامل بالمثل بين الدول مقيد بالفضيلة.

28 المشقة تجلب التيسير.

29 وجوب الجهاد وجوب الوسائل لا المقاصد.

30 الشريعة سوت بين الناس إلا ما قام الدليل على تخصيصه.

31 الشريعة مبناها وأساسها على الحكم ومصالح العباد في المعاش والمعاد.

32 ما كان من حقوق الناس في الحرب المستأمن والذمي سواء.

33 ما لم يكن مالا مضمونا في حق المسلم لم يكن مالا مضمونا في حق الكافر.

34 كل من عمل للمسلمين فله رزقه من بيت المال.

35 الحقوق الموضوعة لدفع الضرر يستوى فيها المسلم والذمي والمستأمن.

36 الصلح جائز بين المسلمين إلا صلحا أحل حراما أو حرم حلالا.

37 التحرز عن الخصومة واجب ما امكن.

38 دفع الظلم واجب بحسب الإمكان.

39 دفع الضرر واجب بحسب الإمكان.

40 قطع المنازعة واجب مع إمكان.

41 متى أمكن الدفع بأسهل الوجوه لم يعدل إلى أصعبها.

42 لا ينعقد الأمان لمن يضر بالمسلمين.

43 الأصل عدم الإكراه.

44 الأصل عدم العدوان.

45 الأصل عدم الخيانة.

46 الضمان على من تعدى.

47 العدوان لايكسب المتعدي حقا.

48 العذاب في مقابل التحريم.

49 الأصل في الدماء والأموال والأعراض العصمة.

XI.   SHARIAH, GENDER AND FAMILY

Qur'an

1 الرِّجَالُ قَوَّامُونَ عَلَى النِّسَاءِ بِمَا فَضَّلَ اللَّهُ بَعْضَهُمْ عَلَى بَعْضٍ وَبِمَا أَنْفَقُوا مِنْ أَمْوَالِهِمْ.

2 وَلَهُنَّ مِثْلُ الَّذِي عَلَيْهِنَّ بِالْمَعْرُوفِ وَلِلرِّجَالِ عَلَيْهِنَّ دَرَجَةٌ وَاللَّهُ عَزِيزٌ حَكِيمٌ.

3 وَمِنْ آيَاتِهِ أَنْ خَلَقَ لَكُمْ مِنْ أَنْفُسِكُمْ أَزْوَاجًا لِتَسْكُنُوا إِلَيْهَا وَجَعَلَ بَيْنَكُمْ مَوَدَّةً وَرَحْمَةً إِنَّ فِي ذَلِكَ لَآيَاتٍ لِقَوْمٍ يَتَفَكَّرُونَ.

4 هُنَّ لِبَاسٌ لَكُمْ وَأَنْتُمْ لِبَاسٌ لَهُنَّ.

5 مَنْ عَمِلَ صَالِحًا مِنْ ذَكَرٍ أَوْ أُنْثَى وَهُوَ مُؤْمِنٌ فَلَنُحْيِيَنَّهُ حَيَاةً طَيِّبَةً وَلَنَجْزِيَنَّهُمْ أَجْرَهُمْ بِأَحْسَنِ مَا كَانُوا يَعْمَلُونَ.

6 إِنَّ الْمُسْلِمِينَ وَالْمُسْلِمَاتِ وَالْمُؤْمِنِينَ وَالْمُؤْمِنَاتِ وَالْقَانِتِينَ وَالْقَانِتَاتِ وَالصَّادِقِينَ وَالصَّادِقَاتِ وَالصَّابِرِينَ وَالصَّابِرَاتِ وَالْخَاشِعِينَ وَالْخَاشِعَاتِ وَالْمُتَصَدِّقِينَ وَالْمُتَصَدِّقَاتِ وَالصَّائِمِينَ وَالصَّائِمَاتِ وَالْحَافِظِينَ فُرُوجَهُمْ وَالْحَافِظَاتِ وَالذَّاكِرِينَ اللَّهَ كَثِيرًا وَالذَّاكِرَاتِ أَعَدَّ اللَّهُ لَهُمْ مَغْفِرَةً وَأَجْرًا عَظِيمً.

7 وَجَزَاءُ سَيِّئَةٍ سَيِّئَةٌ مِثْلُهَا فَمَنْ عَفَا وَأَصْلَحَ فَأَجْرُهُ عَلَى اللَّهِ إِنَّهُ لَا يُحِبُّ الظَّالِمِينَ.

Hadith

8 ما من شيئ في الميزان أثقل من حسن الخلق.

9 أفضل الإيمان هوحسن الخلق.

10 إنما بعثت لأتمم مكارم الأخلاق.

11 إن لكل دين خلقا, وخلق الاسلام الحياء.

12 لا يكون الرفق في شيء إلا زانه ولا ينزع من شيء إلا شأنه.

13 لا تحقرن من المعروف شيئا ولوأن تلقى أخاك وو جهك اليه منبسط, و لو أن تفرغ من د لوك في اناء المستسقي.

14 دينار أنفقته في سبيل الله، ودينار أنفقته في رقبة، ودينار تصد قت به على مسكين، ودينار أنفقته على أهلك، و أعلا ها أجراً الذي أنفقته على أهلك.

Legal Maxims

15 وصف الذ كورة والأنوثة لاتأ ثير له في الوصف المقتضى للحكم.

16 كل شرط للمرأة لها فيه منفعة ولا يمنع مقصود النكاح فهو صحيح لازم.

17 غني الأسرة ينفق على فقيره.

18 شها دة النساء معتبرة بإ طلا ق في سائر الأحكا م إلا ما قيد بد ليل.

19 المراءة كا لرجل في الأهلية.

20 المراءة في مالها كالرجل.

21 المراءة في ملكها كالرجل.

22 لاولاية لأ و لياء المراءة في مالها.

23 العبرة في الفاظ النكاح بالمقصود والمعنى.

24 الطلا ق الصريح لا يفتقر إلى قصد المعنى.

25 لاطلا ق في إغلا ق.

26 كل شرط يخالف مقتضى النكاح يلغ الشرط ويصح النكاح بمهر المثل.

27 النفقا ت المفروضة قضاء أو رضاء لا تسقط إلا بالأداء أو الإبراء.

28 الطلاق يقتضي سابقة النكاح.

29 الرجعي لا يقطع النكاح والبائن يقطعه.

30 ما أثبت التحريم المؤبد إذا طرء على النكاح قطعه.

31 لا حد لأقل المهر ولا لأكثره.

32 استدانة الزوجة بالأمر القاضي بمنزلة استدانة الزوج بنفسه.

33 يحرم على الكافرين ما يحرم على المسلمين.

34 القرابة التي تقتضي التوريث توجب الإنفاق.

35 الولد للفراش.

36 الخلع عقد معاوضة فيقضي سلامة العوض.

37 كناية الطلاق تفتقر إلى نية أو ما يقوم مقامه.

38 الأصل في الطلاق أن يكون رجعيا.

39 الطلاق يفتقر إلى النية في الكناية ولا تفتقر إليها في الصريح.

40 الطلاق لا يتجزأ.

41 الخلع يقتضي البينونة.

42 كل نكاح صحيح بين المسلمين فهو صحيح بين أهل الكفر.

XII.   ISLAMIC BANKING AND FINANCE

Qur'an

1   وَلِلَّهِ مَا فِي السَّمَاوَاتِ وَمَا فِي الأَرْضِ.

2   قُلْ لِمَنْ مَا فِي السَّمَاوَاتِ وَالأَرْضِ قُلْ لِلَّهِ كَتَبَ عَلَىٰ نَفْسِهِ الرَّحْمَةَ.

3   إِنَّ اللَّهَ يَأْمُرُ بِالْعَدْلِ وَالإِحْسَانِ.

4   كَيْ لَا يَكُونَ دُولَةً بَيْنَ الْأَغْنِيَاءِ مِنْكُمْ.

5   وَقَدْ فَصَّلَ لَكُمْ مَا حَرَّمَ عَلَيْكُمْ إِلَّا مَا اضْطُرِرْتُمْ إِلَيْهِ.

6   يَا أَيُّهَا الَّذِينَ آمَنُوا لَا تُحَرِّمُوا طَيِّبَاتِ مَا أَحَلَّ اللهُ لَكُمْ.

7   وَإِنْ كَانَ ذُو عُسْرَةٍ فَنَظِرَةٌ إِلَىٰ مَيْسَرَةٍ.

8   يُرِيدُ اللهُ بِكُمُ الْيُسْرَ وَلَا يُرِيدُ بِكُمُ الْعُسْرَ.

9   يَا أَيُّهَا الَّذِينَ آمَنُوا لَا تَأْكُلُوا أَمْوَالَكُمْ بَيْنَكُمْ بِالْبَاطِلِ إِلَّا أَنْ تَكُونَ تِجَارَةً عَنْ تَرَاضٍ مِنْكُمْ.

10   وَأَحَلَّ اللهُ الْبَيْعَ وَحَرَّمَ الرِّبَا.

11   إِنَّ اللَّهَ يَأْمُرُكُمْ أَنْ تُؤَدُّوا الْأَمَانَاتِ إِلَىٰ أَهْلِهَا وَإِذَا حَكَمْتُمْ بَيْنَ النَّاسِ أَنْ تَحْكُمُوا بِالْعَدْلِ.

Hadith

12   المحتكر خاطئ.

13   المسلمون على شروطهم إلا شرطا حرم حلالا أو أحل حراما.

14   من احتكر حكرة يريد أن يغلي بها على المسلمين فهو خاطئ.

15   من اشترى شيئا لم يره فهو بالخيار إذا رآه.

16   لا تبع ما ليس عندك.

17   لا يحل سلم وبيع ولا شرطان في بيع ولا ربح ما لم يضمن ولا بيع ما ليس عندك.

18   من ابتاع طعا ما فلا يبعه حتى يقبضه.

19   البيعان بالخيار مالم يتفرقا إلا بيع الخيار.

20   أن رسول الله صلى الله عليه وسلم نهي عن بيع الغرر.

21   مطل الغني ظلم.

22   لاضرر ولا ضرار في الإسلام.

Legal Maxims

23 الخراج بالضمان.

24 من ملك شيئا ملك ماهو من ضروراته.

25 المواعيد بصورة التعاليق تكون لازمة.

26 الغرم بالغنم.

27 إذا إجتمع الحلال والحرام غلب الحرام.

28 ما حرم أخذه حرم إعطاؤه.

29 ما جاز لعذر بطل عند زواله.

30 كل ما أضر بالعامة فهو احتكار وإن كان ذهبا أو فضة أو ثوبا.

31 كل ما أضر بالمسلمين, وجب أن ينفي عنهم.

32 العقد يراعى مع الكافر كما يراعى مع المسلم.

33 العبرة في العقود للمقاصد والمعاني لا بالألفاظ والمباني.

34 كل عقد لا يفيد مقصوده يبطل.

35 كل جهالة تفضي إلى المنازعة فهي مفسدة للعقد.

36 كل شرط كان من مصلحة العقد أو من مقتضاه فهو جائز.

37 كل عقد وضع للمعروف و أسس على الإحسان, فالأصل أن لا يمتنع الغرر فيه.

38 الاصل في العقود والشروط الجواز والصحه ما لم يقم دليل شرعي على خلافه.

39 التغرير في المعاوضة سبب الضمان.

40 كل شرط يخالف مقصود العقد فهو باطل.

41 المجهول لا يجوز تمليكه بشيئ من العقود.

42 المقصود من العقد اللزوم.

43 العقود بالقصود.

44 كل ما جاز بيعه جاز رهنه وما لا يجوز بيعه لا يجوز رهنه.

45 من شرط على نفسه طائعًا غير مكره فهو عليه.

XIII.   SHARIAH AND PRIVATE PROPERTY

Qur'an

1 يَا أَيُّهَا الَّذِينَ آمَنُوا لَا تَأْكُلُوا أَمْوَالَكُمْ بَيْنَكُمْ بِالْبَاطِلِ إِلَّا أَنْ تَكُونَ تِجَارَةً عَنْ تَرَاضٍ مِنْكُمْ.

2 وَأَحَلَّ اللهُ الْبَيْعَ وَحَرَّمَ الرِّبَا.

3 يَا أَيُّهَا الَّذِينَ آمَنُوا اتَّقُوا اللَّهَ وَذَرُوا مَا بَقِيَ مِنَ الرِّبَا...فَلَكُمْ رُءُوسُ أَمْوَالِكُمْ لَا تَظْلِمُونَ وَلَا تُظْلَمُونَ.

4 وَلَا تَجْعَلْ يَدَكَ مَغْلُولَةً إِلَىٰ عُنُقِكَ وَلَا تَبْسُطْهَا كُلَّ الْبَسْطِ فَتَقْعُدَ مَلُومًا مَحْسُورًا.

5 وَالَّذِينَ إِذَا أَنْفَقُوا لَمْ يُسْرِفُوا وَلَمْ يَقْتُرُوا وَكَانَ بَيْنَ ذَٰلِكَ قَوَامًا.

6 .وَإِنْ كَانَ ذُو عُسْرَةٍ فَنَظِرَةٌ إِلَىٰ مَيْسَرَةٍ

7 وَالَّذِينَ فِي أَمْوَالِهِمْ حَقٌّ مَعْلُومٌ لِلسَّائِلِ وَالْمَحْرُومِ.

Hadith

8 كل أحد أحق بماله من والده وولده والناس أجمعين

9 لا يحل مال امرئ مسلم إلا بطيب نفس منه.

10 ما أكل أحد طعامًا قط خيرا من أن يأكل من عمل يديه.

Legal Maxims

11 كل ما إنتفع به جاز أخذ البدل منه.

12 لا يجوز لأحد أن يأخذ مال أحد إلا بسبب شرعي.

13 ليس لعرق ظالم حق.

14 الضرر لا يكون قديما.

15 الأمر بالتصرف في ملك الغير باطل.

16 لا يجوز إخراج ملك من يد قد ملكته ملكا صحيحا إلا بحجة لامعارض لها.

17 كل مال ضائع فقد مالكه يسرفه السلطان إلى مصالح.

18 القصد بالبيع تمليك التصرف.

19 الاموال الضائعة يقبضها القاضي حفظا لها على أربابها.

20 الشروط ألتي لا تنافي في مقتضى الوقف يعمل بها في الوقف.

21 من قضى دين غيره بغير أمره لا يكون له حق الرجوع عليه.

22 اليد توجب إثبات التصرف ولا توجب إثبات الملك.

23 من وصل إليه مال في شبهة وهو لا يعرف له مستحقاً فإنه يتصدق به.

24 كل ما ورد به الشرع مطلقا ولا ضابط له فيه ولا في اللغة يرجع فيه إلى العرف.

25 كل ما تلف في يد أمين من غير تعد لا ضمان فيه.

XIV. MODERN BIOETHICAL AND ENVIRONMENTAL QUESTIONS

Qur'an

1 وَاللَّهُ جَعَلَ لَكُمْ مِنْ أَنْفُسِكُمْ أَزْوَاجًا وَجَعَلَ لَكُمْ مِنْ أَزْوَاجِكُمْ بَنِينَ وَحَفَدَةً.

2 إِنْ أُمَّهَاتُهُمْ إِلَّا اللَّائِي وَلَدْنَهُمْ.

3 وَلَا تَقْفُ مَا لَيْسَ لَكَ بِهِ عِلْمٌ إِنَّ السَّمْعَ وَالْبَصَرَ وَالْفُؤَادَ كُلُّ أُولَئِكَ كَانَ عَنْهُ مَسْئُولًا.

4 وَقُلْ رَبِّ زِدْنِي عِلْمًا.

5 وَفَوْقَ كُلِّ ذِي عِلْمٍ عَلِيمٌ.

6 قُلِ انْظُرُوا مَاذَا فِي السَّمَاوَاتِ وَالْأَرْضِ.

7 يَرْفَعِ اللَّهُ الَّذِينَ آمَنُوا مِنْكُمْ وَالَّذِينَ أُوتُوا الْعِلْمَ دَرَجَاتٍ.

8 وَلَقَدْ كَرَّمْنَا بَنِي آدَمَ.

9 لَقَدْ خَلَقْنَا الْإِنْسَانَ فِي أَحْسَنِ تَقْوِيمٍ.

10 وَنَفَخْتُ فِيهِ مِنْ رُوحِي فَقَعُوا لَهُ سَاجِدِينَ.

11 وَتَعَاوَنُوا عَلَى الْبِرِّ وَالتَّقْوَىٰ وَلَا تَعَاوَنُوا عَلَى الْإِثْمِ وَالْعُدْوَانِ.

12 وَلَقَدْ خَلَقْنَا الْإِنْسَانَ مِنْ سُلَالَةٍ مِنْ طِينٍ. ثُمَّ جَعَلْنَاهُ نُطْفَةً فِي قَرَارٍ مَكِينٍ ثُمَّ خَلَقْنَا النُّطْفَةَ عَلَقَةً فَخَلَقْنَا الْعَلَقَةَ مُضْغَةً فَخَلَقْنَا الْمُضْغَةَ عِظَامًا فَكَسَوْنَا الْعِظَامَ لَحْمًا ثُمَّ أَنْشَأْنَاهُ خَلْقًا آخَرَ.

13 يَا أَيُّهَا النَّاسُ اتَّقُوا رَبَّكُمُ الَّذِي خَلَقَكُمْ مِنْ نَفْسٍ وَاحِدَةٍ وَخَلَقَ مِنْهَا زَوْجَهَا وَبَثَّ مِنْهُمَا رِجَالًا كَثِيرًا وَنِسَاءً.

14 قُلْ سِيرُوا فِي الْأَرْضِ فَانْظُرُوا كَيْفَ بَدَأَ الْخَلْقَ.

15 فَاسْأَلُوا أَهْلَ الذِّكْرِ إِنْ كُنْتُمْ لَا تَعْلَمُونَ.

16 سَنُرِيهِمْ آيَاتِنَا فِي الْآفَاقِ وَفِي أَنْفُسِهِمْ.

Hadith

17 الناس سواسية كأسنان المشط.

18 الناس عيال الله احبهم الى الله ارحمهم لعياله.

19 لا يؤمن أحدكم حتى يحب لأخيه ما يحب لنفسه.

20 طلب العلم كان كفارةً لما مضى.

21 الحكمة ضالة المؤمن فحيث وجدها فهو أحق بها.

22 اطلب العلم من المهد الى اللحد.

23 اطلب العلم ولو كان في الصين.

24 الناس رجلان: عالم ومتعلم و لاخير في سواهما.

Legal Maxims

25 الأصل في الأشياء الإباحة.

26 الضرر يزال.

27 المشقة تجلب التيسير.

28 لا ضرر ولا ضرار في الاسلام.

29 الضرورات تبيح المحظورات.

30 الضرورة تقدر بقدرها.

31 الأصل في العبادات التحريم.

32 يختار اهون الشرين.

33 الضرر لايزال بمثله.

34 يتحمل الضرر الخاص لدفع الضرر العام.

35 درء المفاسد أولى من جلب المصالح.

36 إذا ضاق الأمر اتسع.

37 العادة محكمة.

38 اليقين لا يزول بالشك.

XV. FREEDOM OF RELIGION AND THE RIGHTS OF MINORITIES

Qur'an

1 فَمَنْ شَاءَ فَلْيُؤْمِنْ وَمَنْ شَاءَ فَلْيَكْفُرْ.

2 وَلَوْ شَاءَ رَبُّكَ لَآمَنَ مَنْ فِي الْأَرْضِ كُلُّهُمْ جَمِيعًا أَفَأَنْتَ تُكْرِهُ النَّاسَ حَتَّىٰ يَكُونُوا مُؤْمِنِينَ.

3 لَكُمْ دِينُكُمْ وَلِيَ دِينِ.

4 ادْعُ إِلَىٰ سَبِيلِ رَبِّكَ بِالْحِكْمَةِ وَالْمَوْعِظَةِ الْحَسَنَةِ.

5 وَلَا تُجَادِلُوا أَهْلَ الْكِتَابِ إِلَّا بِالَّتِي هِيَ أَحْسَنُ.

6 إِنَّ الَّذِينَ آمَنُوا ثُمَّ كَفَرُوا ثُمَّ آمَنُوا ثُمَّ كَفَرُوا ثُمَّ ازْدَادُوا كُفْرًا لَمْ يَكُنِ اللَّهُ لِيَغْفِرَ لَهُمْ وَلَا لِيَهْدِيَهُمْ سَبِيلًا.

7 يَا أَيُّهَا النَّاسُ إِنَّا خَلَقْنَاكُمْ مِنْ ذَكَرٍ وَأُنْثَىٰ وَجَعَلْنَاكُمْ شُعُوبًا وَقَبَائِلَ لِتَعَارَفُوا إِنَّ أَكْرَمَكُمْ عِنْدَ اللَّهِ أَتْقَاكُمْ.

8 لَا يَنْهَاكُمُ اللَّهُ عَنِ الَّذِينَ لَمْ يُقَاتِلُوكُمْ فِي الدِّينِ وَلَمْ يُخْرِجُوكُمْ مِنْ دِيَارِكُمْ أَنْ تَبَرُّوهُمْ وَتُقْسِطُوا إِلَيْهِمْ إِنَّ اللَّهَ يُحِبُّ الْمُقْسِطِينَ.

Hadith

9   إنما بعثت لأ تمم مكار م الأخلا ق.

10   من آذى ذ ميا فأنا خصمه يوم القيا مة.

11   يا أيها النا س ! إن ربكم واحد و إن أبا كم واحد ، لا فضل لعربي على أعجمي و لا أسود على أحمر إلا بالتقوى.

Legal Maxims

12   القاعدة في النا س الحرية.

13   الذ مم بريئة إلا أن تقوم الحجة بشغلها.

14   اللهو واللعب أصلهما على الإباحة إلا إن قا م الد ليل على المنع والتحريم.

15   الاسلا م د ين الفطرة.

16   لا يرث المسلم الكا فر، ولا الكا فر المسلم.

17   المسلم إذا استولى على مال مسلم آخر لا يصير ملكا له.

18   المسلمون على شروطهم.

19   يحكم لعقود الكفا ر بالصحة وان لم توافق الإسلا م, فإذا أسلموا أجرينا عليهم أحكام المسلمين.

XVI. GOALS AND PURPOSES (*MAQASID*) OF SHARIAH

Legal Maxims

1   إنما الأعمال بالنيا ت.

2   الأمور بمقاصدها.

3   كل تصرف تقاعد عن تحصيل مقصوده فهو با طل.

4 مراعاة المقاصد مقدمة على رعاية الوسائل أبدا.

5 وضع الشريعة على أن تكون أهواء النفوس تابعة لمقاصد الشرعي.

6 الموانع ليست بمقصودة للشارع.

7 من مقاصد الشريعة التيسير.

8 الوسائل لها حكم المقاصد.

9 المقاصد العام للشريعة هو عمارة الأرض و إستمرار صلاحها بصلاح المستخلفين فيها.

10 المعاملة بنقيض المقصود فاسد.

11 مقاصد الشرع تعرف بالكتاب والسنة والإجماع.

12 معرفة أسباب النزول والورود تكشف عن مقصود الشارع.

13 مقاصد الشريعة ومصالحها تعرف بالفطرة.

14 ما لا يترتب عليه مقصود فهو باطل.

15 مقصد الشريعة من تشريع تغير وتقرير.

16 وضع الشرع إنما هو للمصالح الأبد في الآجل والعاجل.

17 النظر إلى مآلات الافعال معتبر مقصود شرعا.

18 قصد الشارع من المكلف أن يكون قصده في عمله موافقا لقصده في التشريع.

19 مقاصد الشارع لا تثبت إلا بالقطع أو بالظن الراجح.

20 الاعتبار بالمقاصد والمعاني في الأقوال والأفعال.

21 مقاصد الشريعة هي المرجع الأبدي لاستقاء ما يتوقف عليه التشريع والقضاء في الفقه الإسلامي.

22 إبتناء مقاصد الشريعة على الفطرة.

23 دلت النواهي الإبتدائية التصريحية على قصد الشرعي.

24 كليات المقاصد إنما تثبت بالإستقراء.

25 جميع وجوه الاجتهاد تحتاج إلى معرفة المقاصد.

26 القصود في العقود معتبرة تؤثر في صحة العقد وفساده.

27 إذا دارت المسألة بين مراعاة اللفظ ومراعات القصد فمراعاة القصد أولى.

28 السماحة واليسر من مقاصد الدين.

29 حفظ الدين مقصد شرعي كلي.

30 حفظ النفس مقصد شرعي كلي.

31 حفظ العقل مقصد شرعي كلي.

32 حفظ النسل مقصد شرعي كلي.

33 عند تعارض مصلحتين او مقصودين يجب تقديم الاقوى.

Bibliography

Abu Dawud, Sulayman ibn al-Ash'ath al-Azdi al-Sijistani. *Sunan Abī Dawud, Kitāb al-adāb: Bāb fi Husn al-Zann*. vol. 4. Cairo: Darul Hadith, 1999.

Agwan, A R. *Islam and the Environment*. New Delhi: Institute of Objective Studies, 1997.

Asad, Muhammad. *The Message of the Qur'an*. Gibraltar: Dar al-Andalus, 1980.

Al-'Awwa, Salim. *Al-Fiqh al-Islami fi-Tariq al-Tajid*. 2nd edn. Ministry of Culture, Jordan, Amman, 2013.

Attia, Gemal al-Din. *Towards Realisation of the Higher Intents of Islamic Law, Maqasid al-Shari'ah: A Functional Approach*. Eng. tr London: International Institute of Islamic Thought, 2008.

Bakar, Osman. 'Environmental Health and Welfare as an Important Aspect of Civilisational Islam.' *Al-Shajarah* 11, no. 1, 2006.

Bassiouni, M. Cherif. 'Evolving Approaches to Jihad: From Self-Defense to Revolutionary and Regime-Change', in *Jihad and its Challenges to International and Domestic Law*, edited by M. Cherif Bassiouni and Amna Guellali, 11–38. The Hague: Hague Academic Press, 2010.

Bellah, Robert Neelly. *Beyond Belief: Essays on Religion in a Post-Traditional World*. California: University of California Press, 1991.

Al-Bukhari, Abu 'Abd Allah Muhammad ibn Isma'il. *Sahih al-Bukhari*. Cairo: Darul Hadith, 2004.

Crane, Robert D. 'A Grand American Strategy of Counter-terrorism'. *Arches Quarterly*, vol. 5 no. 9, Spring 2012, 28–39.

Enayat, Hamid. *Modern Islamic Political Thought*, 2001. Reprint Kuala Lumpur: Islamic Book Trust, 2006.

Esposito, John L. Ed. *The Oxford Encyclopedia of the Modern Islamic World*. New York: Oxford University Press, 1995.

———. *What Everyone Needs to Know About Islam*. New York: Oxford University Press, 2002.

Fadlullah, Sayyid Muhammad Husayn. *Al-Jihad: Dirasah Istidlaliyyah Fiqhiyyah Hawl Mawdu'at al-Jihad wa Masa'iluh*, 2nd edn. Beirut: Dar al-Malak, 1418/1998.

———. *Islamic Lanterns: Conceptual and Jurisprudence Questions for Natives, Emigrants and Expatriates*, trans. S. Al-Samarra'i. Beirut: Dar al-Malak, 1425/2004, 368–69.

Al-Hilli, Jalal al-Din Ahmad b Fahd. *'Uddat al-Daa'i*, Persian translation by Husayn Fashahi. Tehran: Islamiyyah Publications, 1379/1969.

Ibn 'Ashur, Muhammad al-Tahir. *Maqasid al-Shariah al-Islamiyyah*, edited by Tahir el-Messawi. Amman: Dar al-Basa'ir li'l-Intaj al-Ilmi, 1988.

Iqbal, Muhammad. *The Reconstruction of Religious Thought in Islam*. New Delhi: Kitab Bhavan, 2000.

Izutsu, Toshiko. *God and Man in the Qur'an*, 1964. Reprint. Kuala Lumpur: Islamic Book Trust, 2008.

———. *Ethico-Religious Concepts in the Qur'an*, 1971. Reprint. Kuala Lumpur: Islamic Book Trust, 2004.

Jackson, Sherman A. 'Domestic Terrorism in the Islamic Legal Tradition', *The Muslim World*, vol. 91 (Fall 2001): 293–310.

Al-Jawad, 'Abd al-Wahhab 'Abd. *Al-Manhaj al-islami, li-'ilaj talawwuth al-bay'ah*. Cairo: al-Dar al-'Arabiyyah li'l-Nashr wa 'l-Tawzi', 1991.

Kamali, Mohammad Hashim, 'Divorce and Women's Rights: Some Muslim Interpretations of Sura 2:228', *The Muslim World* 74, (1984), 85–100.

———. 'The Citizen and State in Islamic Law', *Syariah Law Journal*, no. 3 (April 1986) Kuala Lumpur, 15–47.

———. 'Islamic Personal Law', *The Encyclopedia of Religion*. Macmillan Publishing Co., New York, 1987, vol. 7, 446–53.

———. 'Madhhab (Legal School)', *The Encyclopedia of Religion*. Macmillan Publishing Co., New York, 1987, vol. 9, 66–70.

———. 'Qiyas (Analogy)', *The Encyclopedia of Religion*. Macmillan Publishing Co., New York, 1987, vol. 12, 128–30.

———. 'Have we Neglected the Shari'ah Law Doctrine of *Maslahah*,' *Islamic Studies* (Islamabad), vol. 27 (1988), 287–305.

———. 'Sources, Nature and Objectives of the Shari'ah', *The Islamic Quarterly* (London), Vol. XXXIII (1989), 215–36.

———. 'The Limits of Power in an Islamic State', *Islamic Studies*, vol. 28 (1989), 323–53.

————. 'Siyasah Shar'iyyah or the Policies of Islamic Government', *The American Journal of Islamic Social Sciences*, vol. 6 (1989), 59–81.

————. 'The Approved and Disapproved Varieties of *Ra'y* (Personal Opinion) in Islam', *The American Journal of Islamic Social Sciences*, Vol. 7 (1990), 39–64.

————. 'Freedom of Religion in Islamic Law', *Capital Law Review* (Columbus, Ohio), vol. 21 (1992), 63–82.

————. 'An Analysis of *Haqq* (Right) in Islamic Law', *The American Journal of Islamic Social Sciences*, 10 (1993), 338–67.

————. 'Characteristics of the Islamic State', *Islamic Studies* 32 (1993), 17–41.

————. 'Freedom of Association: The Islamic Perspective', *IIUM Law Journal* (Int. Isl. Univ. Malaysia), vol. 3, no. 1 (1993), 23–37.

————. 'Freedom of Expression in Islam: An Analysis of *Fitnah*', *The American Journal of Islamic Social Sciences*, vol. 10, no: 2 (1993), 17–41.

————. 'Appellate Review and Judicial Independence in Islamic Law', in ed. Chibli Malhat. *Islamic Public Law*. London: Graham & Trotman, 1993, pp. 49–85.

————. 'The Islamic State and Its Constitution', in ed. Norani Othman, *Shari'ah Law and the Modern Nation State*. Kuala Lumpur: SIS Forum, 1994, 45–69.

————. '*Tas'ir* or Price Control in Islamic Law', *The American Journal of Islamic Social Sciences*, vol. 11 (1994), 25–38.

————. 'Shari'ah and the Challenge of Modernity', *IKIM Journal* (Kuala Lumpur), vol. 2, no. 1 (1994), 1–27. Reprint by *Islamic University Quarterly* (London), vol. 2, no. 1 (1995), 10–37.

————. 'Protection Against Disease: A Shari'ah Perspective on AIDS', *IIUM Law Journal*, vol. 5, (1995), 1–20.

————. 'The Continued Domination of *Taqlid* in Islamic Commercial Law: A Case Study of Futures Trading', *Islamic Thought and Scientific Creativity* (Islamabad), vol. 6, no: 3 (1995), 7–37.

————. *Punishment in Islamic Law: An Enquiry into the Hudud Bill of Kelantan*. Kuala Lumpur: Institut Kajian Dasar, 1995, pp. xi & 178. Reprint by Ilmiah Publishers, K.L, 2000.

————. 'A Comparative Analysis of Social Justice in Western Philosophy and the Shari'ah', in eds. Azizan Bahari and Chandra Muzaffar, *Keadilan Sosial*, Kuala Lumpur: Institute for Policy Research 1996, 16–49.

————. 'Islamic Commercial Law: An Analysis of Futures', *The American Journal of Islamic Social Sciences*, vol. 13 (1996), 197–225.

———. 'Methodological Issues in Islamic Jurisprudence', *Arab Law Quarterly*, vol. 11 (1996), 1–34.

———. 'Fiqh and Adaptation to Social Reality', *The Muslim World* LXXXVI (1996), 62–85.

———. 'Islamic Commercial Law: An Analysis of Options', *The American Journal of Islamic Social Sciences* 14 (1997), 17–39.

———. 'A Shari'ah Perspective on Futures', *New Horizon*, London, no. 64 (June 1997), 3–7.

———. 'Islamic Law in Malaysia: Issues and Developments', *Yearbook of Islamic and Middle Eastern Law*, vol. 4 (1997–1998). London: Kluwer Law International, 1998, 153–80.

———. 'The Scope of Diversity and *Ikhtilaf* (Juristic Disagreement) in the Shari'ah', *Islamic Studies* 37 (1998), 315–38.

———. 'Punishment in Islamic Law: A Critique of the *Hudud* Bill of Kelantan, Malaysia', *Arab Law Quarterly* (1998), 203–34.

———. 'Shari'ah as Understood by the Classical Jurists', *IIUM Law Journal*, vol. 6, no. 1 & 2 (1998), 39–88.

———. *Freedom of Expression in Islam* (2nd revd and enhanced edn). Cambridge, Islamic Texts Society. Reprint by Ilmiah Publishers, Kuala Lumpur, 1998.

———. 'Uncertainty and Risk-Taking (*Gharar*) in Islamic Law', *IIUM Law Journal*, vol. 7, no. 2 (1999), 1–21.

———. 'Law and Society: The Interplay of Revelation and Reason in the Shari'ah', in ed. John Esposito, *The Oxford History of Islam*. New York: Oxford University Press, 1999, 107–155.

———. '*Maqasid al-Shari'ah*: The Objectives of Islamic Law', *Islamic Studies*, 38 (1999), 193–209.

———. *The Dignity of Man: An Islamic Perspective*, 2nd enhanced edn. Cambridge: The Islamic Texts Society, 2002, xvi & 118.

———. 'The Right to Personal Safety and the Principle of Legality in the Shari'ah', *Islamic Studies* 39:2 (2000), 249–89.

———. *Islamic Law in Malaysia: Issues and Developments*. Kuala Lumpur: Ilmiah Publishers, 2000, v & 352.

———. *Islamic Commercial Law: An Analysis of Futures and Options*. Cambridge: The Islamic Texts Society, 2000. Reprint by Ilmiah Publishers of Kuala Lumpur, 2002, xi & 253.

———. 'Issues in the Legal Theory of *Usul* and Prospects for Reform' *Islamic Studies* 41 (2001), pp. 1–21.

———. 'The Johor Fatwa on Mandatory HIV Testing', *IIUM Law Journal*, vol. 9, (2001), 99–117.

———. 'Issues in the Understanding of *Jihad* and *Ijtihad*' *Islamic Studies* 41(2002), 617–35.

———. 'Islam, Rationality and Science', *Islam and Science*, vol. 1, no. 1 (June 2003), 56–77.

———. *Freedom, Equality and Justice in Islam*. Cambridge: The Islamic Texts Society, 1999, and Kuala Lumpur: Ilmiah Publishers, 2002, xi & 184.

———. 'Harmonisation of Shari'ah and Civil Law: The Framework and *Modus Operandi*', *IIUM Law Journal 11* (2003), 149–69.

———. 'Fanaticism and its Manifestations in Muslim Societies', in ed. by Aftab Ahmad Malik, *The Empire and the Crescent*. Bristol, UK: Amal Press, 2003, 175–207.

———. '*Istihsan* and the Renewal of Islamic Law', *Islamic Studies* 43 (2004), 561–81.

———. Civilian and Democratic Dimensions of Governance in Islam *Al-Shajarah 9* (2004), 125–45.

———. *Principles of Islamic Jurisprudence*, 3rd enhanced edn. Cambridge: Islamic Texts Society, 2003, xxvi & 546.

———. 'Beyond the Shari'ah: Siyasah Shar'iyyah and its Application in Malaysia', *Al-Shajarah*, vol. 10, no. 2 (2005), 169–91.

———. 'Islam and its Shari'a in the Afghan Constitution 2004 with Special Reference to Personal Law', ed. by Nadjma Yassari, *The Shari'a in the Constitutions of Afghanistan, Iran and Egypt – Implications for Private Law*. Tubingen: Mohr Siebeck, 2005, 23–43.

———. 'The Islamic State: Origins, Definition and Salient Attributes', in ed. K.S. Nathan and Mohammad Hashim Kamali, *Islam in Southeast Asia: Political, Social and Strategic Challenges for the 21ˢᵗ Century*. Singapore: Institute of Southeast Asian Studies, 2005, 278–98.

———. *A Textbook of Hadith Studies*. Leicester: The Islamic Foundation, 2005, xii & 257.

———. 'Hadith', *The Encyclopedia of Religion*. New York: Macmillan Publishing Co., 2005.

———. *Equity and Fairness in Islam*. Cambridge: Islamic Texts Society, 2005, x & 141. Also, Kuala Lumpur: Ilmiah Publishers, 2006.

———. 'Legal Maxims and other Genres of Literature in Islamic Jurisprudence', *Arab Law Quarterly* 20, no.1 (2006), 77–101.

————. 'Reading the Signs: a Qur'anic Perspective on Thinking', *Islam and Science* 4 Winter (2006), 181–205.

————. 'The Shari'a: Law as the Way of God', in ed. Vincent J. Cornell, *Voices of Islam*, (5 vols), vol. I: *Voices of Tradition*, Wesport, CT: Praeger Publishers, 2007, 149–83.

————. 'Human Dignity: An Islamic Perspective', *Malaysian Journal on Human Rights*, no. 2 (2007), 63–73.

————. 'Shari'ah and Civil Law: Toward a Methodology of Harmonisation', *Islamic Law and Society* 14, 3 (2007), 391–421.

————. *Rights to Life, Security, Privacy and Ownership in Islam*. Cambridge: Islamic Texts Society, 2008, xi & 318.

————. *Shari'ah Law: An Introduction*. Oxford: Oneworld Publications, 2008, viii & 342.

————. 'References to Islam and Women in the Afghan Constitution', *Arab Law Quarterly*, 22 (2008), 270–306.

————. *Maqasid al-Shari'ah Make Simple*. London & Washington. The International Institute of Islamic Thought, Occasional Papers 13, August 2008.

————. 'Halal Industry within Islamic Principles: A Shari'ah Perspective on Halal and Haram', part I, *The Halal Journal*, Kuala Lumpur, July and August 2008, 40–3.

————. 'Halal Industry within Islamic Principles: A Shari'ah Perspective on Halal and Haram,, part II, *The Halal Journal*, Kuala Lumpur, September and October 2008, 36–40.

————. 'Halal Industry within Islamic Principles: A Shari'ah Perspective on Halal and Haram', part III, *The Halal Journal*, Kuala Lumpur, November and December 2008, 36–40.

————. 'Law and Ethics in Islam – The Role of the Maqasid', in ed. Kari Vogt et al., *New Directions in Islamic Thought – Exploring Reform and Muslim Tradition*. London: I B Tauris, 2009, 23–46.

————. 'A Shari'ah Perspective on Aids', in eds Farid Esack and Sarah Chiddy, *Islam and Aids Between Scorn, Pity and Justice*. Oxford: Oneworld Publications, 2009, 76–87.

————. 'Citizenship: An Islamic Perspective' *Journal of Islamic Law and Culture*, 11:2 (2009), 121–3.

————. 'Diversity and Pluralism: A Qur'anic Perspective', *Islam and Civilisational Renewal* (ICR published by Int. Inst. of Advanced Isl. Studies, Malaysia), vol. 1, no. 1 (2009), 27–54.

———. 'Law, Commerce and Ethics: A Comparison Between Shari'ah and Common Law', in ed. Christoph Marcinkowski, *The Islamic World and the West, Freiburg Studies in Social Anthropology.* Zurich: Lit Verlag GmbH & Co. KG Wien, 2009, 243–62.

———. *Civilisational Renewal: Revisiting the Islam Hadhari Approach.* Kuala Lumpur: Arah Publications, 2008. (Revd 2nd edn 2009), xv & 96.

———. *IAIS Malaysia: Exploring the Intellectual Horizons of Civilisational Islam.* Kuala Lumpur: Arah Publications, 2008. (Revd 2nd edn 2009), ix & 118.

———. 'The Halal Industry from a Shari'ah Perspective', *Islam and Civilisational Renewal*, vol. 1, no. 4 (July 2010), 595–612.

———. 'Jihad and the Interpretation of the Quran: Contextualising Islamic Tradition', in ed. M. Cherif Bassiouni and Amna Guellali, *Jihad and its Challenges to International and Domestic Law.* The Hague: Hague Academic Press, 2010, 39–58.

———. 'Constitutionalism and Democracy: An Islamic Perspective', *Islam and Civilisational Renewal*, vol. 2 no. 1, (October 2010), 18–45.

———. 'Islam and Democracy in Malaysia: Women and Minority Rights – A Survey Report', in International Institute of Islamic Thought and Civilization (ISTAC), *Islam and Democracy in Malaysia: Findings from a National Dialogue*, 2010, 105–17.

———. *The Right to Education, Work and Welfare in Islam.* Cambridge: Islamic Text Society 2010, x & 294.

———. 'Maqasid al-Shari'ah and Ijithad as Instruments of Civilisational Renewal', *Islam and Civilisational Renewal*, vol. 2, no. 2 (January 2011), 245–71 (Note: all ICR contents are also available online).

———. 'Classical and Contemporary Approaches to Education: An Islamic Perspective', *Islam and Civilisational Renewal*, vol. 2, no. 3 (April 2011), 447–67.

———. 'Islam's Religious Pluralism in Context, a Viewpoint', *Islam and Civilisational Renewal*, vol. 2, no. 4 (July 2011), 714–16.

———. 'Shariah's Stand on Abandoned Children, a Viewpoint', *Islam and Civilisational Renewal*, vol. 3, no. 1 (October 2011), 187–89.

———. 'Islamic Family Law Reform: Problems and Prospects', *Islam and Civilisational Renewal*, vol. 3, no. 1 (October 2011), 37–52.

———. 'The Principles of Halal and Haram in Islam', *The Modern Compendium of Halal, Vol. 1: The Essence of Halal.* Halal Industry Development Corporation (HDC), Kuala Lumpur, 2011, 10–56.

——. 'Maqasid al-Shari'ah: The Goals and Purposes of Islamic Law', in Samuel O. Imbo, Azizan Baharuddin and S. M. Saifuddeen (eds), *The Role of Universities in Promoting Dialogue Through Philosophy*. Kuala Lumpur: Centre for Civilisational Dialogue, University of Malaya, 2011, 23–50.

——. *Citizenship and Accountability of Government: An Islamic Perspective*. Cambridge: Islamic Text Society 2011, x & 321.

——. *Maqasid Al-Shari'ah, Ijtihad and Civilisational Renewal*, joint publication: The International Institute of Islamic Thought, London, and International Institute of Advanced Islamic Studies (IAIS), Malaysia. Occasional Papers 20, 2012, v & 51.

——. 'Environmental Care in Islam: A Qur'anic Perspective', *Islam and Civilisational Renewal*, vol. 3, no 2 (January 2012), 261–83.

——. 'Constitutionalism in Islamic Countries: Perspective of Islamic Law', in eds Rainer Grote and Tilmann J. Röder, *Constitutionalism in Islamic Countries: Between Upheaval and Continuity*. Oxford: Oxford University Press, 2012, pp. 19–35.

——. 'Exploring Facets of Islam on Security and Peace: Amnesty and Pardon in Islamic Law, a Viewpoint', *Islam and Civilisational Renewal*, vol. 3, no. 3 (April 2012), 527–31.

——. 'Tourism and the Ḥalal Industry: A Global *Shari'ah* Perspective', *Islam and Civilisational Renewal*, vol 3, no. 3 (April 2012), 455–73.

——. 'Ethics and Finance: Perspectives of the *Shari'ah* and Its Higher Objectives (*Maqasid*)', *Islam and Civilisational Renewal*, vol. 3, no. 4 (July 2012), 619–37.

——. 'Child Education and Discipline, a Viewpoint', *Islam and Civilisational Renewal*, vol. 4, no. 1 (January 2013), 147–49.

——. 'Bribery and Corruption from a Shariah Perspective, a Viewpoint', *Islam and Civilisational Renewal*, vol. 4, no. 2 (April 2013), 295–97.

——. 'Peace as a Universal Value' *Islam and Civilisational Renewal*, vol. 4, no. 2 (April 2013), 169–87.

——. Editor, *War and Peace in Islam: The Uses and Abuses of Jihad*, jointly published by Cambridge: The Islamic Text Society and MABDA (The Royal Islamic Strategic Studies Centre, Amman), 2013, xxiii & 521. Kamali wrote a Preface at pp. xi-xvii, and two chapters – one on 'Human Dignity from an Islamic Perspective', 269–81, and the other on 'Dhimmi and Musta'min', 304–14.

———. 'The Religious Thrust of Islamic Civilisation," a Viewpoint, *Islam and Civilisational Renewal*, vol. 4 no. 4 (October 2013), 634–638.

———. 'Tajdid, Islah and Civilisational Renewal in Islam', *Islam and Civilisational Renewal*, vol. 4, no. 4 (October 2013), 484–511.

———. 'Permissibility and Prohibition in Islamic Transactions and Contracts', in eds Mohammad Hashim Kamali and Sheila Ainon Yusoff, *Islamic Law of Transactions and Finance: Principles and Developments*. Kuala Lumpur: IAIS Malaysia & CLJ Publications, 2013, xiii & 472 at 1–28.

———. *The Parameters of Halal and Haram in Shariah and the Halal Industry*, joint publication: The International Institute of Islamic Thought, London, and International Institute of Advanced Islamic Studies (IAIS), Malaysia, 2013, vi & 59.

———. 'A Lifestyle of Moderation, or *Wasattiyah*: The Islamic Perspective', *Islam and Civilisational Renewal*, vol. 5, no. 1 (January 2014), 7–24.

———. 'The Teaching of Islam in Western Universities: Reflections and Impressions', *The Teachings and Study of Islam in Western Universities*. London and New York: Routledge Taylor & Francis Group, 2014, 65–84.

———. 'Separation of Powers: An Islamic Perspective', *Islam and Civilisational Renewal*, vol. 5, no: 4 (October 2014), 471–88.

———. *The Middle Path of Moderation in Islam: The Qur'anic Principle of Wasatiyyah*. New York: Oxford University Press, 2015, xiv & 336.

———. 'Catholics and Muslims in Dialogue: Working Together to Serve Others', *Islam and Civilisational Renewal*, vol. 6, no. 1 (January 2015), 7–24.

———. 'Fiqh Al-Aqalliyat (Jurisprudence of Minorities) in Light of the Higher Objectives (*Maqasid*) of Shariah, a Viewpoint', *Islam and Civilisational Renewal*, vol. 6, no. 1 (January 2015), 114–17.

———. 'Extremism, Terrorism and Islam: Historical and Contemporary Perspectives', *Islam and Civilisational Renewal*, vol. 6, no. 2 (April 2015), 148–65.

———. 'Women in the Workplace: Shari'ah and Contemporary Perspectives', *Islam and Civilisational Renewal*, vol. 6, no. 3 (July 2015), 294–317.

———. 'Amnesty and Pardon in Islamic Law with Special Reference to Post-Conflict Justice', *Islam and Civilisational Renewal*, vol. 6, no. 4 (October 2015), 442–67.

Mavani, Hamid. 'Paradigm Shift in Twelver Shi'i Legal Theory (*usul al-fiqh*): Ayatullah Yusef Saanei', *The Muslim World*, vol. 99, no. 2 (April 2000), 335–55.

————. *Religious Authority and Political Thought in Twelver Shi'ism*. London: Routledge Studies in Political Islam, 2013.

Moussavi, Ahmed Kazemi. *Religious Authority in Shi'ite Islam: From the Office of Mufti to the Institution of Marja'*. Kuala Lumpur: International Institute of Islamic Thought and Civilization (ISTAC), 1996.

Mu'assasah Zayid b. Sultan Aal-Nahyan & Majma' al-Fiqh al-Islami al-Duwali. *Mu'allimah Zayid li'l-Qawa'id al-Fiqhiyyah wa'l-Usuliyyah*, Abu Dhabi, 41 vols, 1434/2013. (Note: this is the main source of most of the legal maxims I have featured in this book. All entries are alphabetical in this extensive Arabic encyclopaedia of legal maxims.)

Muslim, Abul-Hussain bin Hajjaj Al-Qushairi, *Mukhtasar Sahih Muslim*. Ed. Nasrir al-Din al-Albani. 6th edn. Beirut: Maktab al-Islami, 1987.

Mustafa, Namr Ahmad al-Sayyid. *Usul al-Nazar fi Maqasid al-Tashri' al-Islami wa Bayan 'Ilaqat al-Qawa'id al-Fiqhiyyah biha*. 2 vols. Syria, Lebanon, Kuwait: Dar al-Nawadir, 1434/2013.

Muzaffar, Chandra. *Exploring Religion in Our Time (Religion in a Globalising World Series)*. Malaysia: Penerbit Universiti Sains Malaysia, 2011.

Al-Nadwi, 'Ali Ahmad. *Al-Qawa'id al-Fiqhiyyah: Mafhumuha, Nash'atuha, Tatawwuruha, Darasatu Mu'allafatiha, Adillatuha, Muhimmatuha, Tatbiqatuha*. 10th edn. Damascus: Dar al-Qalam-Beirut: al-Dar al-Shami-yah-Jeddah: Dar al-Bashir, 1432/2011.

Nasr, Seyyed Hossein. *An Introduction to Islamic Cosmological Doctrines*. Cambridge MA: Harvard University Press, 1964.

————. 'Shi'ism and Sufism: Their Relationship in Essence and in History', *Sufi Essays*, London: Cambridge University Press, 1972.

————. *Islamic Life and Thought*. Albany: State University of New York Press, 1981.

————. *The Heart of Islam: Enduring Values for Humanity*. New York: Harper Collins, 2004.

Peters, Rudolph. *Crime and Punishment in Islamic Law: Theory and Practice from the Sixteenth to the Twenty-First Century*. Cambridge: Cambridge University Press, 2005.

Al-Qaradawi, Yusuf. *Mushkilat al-Faqr wa-kayfa 'Alajaha al-Islam*. Cairo: Maktabah Wahabah, 1997.

————. *Al-Khasa'is al-'Ammah li'l-Islam*. Cairo: Maktabah Wahbah, 1989.

————. *Ri'ayat al-Bay'ah fi 'l-Shari'at al-Islam*. Cairo: Dār al-Shuruq, 2001.

————. *Hawl Qadaya al-Islam wa'l-'Asr*, 3rd edn. Cairo: Maktabah Wahbah, 1427/2006.

————. *The Lawful and the Prohibited in Islam* tr. of original Arabic *Al-Halal Wal-Haram Fil-Islam*. Kuala Lumpur: Islamic Book Trust, 1985.

Qazwini, Ibn Majah Abu 'Abd Allah Muhammad b Yazid. *Sunan Ibn Majah*, 2nd edn. Beirut: Dar al-Kutub al-Ilmiyah, 1407/1987.

Rida, Muhammad Rashid. *Tafsir al-Manar*, 12 vols. Cairo: Dar al-Manar, 1376/1946.

Sachedina, Abdulaziz Abdulhussein. *The Just Ruler (al-sultan al-'adl) in Shi'ite Islam: The Comprehensive authority of the Jurist in Imamite Jurisprudence*. New York: Oxford University Press, 1988.

Schacht, Joseph. *Origins of Muhammadan Jurisprudence*. Oxford: Clarendon Press, 1950.

Schimmel, Annemarie. *Islam: An Introduction*. Albany: State University of New York Press, 1992.

Shabir, Muhammad 'Uthman. *al-Qawa'id al-Kulliyyah wa'l-Dawabit al-Fiqhiyyah fi'l-Shari'ah al-Islamiyyah*. Amman (Jordan): Dar al-Nafa'is li'l-Nashr wa'l-Tawzi', 1426/2006.

Shahzad, Qaiser. *Biomedical Ethics: Philosophical and Islamic Perspectives*. Islamabad: Islamic Research Institute, 2009.

The Holy Qur'an: Text, Translation and Commentary by Abdullah Yusuf Ali. Leicester, UK: The Islamic Foundation, 1975.

Shah, Raja Nazrin. 'Bridging the Muslim and Western World for Peace and Development', a keynote address at the World Muslim Leadership Forum: Muslim World in the Face of the New World Economic Order, The Cordoba Foundation, London, Occasional Papers Series No. 1, October 2010.

Al-Shatibi, Abu Ishaq Ibrahim. *Al-Muwafaqat fi usul al-ahkam*. Annotated by M. Khidr al-Husayn, Cairo: Al-Matba'ah al-Rahmaniyyah, 1341H.

al-Tabrizi, 'Abd-Allāh al-Khatib. *Mishkat al-Masabih*. 2nd edn. E. Muhammad Nasir al-Din al-Albani. Beirut: Al-Maktab al-Islami, 1399/1979.

Talal, Ghazi Ibn Muhammad ibn. (Compiler). *Kitab Ihtiram al-Madhahib*. Revd edn. Amman: Aal al-Bayt Institute for Islamic Thought, 1427/2006.

Umar, Muhammad Suheyl. *The Religious Other: Towards a Muslim Theology of Other Religions in a Post-Prophetic Age*. Lahore: Iqbal Academy, 2008.

Winer, Rabbi Mark L. 'Fundamentalists vs Moderates: The War Within Judaism', *Arches Quarterly*, vol. 5, no. 9 (Spring 2012), 116–23.

Wizarat al-Awqaf wa'l-Shu'un al-Islamiyyah. *Al-Mawsu'ah al-Fiqhiyyah*. 3rd edn. Kuwait: 1426/2005.

Al-Zarqa, Mustafa Ahmad. *Sharh al-Qawa'id al-Fiqhiyyah*. 2nd edn. Damascus: Dar al-Qalam 1414/1993.

Zaydan, 'Abd al-Karim. *Al-Wajiz fi Sharh al-Qawa'id al-Fiqhiyyah.* Tab'ah Jadidah Munaqqahah wa Musahhahah. Beirut: Risalah Publishers, 1425/2004.

———. *Synopsis on the Elucidation of Legal Maxims in Islamic Law.* Eng tr. of 'Abd al-Karim Zaydan's *al-Wajiz fi Shah al-Qawa'id al-Fiqhiyyah fil-Shari'ah al-Islamiyyah* by Md. Habibur Rahman and Azman Ismail. Kuala Lumpur: IBFIM & CIMB Islamic, 2015.

Al-Zuhayli, Wahbah. *al-Fiqh al-Islami wa Adillatuhu.* 8 vols. Damascus: Dar al-Fikr, 1985.

———. *Al-Fiqh al-Islami wa Adillatuhu.* 11 vols. Damascus: Dar al-Fikr, 1997.

———. *Qadaya al-Fiqh wa'l-Fikr al-Mu'asir.* Damascus: Dar al-Fikr, 1427/2006.

———. *"al-Tatarruf fi'l-Islam,"* in Mu'assasah Aal al-Bayt al-Islami, *Mustaqbal al-Islam fi'l-Qarn al-Hijri al-Thamin al-'Ashr.* Jordan: Amman, 1425/2004.

Glossary

'*Aam*: general, a general or unqualified word or sentence.

'*Adl, also '*Adālah*: justice, just and upright character.

'*Afwa*: forgiveness.

Ahad: solitary hadith, report by a single person or odd individuals.

Ahliyyah: legal capacity.

Amānah: trust, trusteeship.

'*Aql*: rationality, human intellect and reason.

'*Aîr*: late afternoon, late afternoon prayer.

'*Asabiyyah*: fanaticism, also group solidarity as in the works of Ibn Khaldun.

Asbāb al-nuzūl: the occasions of revelation, phenomenology of the Qur'an.

Athar: imprint, precedent, especially of Prophet Muhammad's Companions.

'*Awrah*: private parts (that need to be covered especially in ritual prayers).

'*AzÊmah*: original unmitigated Shariah command or requirement, one which is not reduced by concessionary circumstances.

Bay 'al-Mu'ajjal (also *bay bi-thaman aajil* or BBA): deferred payment sale.

Bid'ah: pernicious innovation - as opposed to Sunnah.

Bulugh: majority, the age of majority.

Dabitah: (pl. *dawabit*): controlling rules.

Darar: harm, prejudice.

Darar Fahish: exorbitant harm.

ÖarÊrah: dire necessity.

Daruriyyat: necessities, essential purposes or *maqasid*.

Dhikr: invocation and remembrance of God.

Dhimmah: (contractual) commitment.

Dhimmi: non-Muslim citizen (now *muwatin*).

Diyyah: blood money.

Faìā'il (sing. *faÎÊlah*): virtues, excellent qualities.

Fajr: early morning, early morning prayer.

Fasad: corruption.

FalÉÍ: salvation, deliverance.

Faqih: jurist, one knowledgeable of *fiqh*.

Fard 'ayn: personal obligation.

Fard kifa'i: collective obligation.

Fasad: corruption, mischief-making.

Fatwa: juristic opinion or verdict.

Fiqh: lit. Understanding, Islamic law.

Fitnah: tumult, sedition.

Fitrah: pristine/enlightened human nature.

FiÏrah: sound human nature.

FiÏr: religious charity (*ÎadaqÉt al-fiÏr*) paid at end of Ramadan.

Furu': subsidiary matters or rules.

Gharar: excessive risk-taking especially in financial contracts and transactions.

Ghaybiyyat: invisible, unseen, transcendental.

Hadith: saying of the Prophet Muhammad.

HÉjiyyat: needs, complementary purposes or *maqasid*.

Halal: lawful, permissible.

Haraj: hardship, difficulty.

Haram: forbidden, illegal. Act or conduct that incur both blame and punishment.

Haqq: right, truth, that which is proven and justly deserved.

Haqq al-Adami: private right, that which belongs to the individual. Haqq Allah: God's Right, public right, right of the community.

Hibah: gift, donation, unconditional transfer of assets to another person or institution.

HifÄ al-bay'ah: conservation of the natural environment, taking care of one's living environment.

HifÄ al-nafs: Protection of life, which is one of the higher objectives of Shariah.

HifÄ al-mÉl: protection of property, which is one of the higher objectives of Shariah.

Hijab: veil.

Hijr: interdiction by court order.

Hikmah: wisdom, balanced judgement, rationale.

HÊlah (pl. *hiyal*): trick, stratagem, ingenious legal tampering.

Hirabah: banditry, terrorism, highway robbery.

HiwÊr: dialogue that seeks to reconcile diverging views and interests.

HudËd (sing. *Íadd* lit. limit): prescribed penalties for specified offenses in the Qur'an.

Hukm (pl. *aÍkÉm*): ruling, judgement, Shariah value.

Iftar: breaking of fast.

ÔmÉn: faith, belief, referring to a state of mind in contradistinction with Islam which mainly refers to conduct.

IÑmÉr al-arÌ: building the earth, building a human civilisation in the earth.

'IbÉdÉt (sing. *ÑibÉdah*): matters of worship, ritual performances.

Ibahah: permissibility.

'Iffah: purity, ethical rectitude.

IfrÉÏ: exceeding the limits.

Ihsan: beauty, goodness, being g good to others.

Ijab: offer as in a contract.

Ijarah: lease and hire.

I'jaz: inimitability in reference especially to the Qur'an.

I'tidal: moderation, avoidance of excess.

Ijmā': general consensus of the community or scholars.

Ijtihad: independent interpretation, independent reasoning.

IkhtilÉf: reasoned disagreement, differential interpretation.

IjtihÉd: independent reasoning or interpretation.

IkhlÉÎ: sincerity.

'Illah: effective cause.

'Ilm al-'aqa'id: dogmatic theology, also known as *'Ilm al-Kalam*.

Iltizam: unilateral obligation.

Islah: reform, rectification, change for the better.

Isrāf: extravagance and excess.

Istidlal: open reasoning not regulated by any particular methodology.

Istihsan: juristic preference, also equity. When enforcement of normal rules in a particular case fails to provide a satisfactory solution, the judge or jurist should attempt to provide a preferable or equitable solution.

IstiÎlÉh: considerations of public interest.

Ithm: sin, transgression, blame.

JamÉl: beauty – both manifest and aesthetic beauty.

Jāhiliyyah: ignorance, age of ignorance (In reference particularly to pre-Islamic Arabia).

JihÉd: Effort, struggle in a comprehensive sense that may involve struggle against the base elements in oneself, and struggle against injustice in society, or indeed military struggle.

Jihad al-nafs: jihad of self, struggle for self-education and refinement.

Jihad fi-sabil Allah: jihad in the way of God.

Kaffarah: expiation, self-imposed punishment.

KalÉm; (lit. speech), dogmatic theology (also *'Ilm al-Kalam*).

Khabar: news, also another term for hadith as used by the Shia sources.

Khass: particular, specified – as opposed to *'aam* vicegerency of humankind in the earth. It also refers to the historical caliphate.

KifÉyah: sufficiency – enough e.g., to satisfy one's basic needs.

Khiyar al-'ayb: option of defect.

Khul': a form of divorce initiated by the wife.

Khulafa' rashidun: rightly-guided caliph- referring to the first four caliphs of Islam.

Kufr: infidelity, unbelief, rejection of Islam.

KhurÉj: lit. exit challenging the legitimacy of rule, or of a constitutional government.

MahÐËr: forbidden.

Manat al-Hukm: case of a ruling – synonymous with *'illah*.

MandËb: recommended, commendable. It is one of the value points in the Shariah scale of Five Values.

Ma'siyah: sin, transgression.

Maslahah (pl. *Masalih*): public interest, benefit, welfare.

MafÉsid: harms, as opposed to *masalih*.

Maghrib: dusk prayer after sunset.

Mahram: close male relative with whom marriage is not permissible.

MaqaÎid (sing. *maqsad*): purposes, objectives.

Madhhab (pl. *madhÉhib*): school of thought, legal or theological school.

MakrËh: reprehensible, abominable – as opposed to *mandub*.

Marja Ñ-e taqlÊd: (lit. locus of imitation) highest ramming religious authority in ShiÑism to be followed.

Maysir: gambling.

Mudarabah: commenda, sleeping partnership.

MuftÊ: jurisconsult, one qualified to give fatwa.

MuÑÉmalÉt (sing. *muÑÉmalah*): civil and commercial transactions.

Mujahadah: jihad of the self as in the Sufi tradition.

Mujtahid: jurist, one capable of exercising ijtihad.

Mukallaf: a competent person.

Muqaddarat: quantified (Sharial duties).

Murabahah: cost plus profit sale.

Musharakah: partnership.

Muqallid: an imitator who simply follows the opinion of others – one who practices *taqlid*.

Mutaghayyirat: changeable (rules).

Mutawatir: proven by continuous testimony (a variety of hadith).

Mutlaq: absolute, unqualified.

Muwatinun: compatriots.

Muwatanah: citizenship.

Nafs: living soul, self.

Nazariyyat (sing. *Nazariyyah*): theories.

Nihlah: free gift.

Niqab: veil that covers the face except for the eyes.

Nushuz: disobedience, rebellion.

Qabul: acceptance (such as of an offer).

Qaʿidah (pl. *qawaʿid*): principle.

Qaʿidah kulliyyah fiqhiyyah: legal maxim.

QaÏᴺī: definitive, decisive that needs no interpretation.

Qadhf: slander, slanderous accusation.

QawÉmah: supervision, overseeing, support.

Qiblah: direction of prayer for Muslims.

Qimar: gambling.

Qisas: just retaliation.

QiyÉs: Analogy, analogical reasoning.

RafÑ al-Íaraj: removal of hardship.

RafÑ al-Íarar: elimination of harm.

RibÉ: usury, banking interest.

Rifq: gentleness, kindness.

RukhÎah (pl. *rukhaÎ*): Shariah concession in view of mitigating circumstances.

Rushd: maturity.

Îabr: perseverance, patience.

Sadaqah: charity.

Sadd al-dharaʾiʿ: blocking the means (to an evil or unlawful end).

SafÊh: idiot, stupid.

ØalÉh: ritual prayer.

Salam: forward sale.

SamÉÍah: forbearance, tolerance, easy encounter.

SamÍ: lenient, tolerant.

ShajāÑah: courage, prowess.

SiyÉsah sharÑiyyah: judicious policy, shariah-oriented policy.

Shubha: doubt.

ShËrÉ: consultation.

Sihah Sittah: usually refers to the six major collections of hadith.

Siyasah Shar'iyyah: shariah-oriented policy.

Sunnah: saying and exemplary conduct of Prophet Muhammad.

Tabarru': charitable giving.

Tadarruj: graduality.

Ta'wil: allegorical interpretation.

Tafsir: interpretation, also refers to Qur'anic interpretation.

TaÍkÊm: arbitration.

Talaq: divorce.

Tanjim: graduality, synonym is *tadarru*.

Taqiyyah: dissimulation.

TarhÊb: scare-mongering, frightening.

TashdÊd: sternness, severity.

TaÑsÊr: opting for hardship, making matters difficult.

TaÑzÊr: deterrent punishment.

TaÍsÊniyÉt: enhancements, embellishments.

TajdÊd: renewal, restoring to original state.

TakfÊr: charging a Muslim with disbelief.

Takhyir (also *takhayyur*): selection, principle of selection.

TaklÊf: duty, liability, obligation.

Taqlid: imitation, blind following.

TaÎarrufÉt: legal dispositions.

TashrÊf: treating with dignity, honouring.

TawÉzun: balance, equilibrium.

TawassuÏ: opting for the medium average.

Tawbah: repentance.

TawÍÊd: Divine Oneness, monotheism.

TaysÊr: bringing ease.

Thawabit: fixed, unchangeable (rules and principles).

Tazkiyat al-nafs: purification of the self.

ÑUlamā' (sing. *'alim*): scholars, learned persons.

'Uli al-amr: those in charge of the management of community affairs.

Ummah: Muslim community worldwide.

ÑUrf: general custom, usage.

Usul al-Fiqh: science of the sources of Islamic law; Islamic jurisprudence.

WÉjib: obligatory.

Wajib 'ayni (personal obligation); *wajib kifa'i* (collective obligation).

Waqf (pl. *awqaf*): charitable endowment, endowment in perpetuity.

WasaÏiyyah: moderation, the middle path.

WalÊ (pl. *awliyÉ'*): guardian, supporter.

WilÉyah: authority, guardianship.

WilÉyah ÑÉmmah: public authority.

WilÉyah khÉÎÎah: private authority.

Zakah: legal alms.

Úannī: speculative, open to interpretation.

Úulm: oppression, injustice.

Úuhr: early afternoon, early afternoon prayer.

Index